What they said about the book ...

'I have worked with accountants for a large part of my career and have often "felt the fear" of being bamboozled by jargon. As an operational lead in a technical and financial charity, this book has really helped me to feel comfortable digesting the digits. The glossary of terms was completely invaluable to me, and I found the book to be both technically excellent and completely accessible.'
Emma Barklamb, Head of Member Services, Chartered Institute of Taxation and Association of Taxation Technicians

'As a long-standing finance professional, I thoroughly recommend this book for its promotion of ethical governance but, above all, for its wonderful demystifying of the world of finance.'
Paul Fitzsimons, Manager, Internal Audit, Canberra Region Joint Organisation

'An insightful, humorous and no-nonsense summary of the world of charity finance. This book is wonderfully written with real background and personal comments on a human-to-human level. Caron caters to everyone involved in charity finance and sets out every aspect from a balanced and experienced view, without overwhelming the reader. I will certainly be getting copies for existing charity clients and trustees who are new to the world of charity finance.'
Samantha Green BFP ACA, Partner, George Hay Chartered Accountants

'Worried about understanding financial conversations at your charity? Worry no more – Caron Bradshaw has got your back! This accessible and highly engaging guide will enable you to understand all aspects of your charity's finances in your organisation.'
Andrew Hind, former CEO of the Charity Commission for England and Wales and Senior Visiting Fellow at Bayes Business School

'Caron has succeeded brilliantly in painting in glorious technicolour the world of charity finance. She spends satisfyingly little time on the numbers themselves and rightly focuses on understanding the processes that lead to good decisions. I wish this invaluable guide had been available when I first came to the charity sector!'
Bob Humphreys, Chair of the Audit and Finance Committee, Education Development Trust

'This book addresses the "nightmare with the numbers" by placing charity finance in context, showing readers how those numbers can help them in their roles – both governance and operational. It is full of excellent advice and written in an accessible style, using many helpful examples drawn from practice.'
Laura F. Spira, Emeritus Professor of Corporate Governance, Oxford Brookes University

Caron Bradshaw

IT'S A NIGHTMARE WITH THE NUMBERS

The no-fibbing guide to charity finance

In association with:

Published by the Directory of Social Change (Registered Charity no. 800517 in England and Wales)

Registered address: Directory of Social Change, First Floor, 10 Queen Street Place, London, EC4R 1BE

Tel: 020 4526 5995

Visit www.dsc.org.uk to find out more about our books, subscription funding website and training events. You can also sign up for e-newsletters so that you're always the first to hear about what's new.

The publisher welcomes suggestions and comments that will help to inform and improve future versions of this and all of our titles. Please give us your feedback by emailing publications@dsc.org.uk.

It should be understood that this publication is intended for guidance only and is not a substitute for professional advice. No responsibility for loss occasioned as a result of any person acting or refraining from acting can be accepted by the author or publisher.

Print and digital editions first published 2024
Copyright © Directory of Social Change 2024

All rights reserved. No part of the printed version of this book may be stored in a retrieval system or reproduced in any form whatsoever without prior permission in writing from the publisher. This book is sold subject to the condition that it shall not, by way of trade or otherwise, be lent, re-sold, hired out or otherwise circulated without the publisher's prior permission in any form of binding or cover other than that in which it is published, and without a similar condition including this condition being imposed on the subsequent purchaser.

The digital version of this publication may only be stored in a retrieval system for personal use. No part may be edited, amended, extracted or reproduced in any form whatsoever. It may not be distributed or made available to others without prior permission in writing from the publisher.

The publisher and author have made every effort to contact copyright holders. If anyone believes that their copyright material has not been correctly acknowledged, please contact the publisher, who will be pleased to rectify the omission.

The moral right of the author has been asserted in accordance with the Copyrights, Designs and Patents Act 1988.

ISBN 978 1 78482 135 7 (print edition)
ISBN 978 1 78482 136 4 (digital edition)

British Library Cataloguing in Publication Data
A catalogue record for this book is available from the British Library

Cover and text design by Kate Griffith
Typeset by Marlinzo Services, Frome
Printed and bound in the UK by Page Bros, Norwich

For Ian Theodoreson – I owe you so much

Contents

About the Directory of Social Change — viii
About the author — ix
Acknowledgements — x
Foreword by Pesh Framjee — xi
Preface — xii

Chapter 1   Before we get started — 1

Chapter 2   It's so much more than keeping the score — 11

Chapter 3   The building blocks of financial management — 21

Chapter 4   Risky business — 53

Chapter 5   'Rainy day' reserves — 83

Chapter 6   Narrative reporting — 101

Chapter 7   Numbers and notes — 111

Chapter 8   Investments — 131

Chapter 9   External scrutiny — 147

Chapter 10   Pearls of wisdom — 167

Appendix 1   Table of thresholds — 173

Appendix 2   Glossary of terms — 183

References and notes — 193

Index — 203

About the Directory of Social Change

At the Directory of Social Change (DSC), we believe that the world is made better by people coming together to serve their communities and each other. For us, an independent voluntary sector is at the heart of that social change and we exist to support charities, voluntary organisations and community groups in the work they do. Our role is to:

- **provide practical information** on a range of topics from fundraising to project management in both our printed publications and our e-books;
- **offer training** through public courses, events and in-house services;
- **research funders** and maintain a subscription database, *Funds Online*, with details on funding from grant-making charities, companies and government sources;
- **offer bespoke research** to voluntary sector organisations in order to evaluate projects, identify new opportunities and help make sense of existing data;
- **stimulate debate and campaign** on key issues that affect the voluntary sector, particularly to champion the concerns of smaller charities.

We are a registered charity ourselves but we self-fund most of our work. We charge for services but cross-subsidise those which charities particularly need and cannot easily afford.

Visit our website **www.dsc.org.uk** to see how we can help you to help others and have a look at **www.fundsonline.org.uk** to see how DSC could improve your fundraising. Alternatively, call our friendly team at **020 4526 5995** to chat about your needs or drop us a line at **cs@dsc.org.uk**.

About the author

Caron studied law at the University of Westminster, gaining an LLB (Hons), and went on to train as a barrister. She was called to the Bar as a member of the Honourable Society of Lincolns Inn.

She fell into working with finance professionals when she joined the Institute of Chartered Accountant in England and Wales (ICAEW) as a conciliator. After 16 years working for the ICAEW, latterly as Head of the Charity and Voluntary Sector, she joined Charity Finance Group as its CEO in 2010.

Caron has been involved with voluntary and social change work for as long as she can remember. Starting in her teenage years and continuing into her adult life, alongside her career, Caron has been involved with and supported a number of small charities and community organisations.

As part of an increasing portfolio of roles, Caron is a non-executive director of the Lending Standards Board and of Origin Housing. She's a member of the Church of England Pension Board's Audit and Risk Committee and the Finance and Risk Committee of the British Asian Trust. She is a member of the University of Westminster's Industry Advisory Board and a former chair of trustees of the Directory of Social Change. She is a keen hockey player and – you guessed it – was chair of her local hockey club.

Caron has been a member of the NCVO's National Assembly and the Charities SORP Committee, and has sat on a number of government working parties. She is an avidly social CEO and has been named in the top 30 social CEOs in 2013, 2014 and 2015.

Caron was honoured with an OBE for her services to charity in the New Year's Honours lists in 2021.

Acknowledgements

This book wouldn't have been possible without drawing on the expertise and time of a wide range of people.

In particular, I would like to thank Rachel Cooper, Hilary Seward and Simon Hopkins for allowing me to share their ideas. I'm grateful to others who contributed to the book their pearls of wisdom: Nicki Deeson, Rui Domingues, Andrew Hind, Bob Humphreys, Joyce Materego-Woodall, Kevin O'Brien and Ian Theodoreson. Rui deserves a special mention for holding my hand with the fictious examples – making sure they made sense and were correct.

A special mention also goes to Nigel Davies for helping me cover content on the different jurisdictions in the UK. Huge thanks to the people, including those already mentioned, who reviewed some or all of the chapters and gave me feedback that ultimately made this a better book than I would have written alone: Harriet Hardie, Tom Phillips, Richard Sagar, Vicky Smith, Genny Jones and Ian Pembridge. And those who read the final copy (again, including some already mentioned) and said such nice things: Sammie Green, Paul Fitzsimons, Emma Barklamb and Prof. Laura F. Spira – thank you so very much.

The marvellous team at CFG, including Emma Abbott, Sarah Lomax and Clare Mills, who have been super supportive, providing me with input and giving me time and headspace to make this book happen. In particular, Pesh Framjee (CFG's special adviser, author of the foreword to this book and someone who has forgotten more about charity finance than I will ever know) has been invaluable in answering my questions and making sure the content both is technically accurate and avoids the technical precision and jargon that is so often present with this topic (not an easy balance to achieve!).

I want to thank Debra Alcock Tyler who is such a phenomenal person – insightful, funny, kind and all round brilliant – for giving me the opportunity to muscle in on her exceptional '*It's a…*' series of books (if you've not read them all, go and buy them now!). And the awesome DSC team, in particular Gabi Zagnojute, John Martin and Hazel Bird. I hope I was as easy to work with for you as you were for me.

Lastly, I want to acknowledge and thank my lovely husband who has put up with me whinging about how challenging it is to write a book, provided me with endless cups of fruit tea as I sat in front of my laptop tapping away and is in all ways the very best of men. Peter Bradshaw – you are my rock.

Foreword

Charities play a pivotal role in addressing some of society's most pressing issues. However, their effectiveness and sustainability depends not just on the passion and dedication of their teams but also on sound financial management and robust accounting practices. Now, more than ever, charities are faced with the difficult task of satisfying short-term needs against the pressure of maintaining resources to achieve long-term impact.

For those tasked with navigating these choppy waters, the journey can be daunting, filled with technical jargon, regulatory requirements, and the ever-present need to ensure transparency and accountability. Having been auditing and advising charities on matters related to charity finance, strategy and governance for over 35 years, I have seen the need for a book such as this to demystify these complexities for anyone who comes in contact with charity finance.

I often say that charity finance and accounting incorporates all the complexity of private and public sector accounting and more. It needs to recognise both the financial reporting standards and the important principles of trust law. Ironically, to meet these complicated and ever-increasing requirements charities often have fewer resources than their counterparts in other sectors. Therefore, understanding the financial principles and their practical application is crucial for those involved with a charity.

In 1987, I was one of the six individuals who set up the Charity Finance Group (CFG) to inspire a financially confident, dynamic and trustworthy non-profit sector. Today, CFG does this by championing best practice, nurturing leadership and influencing policy makers. It helps its more than 1,400 members to develop their finance management knowledge and skills. As CFG's CEO, Caron sees firsthand the challenges that so many have in managing charity finance and preparing accounts that tell the charity's story.

Applying all of her experience and expertise, Caron has written this book to break down the sometimes intimidating world of charity finance into understandable and actionable insights that are accessible to everyone.

I welcome you to a clearer, more confident understanding of charity finance and accounting!

Pesh Framjee

Special Advisor to the Charity Finance Group and Founder of Consulting for Purpose

Former Global Head of Social Purpose and Non-profits at Crowe, Deloitte and Arthur Andersen

Preface

I have been privileged to work with DSC for over a decade, and for a decent chunk of that time I have served as either the chair or a trustee. I am delighted to have been granted the opportunity to write this book.

I have worked with and for charities and community organisations of all sizes. What I have picked up along the way has shown me that great financial management is essential for all well-performing social change organisations.

The recent past has underlined the need to reconsider, reimagine and reflect on the ways we have financed our charities as we have dealt with the perfect storm of a global pandemic, a cost-of-living crisis, and global political, economic and social uncertainty. Demand has risen as incomes have been shattered. Life has thrust its metaphorical hand under the tray of our income and expenditure models, sending all the pieces flying into the air. Understanding the numbers is therefore critical to running effective social change organisations.

Charity finance is not as inaccessible as many would have you believe. Once the veil of accounting language and assumed cerebral superiority is lifted, I hope you'll see that it's a tool which can drive greater impact.

This book is not a technical text for finance people. It's a no-nonsense, plain-speaking, honest insight into all things charity finance for pretty much anyone who needs to understand the numbers in their charity. I hope you will find it a helpful guide whatever your role – CEO, trustee or non-finance member of staff – and whatever the size of your charity.

And, even if you are a finance person, do read on. You might still find it helpful to consider a different perspective on the numbers so you can better interpret or translate figures for people you work with.

I hope that this book will help you awake from having a nightmare with the numbers.

1 Before we get started

Charity accounting used to be like the Wild West – anything went. Ian Theodoreson

It was my privilege to serve under Ian Theodoreson when he was chair of Charity Finance Group (CFG), and he often pointed out that charity finance in the UK had come a long way since 1987, when the organisation was founded. Then there was no formal accounting practice or official guidance, no consistent or transparent approach to reporting, and the majority of senior finance people in charities did not hold a formal accounting qualification.

Like the Wild West, reporting was untamed and unruly.

While we now have significantly higher levels of professionalism and the larger charities employ skilled charity finance professionals, the numbers continue to be a nightmare for many. They can feel like a compliance burden – an inaccessible dark art or something that is just not *our* responsibility.

This chapter explains what underpins charity accounting in the UK and outlines its purpose beyond ticking the compliance box. We'll explore why people are afraid of numbers and how the hat you wear, whether operational or governance, may change your perspective and/or areas of responsibility. So, grab your Stetson...

> **Outcomes**
> After reading this chapter you will:
> - See the benefit of getting to grips with the numbers as a trustee or non-finance staff member
> - Understand the origin of the modern charity accounting framework in the UK and its purpose
> - Understand who is responsible for what when it comes to charity finance

Feel afraid, feel very afraid?

In my years of speaking to trustees and staff of charities, I have heard fear expressed in a number of ways – from the 'ah yes, but we have an accountant/treasurer, so I don't need to worry about the numbers' to the 'I'm a cause person, not a numbers person'. However it is dressed up, fear is often the common denominator. Whether you're one of the 'why have a dog and bark yourself?' brigade or the 'I don't need to know' tribe, please recognise that numbers are important to us all. I have often heard this beautifully encapsulated in the idea that you cannot change the world unless you can balance the books! Money may not be the end in itself, but without it your charity's achievements may be limited. Your charity doesn't exist to generate a profit to return to shareholders, of course. But, if you can generate the right level of resources, if you can understand your business model, if you can get to grips with the numbers, you stand a greater chance of getting ahead of risks and problems – ultimately making your charity more sustainable.

Knowing your way around the numbers helps you to make better decisions as a member of staff or in the board room. And there is another reason to savvy up – the level of responsibility that may come with your role. Rarely will 'not knowing' or 'not asking' provide you with protection if the proverbial hits the fan.

You might have read of charities that got into trouble with the Charity Commission for England and Wales or another regulator because of poorly run finances. In extreme instances, trustees can be taken to court. In such cases a defence of 'it was the finance committee's job so we're not to blame' wouldn't cut it. All the trustees would be required to demonstrate that they understood the finances of the charity regardless of their skill. So, you have to understand what your charity's financial records are telling you, even if you don't know how to produce them.

It's OK to feel afraid, scared witless or just uncomfortable around numbers. And it doesn't say anything about your intelligence or mathematical ability. I'm a trained lawyer – numbers are not my discipline. In the early days, I would look at accounts and financial information with a knot in my stomach. I may as well have been looking at a different language or computer code. Look at me now – I run an organisation (CFG) whose central mission is to drive up the standards of charity finance and I sit on the committee (the Charities SORP Committee) which writes the recommended practice on accounting rules for charities. Finance isn't as inaccessible as you might think.

Maybe our fears surrounding the dark art of finance have been played to over the years by individual finance staff wanting to hold the purse strings or a specific treasurer wanting to be the score-keeper. Information is knowledge and knowledge is power, after all. It is probable that over the years it has served some individuals well to make financial information hard to navigate and knowledge difficult to come by, resulting in folk being excluded from decision-making. However, certainly during my time as CEO of CFG, I have found such behaviour to be the exception. Nowadays, the finance professionals I meet, whether staff or volunteers, want all areas of their charity and all their colleagues to understand and contribute to the charity's finances. They are trying hard to change the stereotypes associated with them. No more do they wish to be seen as the 'budget police' or enforcers of the rules – the person wielding the hatchet or a 'bean counter'. They want to create maximum impact from the resources available. They see the benefit of making the numbers accessible and understandable. They have chosen to work in our beloved sector not because they want to wave technically accurate accounts in the faces of their friends at dinner parties but because they want to change the world too – they just happen to be accountants.

The UK accounting framework

Charities have been around for centuries, and accounting terms – which go by odd and uncomfortable-sounding names like 'double-entry bookkeeping' – are equally long in the tooth. However, until relatively recently there was little focus on how charities should account for the money they raise and spend on delivering their charitable objects.

In the early 1980s, the Institute of Chartered Accountants in England and Wales published an important research report by Peter Bird and Peter Morgan-Jones. In it, the authors expressed horror at the state of charity financial reporting. So strong were the concerns they raised – about the impact the apparently dubious and creative tactics used at the time might have on trust and transparency if left unfettered – that the report changed the face of charity accounting forever. They showed that, in the absence of a proper set of rules, there was huge scope for charity personnel to manipulate figures – for example, by pushing expenditure into the future, bringing future income into the present, hiding costs or not disclosing inconvenient information. The paper set us on the path to formal codification of recommended accounting practices and financial reporting for charities, including the now well-established Charities Statement of Recommended Practice, or SORP. In addition to laying down rules for charity financial reporting, the SORP has had a real influence on good practice – for example, by asking trustees to report on their policies around risk management, reserves and recruitment of trustees. Because the SORP requires charities to report on these matters, they are nudged into considering them.

There are two things which I believe it is incredibly important for you to bear in mind from the outset of this book. They will help you to understand how some of the complexity and difficulties your charity might experience are built into the financial reporting framework and rules.

Firstly, the accounting and reporting standards used in the UK (referred to as the Generally Accepted Accounting Principles, or GAAP) were developed with the for-profit sector in mind. As I've already noted, charities' actions are not geared towards making a profit to distribute to shareholders. What is of most importance to charities (like increasing impact) can be quite different from what is of primary importance in the traditional private sector (by which I mean companies that are not set up to deal with environmental, social and governance matters, or ESG – we'll explore ESG further in chapter 8). Also, the nature of transactions and resources within charities (for example, the goods and services people donate to us) may not have straightforward comparisons in the for-profit space.

Secondly, many people use the term 'sector' to describe what are more realistically multiple sub-sectors of wildly varying sizes, natures and causes loosely held together by their desire to bring about positive social change. The vast majority of charities are small in size. Conversely, a tiny minority of charities account for the lion's share of the money. Entities can be entirely voluntary with simple delivery methods, or global enterprises with complex business models, thousands of employees and multimillion-pound turnovers – and of course everything in between.

These two points present us with challenges. Imagine you have bought one of those 'one-size-fits-all' flexible dish covers (in case you don't spend as much time as me in the kitchen, these are silicone stretchy circles designed to snugly sit over bowls of different sizes and they feature in those gadget magazines that drop through your door). When you get a cover out of the packaging, you'll find it is developed for round containers of a limited diameter range. You open your cupboard and reflect that, with the odd exception, all your dishes are square, rectangular and other non-round shapes. For all your little pots, the cover is way too big, flops over the top and serves little purpose, perhaps even getting in the way. For the bigger ones, whatever direction you tug and however hard you pull, the blooming gizmo is never quite going to fit!

Larger charities and some others are required to follow the SORP (the thresholds can be found in appendix 1, and I'll cover broadly which rules apply to which charities as we go along). For these charities, the SORP – like the one-size-fits-all cover – is not a perfect or easy fit, but significant effort has gone into improving it over the years. Despite criticisms, it has evolved into a pretty good tool. It's a chunky tome which sets out how financial reporting standards are translated into the charity context. Over time, the content has increasingly provided not just guidance on the technical accounting approach to various aspects of charity finance but also direction on the non-financial reporting that sits alongside the numbers.

For a significant proportion of charities (smaller unincorporated charities with under £250,000 in annual income), the pages of the SORP are likely to remain firmly shut because they are not required to apply it. These charities may apply the simple accounting practice of recording money in and money out ('receipts and payments' accounting) and never trouble themselves with how the UK GAAP should be interpreted. If you are one of those charities, however, definitely read on, as this book goes far beyond the SORP. It aims to help you manage your charity's finances better and help you see why nailing the numbers can improve your stewardship, focus on impact and be more sustainable irrespective of the accounting framework you follow.

The SORP – so what?

As mentioned, the SORP doesn't apply to all charities in the UK. However, irrespective of whether your charity needs to apply the SORP right now or not, it's useful to understand what it (and changes relating to it) aims to achieve.

The intended primary users of the SORP are the people involved in preparing a charity's accounts and trustees' annual report. Additionally, the SORP is intended to help accountancy firms, auditors and those involved in scrutinising accounts. The document assumes a level of familiarity with accounting concepts, principles and terminology. So, you might be forgiven for concluding that its purpose is to help people who already have a reasonable level of knowledge about accounting. However, in my view, this tells you about its pitch, not its purpose.

The SORP exists to drive up standards of charity accounting to enhance the understanding and use of financial information for stakeholders. It does not just focus on the numbers, although these are incredibly important, but also helps charities identify what they ought to include in the trustees' annual report. In the context of charities, I would argue that this narrative stands shoulder to shoulder with the raw numbers.

In his paper *The Charities SORP: An 'engine' for good?*, professor and long-serving Charities SORP committee member Noel Hyndman describes the SORP as a bespoke framework that is designed to steer charities and that can be deployed to 'provide the basis for a more legitimate, better-managed, more-accountable and healthier sector'.

The SORP therefore has two functions. It is a how-to guide which aims to make the numbers in charities' reporting more relevant, comparable and understandable. And it is a tool for improving the transparency and accountability of the sector to our beneficiaries, shaping how we share our achievements, activities and lessons.

Which hat are you wearing?

Let's look at roles and responsibilities – what are the broad types of hat you might wear when engaging with a charity's numbers? There are two main types of hat you can wear: the governance hat and the operational (or delivery) hat.

The governance hat

You may be expecting a sub-division here into 'treasurer's hat' and 'other trustees' hat', but I'm not going to distinguish between the treasurer and other trustees. It is a common misconception that the treasurer holds greater responsibility in matters of charity finance within the board of trustees. Not only do all trustees hold the same level of responsibility for the governance of their charity but also, increasingly, charities are questioning whether they need the role of treasurer.

Should you have a treasurer?

In my view there are pros and cons to having a named treasurer. Practically speaking, it can be valuable to have a single person who acts as the focal point for all things financial (a pro). However, there is also an argument that doing so can lead to the erroneous belief that a single individual is more responsible than the others, with the others consequently feeling they can afford not to engage with the numbers (a con). After all, it is a *trustees' annual report* you produce, not a *treasurer's annual report*.

> **Two examples of charities without a treasurer**
>
> At **Charity Finance Group (CFG)**, where I am the CEO, our governance structures include a sub-committee of the board whose remit is finance and audit. The chair of that sub-committee is the closest that you'd get to a traditional treasurer. Their role is to chair the meetings at which the sub-committee considers the facts and figures relating to CFG's financial management and reporting in more detail, and to help the full board understand the breadth and depth of conversations had during such meetings if required. This person acts as a governance-level contact point for the external auditors too. But they are not more responsible than the rest of the trustees for our numbers.
>
> Similarly, at the **Directory of Social Change (DSC)**, the trustees take equal responsibility for understanding the numbers and using the financial and non-financial information to make appropriate decisions. Individual trustees may lead on topics they are more experienced or expert in through working groups and task forces (which rise up to deal with specific issues and close down when those matters are put to bed). There is no finance sub-committee or named treasurer.

You could argue, of course, that a qualified finance professional would be expected to have a greater level of understanding of financial information. This could be relevant if they were called upon to explain their actions to a court in, say, a prosecution for wrongful trading (where a director is accused of carrying on trading after they should have known the company couldn't avoid going bust owing people money it couldn't pay back). Similarly, this could be true if their professional body received a complaint about their competence. However, I would argue that this is less to do with whether they are named as treasurer and more about holding them accountable for potentially duff decisions given their training. Their level of assumed knowledge will be greater in relation to financial matters, just as a trustee with a medical background might be assumed to have a greater level of technical understanding regarding medical issues in a health charity. But, in governance terms, no greater responsibility comes simply from being a treasurer – when it comes to the numbers, the considerations for *all* trustees are equal.

There is no legally right or wrong answer to the question of having a treasurer. Consider who sits on your charity's board and whether the presence or absence of a treasurer is encouraging engagement or lack of responsibility.

1. Before we get started

My advice is not to stick with an approach simply because that's how it's always been done – actively think about what works for your charity.

So, when I talk about the governance hat, I am referencing the decisions and considerations that *all* trustees need to take on board. There is no fixed line between people involved with governance and people involved with operations that applies to all charities irrespective of their size, nature or business model. Practical considerations may mean that a trustee steps beyond their governance responsibilities into delivery. For example, I used to be the operationally active chair of a tiny pre-school. Within that charity, the paid staff were focused on the provision of early-years services, and the trustees did what in a larger organisation a range of paid staff might undertake. We pulled the accounts together, created the accounting records, recorded the transactions and much more. These practical necessities don't change what governance is, but you may need to wear the operational hat simultaneously with the governance hat, or switch between the hats in short order.

I can do no better than quote *It's a Battle on the Board* here, because the author, Debra Allcock Tyler, sums the reality up perfectly:

> The hat you wear as a trustee is quite a specific one – and it is not the same hat that your executive, staff or volunteers wear ... Whatever the size of your charity, when you have your trustee hat on, your job is to ask questions. Big questions, strategic questions.

Try to keep this context in mind and reflect on the various perspectives and questions you should consider.

Governance hat: financial responsibilities at a glance

When thinking specifically about the numbers, if you are a trustee, you need to:

- understand your charity's objectives and how it operates (its business model), and keep the charity's best interests as your central focus when making decisions;
- identify any conflicts of interest, particularly those with a financial implication;
- meet your legal responsibilities – in other words, ensure your charity carries out its charitable objects, manage your charity's resources responsibly, and comply with your governing document and the law;
- understand and meet your legal financial reporting requirements (the trustees' annual report and accounts, reports to the regulator, etc.) – see chapters 6 (on narrative reporting) and 7 (on numbers and notes);
- have a clear plan for how you will finance your activities (otherwise known as a 'financial strategy') and put in place measures to check in on how you are performing – see chapter 3 (on the building blocks of financial management);
- have a mechanism for considering the risks and opportunities facing your charity – see chapter 4;

- have a mechanism for ensuring you understand and agree the financial policies your charity adopts and that they do what they are supposed to do (are fit for purpose) – see chapter 3;
- appoint an external auditor or independent examiner – see chapter 9 (on external scrutiny).

The operational hat

So, if the governance hat requires you to ask the big, strategic questions, what does wearing the operational hat mean in terms of charity finance?

The CEO, finance lead or other members of the senior management team will have the responsibility for using resources in furtherance of your charity's cause in a sustainable way. And they will need to report on the ebbs and flows of resourcing to the board (among other stakeholders). Different tools – such as management information, including cash flows, budgets and forecasting (all of which will be covered in the following chapters) – will be deployed to manage these responsibilities.

You might be wondering about the place of other individuals who are responsible for budgets and who make decisions which have an impact on the financial and charitable performance of your charity, but who have not been mentioned so far (such as volunteers deployed in operational delivery). Where do they fit in? An example is a member of staff who has responsibility for delivering activities to an agreed budget but is not part of the executive and may not have played an extensive role in strategic decisions or setting that budget. While these individual staff members and volunteers may have less authority, they will still need to understand the numbers. This book includes such people within the scope of the operational hat.

Depending on the size of the charity, operational functions can be concentrated in very few people (or even a single individual) or organised into specialist teams, each taking responsibility for different parts of running the charity. In very small charities, as in the pre-school example I gave above, the trustees may roll up their sleeves to undertake these operational functions.

The trustees may have documented which decisions and financial level of decision-making they have delegated to the senior staff, sometimes called 'the executive'. Such documentation is often referred to as a 'scheme of delegation' (see more in chapter 3). For example, in one charity I know of, the CEO has the power to authorise invoices up to £5,000, but anything over that amount has to be signed off by the trustees. However, while the functions and activities can be delegated, the responsibility cannot be. In the charity context, the buck always stops with the trustees, whatever the practical arrangements in place. This can lead to trustees getting sucked down into the weeds and detail despite having an executive in place. In my experience, having the right level of information available and mechanisms in place to monitor how the charity is performing can help keep trustees wearing their governance hat.

To summarise the operational hat, I'll quote Debra again. The role of the executive is 'to put plans in place to achieve the vision, mission and objectives of the charity' and to 'ensure that the charity's finances are stable and sustainable'. Again, try to keep this context in mind whenever this book refers to the operational hat, as doing so should help you reflect on the various perspectives and questions you should consider.

Operational hat: financial responsibilities at a glance
The executive and staff will typically be responsible for the following:
- producing budgets which support your charity's strategic goals;
- producing monthly management information (including forecasting how your charity's financial performance could look by the year end based on what is known to date);
- drafting the trustees' annual report and accounts for approval;
- managing day-to-day risks, opportunities and performance (including managing the cash flow) of your charity and keeping the trustees aware of how things are going.

The Society of Oneirocritics

I have dreamt up – pun intended – a fictious charity: the Society of Oneirocritics (oneirocritics interpret dreams). It is a small charity (as defined by the Charity Commission, having an annual income under £1 million) and has a 31 March year end. It carries out work which spans education and training, a nightmare counselling service, and policy work. Its biggest bill, as with many charities delivering services, is its people, and it has other modest costs relating to premises and IT. In terms of income, the charity receives a mixture of grants for educational work and providing nightmare counselling, donations (from people who like to read about what dreams mean), some fees from online services and courses, and a bit of fundraising income. I'll call on this charity to help us make sense of some of the more tricky, technical or dry content that the topic of finance forces us to confront.

Feel the fear and do it anyway

Irrespective of the hat you wear, nailing the numbers and feeling comfortable digesting the digits bring benefit to all.

If you're wearing the governance hat, being able to ask the right questions – and not being put off by thinking the finances are for someone else – will enable you to discharge your duties better. In times like these, when conditions are tough and charities are coping with rising demand and squeezed income, having a greater grasp of the finances should enable you to make the appropriate decisions about the big stuff, leaving the executive and staff to focus on the detail.

If you have donned the operational hat, you might previously have been able to get away with not really knowing the relevant numbers and leaving them to 'the finance person'. However, the professionalism of the sector has grown and the expectations around charity reporting and accountability have increased, such that you really can't get away with not knowing now. It's not the finance person's job to splosh a dose of realism on your plans or enforce financial prudence. It is their job to help you undertake activities which sustainably deliver impact.

And a final 'footnote' for the finance bods among you – understanding what holds others back from getting a grip on the numbers should help you share your knowledge in a more accessible way. Unlocking this information improves discussions and helps put finance at the heart of effective decision-making.

Main chapter takeaways
- The trustees have ultimate and equal responsibility for understanding the numbers and making decisions which deliver on the strategy of your charity.
- Understanding the numbers, whatever your role, enables you to make better and more sustainable decisions which can lead to greater impact.
- Understanding the financial impact of the things you do helps your charity be more sustainable.

2 It's so much more than keeping the score

You can't change the world without balancing the books. Dame Julia Cleverdon

I had the pleasure of listening to the marvellous Dame Julia Cleverdon deliver an after-dinner speech in 2018. She was addressing a room full of finance professionals at the Charity Finance Group (CFG) annual fundraising dinner and told them their work was important and went beyond making the numbers stack up. She was so right – social change requires great financial management. But it's more than that. Money is one of the means by which you can accomplish your vision. It's a mechanism for enabling you to do your work – not the reason for the work. In a traditional private sector company, the money (i.e. being profitable and generating a financial return) is the motive. This doesn't mean that companies are evil, unethical or not driven by a purpose, just that profit is the primary driver. In our sector, in contrast, the money is only the mechanism.

Additionally, there are differences and nuances between the for-profit and the not-for-profit contexts – not just in terms of what specific words mean but also in terms of which words might be used. For example, some have an aversion to saying 'profit' because it implies dividends. Charities are more likely to talk about 'surpluses' or 'contributions' because such money is not distributed to anyone (e.g. shareholders). It's a common misunderstanding that charity finance is the same as business finance – although there is a lot in common, there are also fundamental differences, especially relating to reporting and decision-making. For example, restricted funds (money a charity can spend only on specific things because the donor gave it for those specific activities) are likely to be an unfamiliar concept to those operating in the private sector.

In this chapter, I'm going to tackle the problem of jargon (and refer you to this book's glossary of common terms and phrases) and introduce you to the various facets of finance present in those charities that nail the numbers.

> **Outcomes**
> After reading this chapter you will:
> - Know how to unpack the jargon used in charity finance
> - Understand the different skills and processes required in a well-functioning finance team
> - Have a model to apply when assessing the financial resources available to your charity

Unpacking the jargon

We need to acknowledge that the accounting profession is a bit guilty of using jargon. There are many terms you may come across which may leave you puzzled. Rather than include definitions within this chapter, I have created a glossary for you to use (see appendix 2). Before you read on, I'd like you to consider which terms you have come across in your charity and whether you know what they mean. You might also want to take some time to read through the glossary in its entirety before moving on. In it I've provided some plain-speaking definitions to help you make sense of this language. I hope the glossary will serve as a reference point for you, demystifying words commonly used in finance and perhaps challenging your understanding of others. Maybe you are unclear about the meanings of some terms but have not asked for clarification because you assume you're the only one who doesn't know. Believe me – if you're thinking it, someone else will be too. There is no such thing as a stupid question.

For those more seasoned finance people reading this book, the glossary's definitions might help you make your work more accessible to your peers by giving you a less technical and more accessible way of explaining concepts. I appreciate that you may find the general absence of technical jargon jarring and sense a lack of precision in the language, and thus you might think the definitions are not strictly technically accurate. But the definitions are geared towards improving understanding of the concepts, intent or actions behind the terms, not technical precision.

What is 'finance'?

A wonderful friend, senior finance leader and author of a toolkit called The Finance Journey (which I will introduce you to in this chapter), Simon Hopkins, was once told by a senior colleague that finance was all about 'keeping the score'. On one level, of course, that's right: it is helpful for those running a charity to have accurate financial information telling them what money has come in and what is going out. But this is just a sliver of the bigger picture. The finance function is about how you manage your resources (money, people, physical assets, intellectual property) in order to achieve your objectives. It isn't about job roles or technology, the size of the charity, or the number of staff working on financial matters. It is about a process of correctly targeting resources to achieve your charity's aims and objectives. What's more, you don't need to be an accountant or have a qualification to tackle finance!

Imagine a big cook pot – what words would you put into the soup to make up the ingredients of this thing called 'finance'? Just take a minute and scribble down your ideas before you read on.

Do you have words like 'debit' and 'credit' on your list? Maybe there are words like 'transactions' and 'processing'?

While these are all legitimate and important elements, they focus on the number-crunching bit of finance. My invitation is to think wider.

What makes good financial management goes further afield. It includes planning different scenarios and testing any assumptions against them (called stress-testing). It requires risk management and financial controls. Being able to understand how much your charity needs to keep back for a rainy day or to help it invest in change is essential. I would also include how you use data to enable you to spot and take advantage of opportunities, and to manage and drive up performance. These concepts are all part of my recipe for finance soup. It's so much more than keeping the score!

In other words, nailing the numbers, dominating the digits and being clear with the calculations is not just about the technical accounting bit. It's about understanding your charity's business model and getting as much bang for your buck as possible.

Future chapters will focus on how to do that, but let's first consider what makes a good finance function.

The Finance Journey

Let me introduce you to Simon's model, which CFG first published in 2014. This way of thinking about the different disciplines, skills and processes within a well-balanced finance function has been supporting finance professionals ever since (a second edition was published in 2021). But I think it is helpful for a wider audience too. Whether you are wearing the governance or the operational hat, thinking about what the different bits of a finance function are and who does what can help you to allocate resources wisely. I encourage you to think about what resources and roles your charity needs to make great financial management part of your charity. This is a summary of the model and how you might apply it. I've stripped back the detail to make it useful to a non-finance audience but the full content can be found on the CFG website (www.cfg.org.uk).

The model sets out the various parts of the optimum finance function as levels in a pyramid. Each level links with the next and together the levels support a healthy finance function.

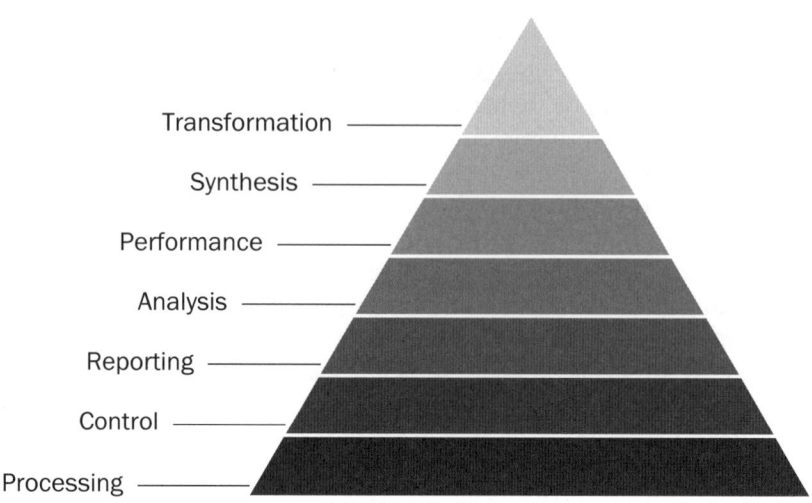

Let's walk through the layers.

Firstly, **processing** – this is the bit of finance that looks at individual transactions, such as expenses, supplier invoices and customer transactions. Because it is necessary to record and complete individual transactions, getting this bit right provides a solid foundation on which everything else sits. If things aren't processed accurately, then everything else is a bit wobbly and unreliable. Processing requires systems (not necessarily software) to capture what your charity is doing in great detail. Every item purchased, every bill paid, every expense claimed – these all provide the basic data required, not just to enable accurate accounting records but also to enable you to move beyond producing spreadsheets of numbers to making sure the numbers drive decisions and increase impact.

There is a close relationship between this first element and the next: **control**. Great processes can help to identify the appropriate controls and, conversely, strong controls can identify ways to improve processes, making them more productive, quicker or more reliable. If we understand the logical flow of transactions, we can identify extra checks and reviews that will help to prevent problems. For example, if you know that Vera receives the cash from the raffle, counts it, writes the amount down and banks the cash at the Post Office, you can also identify improvements and appropriate controls. In this situation, if Vera opens the cash box alone, not only is there a chance for error, there is also the chance that Vera will be tempted to pop some in her pocket. A good process, with effective controls, might therefore include having a second person to open the cash box, count with her, bag up the money and deposit it at the Post Office. The control layer can ensure accuracy in the processing but it can also help to address the elements of the processing layer which are most susceptible to error, omission, fraud or other undesirable events. In this way, we can improve the processing through the amount of control we have.

Control, therefore, represents the checks and balances we put in place to make sure the processing layer is doing what it should. It is the things that give us assurance that the systems we have established have integrity. Control is about the application of healthy scepticism and the ability to contemplate how mistakes or problems can arise. If those responsible for managing the finances at your charity can see potential flaws or risks in processing, it is a pretty good indicator that you have achieved this basic level.

So, the data has been processed and the executive and trustees are content that suitable controls are in place – now you need good reports. **Reporting** is about the creation and sharing of data: management information, accounts, annual reports, ad hoc reports and so on. The key word here is 'meaningful'. So, if processing and control are about the quality of the data in the system, reporting is about getting that data out, turning it into information and doing something with it to help your charity perform.

There have been significant improvements in accounting packages and technology which will aid the development of reports, but reporting does not have to be reliant on software packages. If your charity is a tiny organisation that relies on spreadsheets or even paper, you will still need meaningful reports – the process will simply be manual rather than automated.

The next layer is **analysis**. This is about interpretating your reports so as to understand what is really going on behind the figures and why it is happening. Analysis is all about trying to understand *why* things happen, as opposed to *what* happens (which is reporting). Again, it's not just about the financial numbers. Analysis requires more than a bit of commentary to confirm that one number is bigger or smaller than what is in your budget. This level of financial maturity is about understanding what the information is telling you. For example, your finance person – whether a staff member, an external accountant or a volunteer (or, if your charity is large, a team of people) – might tell you that the figures relating to income from grants are looking too low because you were anticipating receiving a payment earlier. They might be able to say you don't need to worry as it will be arriving next month instead – i.e. the apparently low figure is a timing blip. Conversely, they might diagnose an underlying trend – for example, there might be fewer bookings across the board for your training courses and people might seem to be tightening their belts, leading to the risk of substantial under-performance over the full year. Can your finance person tell you when the numbers reveal something concerning about the underlying data itself? Do they spot when the numbers just don't look right? Having the right support and analysis can really help to reduce the numerical nightmare and give you confidence. It can help you anticipate and get ahead of problems before they really become a worry.

If analysis is about pinpointing why things are happening, **performance** is about using what you have learned to drive improvements across your charity. A compelling report has been produced, the executive and trustees are confident that the figures are reliable, and your finance person has given good insights into why something isn't working. Now you need to be confident that this insight is going to lead to action.

This layer of the model highlights the need for more than technical skills and knowledge. Well-managed finances need people who can also influence change. People thinking about their organisation's finance functions will often finish here – good information, processed effectively and reliably, clear reports, identifying the need for change and taking action. Sounds like a good, solid finance function, doesn't it? But there is more your charity can get from nailing the numbers.

The penultimate layer of the Finance Journey is **synthesis**. This represents a group of activities that help you to visualise what the future could be like. Often, examining your numbers means looking back. Instead, synthesis means taking what is known and looking forward. It is about being strategic – creating something new (or more sophisticated) from simpler elements. Synthesis requires you to take what you know and expand it or build on it to define what the future might look like.

At its simplest level, synthesis means predicting what the future financial picture might be (forecasting) or developing a plan of income and expenditure for a period (a budget). At the more sophisticated level, it means producing a compelling and realistic vision of your charity or its impact at some point in the future. This vision might be a long-term 'what if?' financial or investment scenario, a new business model or way of working, or a new system. It might be a tool which would let you take a significant jump forward in terms of productivity, quality or effect. For example, the finance function might prompt the executive to consider new artificial intelligence (AI) tools, chat bots and the like, to deal with more routine queries and free up staff to provide more tailored and detailed support.

Finally, **transformation** represents the process of substantially changing your charity's impact or way of working so as to deliver on the future that the executive and trustees imagined as part of the synthesis level. Taking our AI example, a transformational finance function wouldn't just make the suggestion – they would lead the change project to implement the new way of working, leading to increased productivity and better impact. This is where all the levels of the Finance Journey come together:

- understanding how things work at the operational level (**processing** and **control**);
- understanding what causes things to improve for the charity's beneficiaries, and how to make that happen (**reporting**, **analysis** and **performance**);
- articulating a vision for the future that is credible and built on evidence (**synthesis**);
- implementing a change to deliver that vision (**transformation**).

But how do you know if it's working well?

You may be reading about the Finance Journey and thinking it is designed solely for the largest charities. However, this model works brilliantly as a tool for identifying not only the maturity of your charity's finance function but also the resources needed to unlock the numbers. Let me reassure you – this model is great for charities big and small.

None of the levels within the model represent an individual or job role. Indeed, several layers of the model may be included within the job role of a single individual. The people undertaking the different elements of the model don't all have to be employed by your charity either – they may be volunteers.

In a small charity, for example, **processing**, **control** and **reporting** might be undertaken by a bookkeeper; staff and trustees might work together on **analysis**; and the **performance**, **synthesis** and **transformation** levels might be provided by the CEO working with the board.

A larger charity might have several financial roles deployed to undertake the various aspects. For example:
- data-entry personnel processing transactions;
- specific roles overseeing controls (e.g. a financial controller);
- members of the management team (a finance director) and the most senior leaders sitting alongside the chief executive (a chief finance officer) to handle the layers from analysis upwards;
- trustees casting a governance eye over all the levels and asking the big strategic questions about vision and opportunities.

Using the table below, consider each layer of the Finance Journey and mark your charity on a spectrum of 1–10, with 1 being not at all and 10 being exceedingly well. Think about things like the systems you have in place and the performance of your charity at each level.

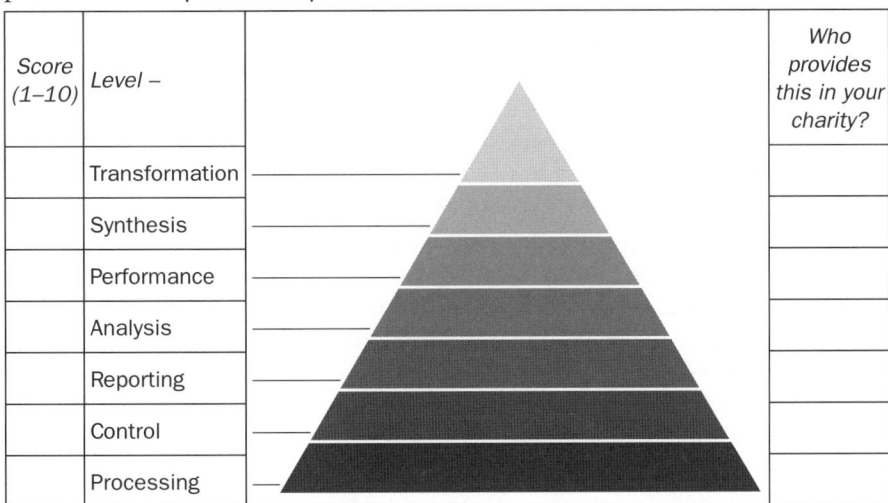

Score (1–10)	Level –		Who provides this in your charity?
	Transformation		
	Synthesis		
	Performance		
	Analysis		
	Reporting		
	Control		
	Processing		

Next think about who undertakes the work in each layer:
- Think about the skills the individuals have.
- Are there training needs and development opportunities (remembering that training is not just for technical skills but can include leadership, influencing and communication skills)?

- Do any challenges or problems you face stem from a mismatch between what your charity needs from its staff and trustees and the roles it has in place?

A successful finance function has many layers, and the knowledge and qualities required for each layer are different. Your charity is likely to require a blend of skills and inputs from a range of different individuals. You may be lucky and have a finance person who is great with strategy and who is also happy to input data, or conversely a bookkeeper with great insight. However, the market rates associated with these different elements mean your charity may benefit from rethinking the resources available to it. You might be paying for someone with strategic skills (which attracts a higher salary than the more transactional activities of processing and controlling) to do it all – meaning you're both spending more for the more operational activities and probably not playing to your employees' strengths. Consider:

- Do you need a single full-time role that spans all layers or a combination of part-time posts? Has too much been packed into your finance role (or roles if you have more than one person)?
- Are staff required to cover all layers or could an outsourcing service be used? Could the 'number-crunching' part be outsourced, and a more strategic brain employed to help staff and trustees unlock the power of the numbers?

If you are a trustee, reflect on whether you spend too much time checking the accuracy of the inputs and the effectiveness of the controls in your charity. This might mean you are failing to think about the 'So what?' and missing opportunities to increase your impact. Trustees can easily get caught up in whether an area of their charity is performing to budget rather than whether the charity is using its resources wisely. For example, I was once asked for advice by a charity that thought it needed to modernise its finance processes. What I discovered was that the processes were fine. The problem was that the trustees were caught up with the detail of the figures and had lost sight of the strategic picture. At a board meeting I observed them spending over 45 minutes poring over really small details in the management information and completely missing the bigger picture. They looked at things line by line rather than in the round. They spent so long talking about the money allocated to computer replacements that they completely missed that there wasn't enough money in the fundraising budget to market their major event so it would attract enough donors. Seeing the bigger picture might have helped them to make better choices about where to spend their resources to deliver for their beneficiaries.

In the next chapter, we will dig around in what effective financial management means for the systems and processes your charity has put in place. We will also look at how financial information can be usefully presented. But I hope in the meantime this chapter has prompted you to think more about the resources your charity deploys on its finance function and how far along the Finance Journey your charity has travelled.

Main chapter takeaways
- Jargon is plentiful in accounting – don't be afraid to ask for explanations.
- A successful finance function has many layers, and the skills and qualities required for each layer are different. Your charity is likely to require a blend of skills and inputs from a range of different individuals.
- Use the Finance Journey to assess your charity's finance function.
- Think about the skills your charity has on the board and executive.
- Ensure you have the right spread of resources, skills and knowledge.

3 The building blocks of financial management

It's all very well to be able to write books, but can you wag your ears? J. M. Barrie

You might be wondering what the author of a children's novel has to do with finance, and the honest answer is nothing! But I love this quote because it sums up for me the essence of what good financial management is about: it's a means to an end and not an end in itself. It also highlights the importance of perspective. It will be fabulous if you can get really technically good with spreadsheets, accounting terms and accounting policies. If you master the numbers like a finance professional, good on you – there can never be too many financial gurus in my book. However, I am not seeking to turn you into an accountant. This chapter is about helping you, whatever your role, to manage your charity's finances as part of the big picture of social change.

The chapter sets out the 'how' of managing finances, from thinking about what resources your charity needs to monitoring how it's doing. It draws heavily on the work of others – such as Rachel Cooper, a trainer specialising in small charities, who delivered the Small Charities Programme for Charity Finance Group (CFG) (a programme delivering training and resources to small charities to build their financial skills; see http://smallcharityfinance.org.uk). The chapter represents a collection of the bits of other people's thinking that landed best with me as a non-finance person. I'll give you my take on and delve into the financial management tools at your charity's disposal, from budgets to management information. I'll also explore different ways of communicating financial data internally, to staff and trustees, that might help your charity to make better decisions and achieve greater impact.

Although this chapter is by its nature inward-looking, focusing on how your charity manages its performance rather than how it tells its story to external stakeholders, try to maintain a sense of perspective and keep your beneficiaries in mind. Don't become obsessed with every cost code and calculation – keep the wider picture firmly in view. Whatever your role might be, your job is to be a competent writer of books and still be able to wag your ears!

> **Outcomes**
> After reading this chapter you will:
> - Understand forecasting and the principles of constructing a good budget
> - Have a grounding in the tools needed to manage your charity's finances, such as cash-flow forecasts and management information
> - Be better equipped to think about effective presentation of financial and related data

Processes, controls and authorities

Before I get into the key tools essential for good financial management, let me share a few thoughts on processes, controls and authorities. In the previous chapter I introduced you to the Finance Journey – a pyramid of skills required for effective financial management. The first level of this pyramid relates to processing. It's important that your charity gets its processes right. Questions to think about include:

- Who is ensuring that all transactions are captured – in other words, that the data in the systems is complete irrespective of whether technology or a physical accounting ledger is being used?
- Are there recognisable steps that staff, or where appropriate volunteers, can apply when spending or raising funds within your charity?
- Who is involved in the conversations across the charity?
- Do these people understand what the limits of their permissions are for committing the charity to expenditure? These are some important questions that underpin all of the topics discussed in this chapter, so try to keep them in mind.

Delegation ... that's what you need

If you're not humming the theme tune to the children's TV show *Record Breakers* ('Dedication' by Roy Castle) then I'm seriously disappointed (and old)! Boards may well be the ultimate decision makers and responsible for charities' performance, but on a practical front the powers that trustees have in relation to what the charity can and cannot do are often delegated to others. Documenting what has been delegated is really important. This document is often referred to as a 'scheme of delegation', and it can deal with matters beyond the budget, such as the power to hire staff. Knowing who can do what is inextricably linked, in my view, to budgeting and monitoring subsequent performance or decisions that may be required. A good scheme of delegation will recognise the distinction between governing, on the one hand, and doing or managing, on the other. It will also clarify the boundary between the two by establishing the extent of the powers and responsibilities delegated to the chief executive, directors and other staff members by the board. A good policy will result in faster, more effective decision-making, quality control of service delivery, and a highly motivated executive and staff.

For example, your scheme might say that the CEO can authorise expenditure up to a certain total spend but other staff can only spend a much lower sum without express authority. In one charity I know of, for big ongoing contracts (such as regular payments to advertisers or external fundraising suppliers), the CEO can authorise up to £50,000. However, for more irregular payments (such as an IT project) the figure is set lower, at £30,000. Setting these levels is about assessing the perceived risk and where your charity's trustees want to draw the line.

Any scheme of delegation must reflect the powers set out in your charity's governing document. When it comes to setting budgets, it is essential that processes are aligned to ensure that staff and trustees understand who has the power to do what and individuals don't overstep their authority. Additional time required for decision-making, alongside thinking about certainty, risks and opportunities, should be factored in.

If your charity doesn't have a scheme of delegation, think about putting one in place. It will definitely help you to solidify the overall picture of your financial (and other) management. Here are some guiding steps:

1. Start with your charity's governing document. Which powers are the trustees allowed to delegate to others and which matters are only for the board to decide upon (known as 'reserved to the board')?
2. Then think about the practicalities of day-to-day management:
   a. How much can they spend without coming back to the board for permission?
   b. Does your charity have premises? If so, what are the limits of the team's authorities on negotiating terms for major contracts or leases?
   c. What about hiring staff – do the trustees require sign-off on new posts or is there greater flexibility as long as an agreed total wages budget is not exceeded?
3. Are there elements of your charity's business model that would function more smoothly if the staff could make more decisions? For example, CFG is a membership organisation and the trustees have delegated the power to admit new members to the executive and staff. The alternative of the board examining each new member's application would add no value and delay the process unnecessarily.

It's important to have processes and understand who is allowed to do what. Staff and trustees should also reflect on the adequacy of the controls that are in place for the various areas that might impact the use of and access to funds – whether dealing with how the charity's post is opened, checking that what's spent on a 'company' credit card is all appropriate expenditure, or deciding how many bank signatories your charity should have.

I am not going to run through those wider processes or controls as that would take us into the nuts and bolts of finance, beyond the scope of this book. If you are interested, however, the Charity Commission for England and Wales guidance *Internal Financial Controls for Charities* (CC8) gives some comprehensive information. Instead, I am going to concentrate on the principles to apply and questions you might like to ask irrespective of the processes and controls your charity has in place. And I'll throw in some suggestions to get you thinking about how to decide on appropriate processes and controls within your charity. So, let's take a look at the first of the tools in your financial management toolkit.

Budget basics

What is a budget and why does it matter? I'd describe a budget as the financial expression of the things – money, staff, rent, etc. – required to operate for a set period of time or for a specific project. It gives the best guess of how much money will come in from all sources and how much money will be spent in total to deliver your plans.

Translating your charity's strategy and plans into monetary terms helps you identify whether you can afford to deliver them. It also helps you to allocate resources appropriately, from staff time to thinking about where your office is located, and can aid tracking of performance. Finally, it may be required by your charity's funders. In the most successful organisations, there is a clear link that flows from the high-level strategic picture to the detailed activities expressed in the budget.

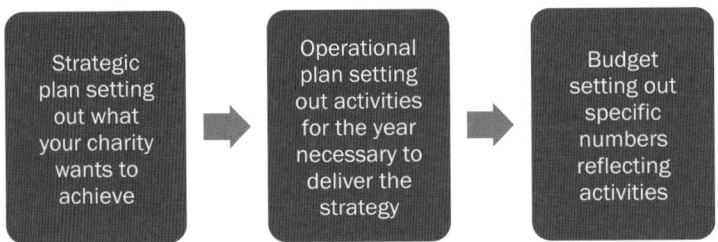

It can also be helpful to model the possible outcomes of an activity. For example, if you are planning a new activity, your charity could imagine how various scenarios might play out, so as to be able to understand its possible financial outcomes. Being realistic about these scenarios, rather than theoretical, can help you to refine your numbers.

The key element often identified when budgeting is ineffective is a disconnection between planning and budgeting processes. Budgets produced prior to detailed plans are unlikely to accurately reflect the needs and intentions of teams. Think of this as a cycle. The flowchart below sets out a thought process for starting to make budget discussions.

3. The building blocks of financial management

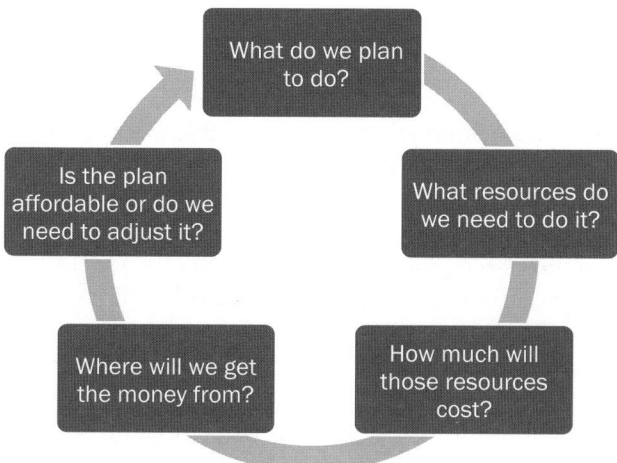

If you have multiple teams, it's important that each one feeds into the process. How might you gather views and ensure you're consistently receiving the right information? Your charity's finance team, if you have one, might want to provide templates for your other teams to fill in which break down anticipated income and expenditure into manageable units reflecting the structure of the financial information in the underlying accounts. Each team should complete the templates in the same way so that information is consistently collected. If this is your approach, it's preferable if the template prompts teams to think about *what* the numbers represent, perhaps using the questions from the cycle above to help staff avoid the temptation to simply bung down a few figures. So, for example, the fundraising team needs to say how much the annual fundraising dinner will generate in donations, how much it will cost to advertise and how much it will cost to run. This will help you to decide if it's worth the money being spent on it.

Whether they use a template or not, those submitting their figures for inclusion in the budget should make notes on the assumptions behind the figures. Specifically, they should capture what has been included and why, whether there are any uncertainties behind their assumptions and any other commentary. It's like a maths exam – show the working out!

A charity I work with always starts its budgeting process by discussing wider assumptions about the economy, the funding climate, the likely cost of inflation, what is happening to the local authority's budget and so on. The executive then discusses their assumptions about where they are likely to get funding from and what the competition might be, what staff turnover they might have, what equipment might need to be replaced, how much of an increase in salary they think is likely or appropriate, and so on. These high-level assumptions are then presented to the trustees, who decide whether they agree with them. Only once the assumptions have been approved does the charity put the details of the numbers into its budget. This approach works because it means the trustees don't need to get involved in the detail: as long as the budget follows the assumptions agreed, it will provide boundaries that inform the detailed discussions and, when the staff present the budget, the board will already understand the rationale behind it. In this charity the executive and staff also produce a budget paper providing a narrative that explains the thinking behind all areas of income and expenditure. The paper also includes the underlying assumptions on which the budget is based, information on risks, and any information relating to sums already secured (for example, in bookings) and costs that can be varied if required.

Using some kind of template and/or getting the trustees to approve a set of budget assumptions can make the process of agreeing a budget and negotiating or amending the figures to reach an agreed position that much easier. It is essential to retain this information for future use; knowing what people were thinking and why certain assumptions were made the year before, when setting the budget, can help you to reflect on whether your charity's plans were overly optimistic or pessimistic. It also provides a record of the thinking that underpinned the numbers so you can make logical decisions throughout the year that strike a balance between your aspirations and the resources available to you.

While a budget helps you understand where you want to get to and what that might look like, you should treat it as a road map that informs, not an instruction manual that dictates every step. Your charity's approach should be akin to how you use a sat nav when unforeseen things happen when driving – such as a road being closed unexpectedly, heavy traffic slowing you down or needing to find a garage because someone needs the loo. If you used your plotted route as a diktat and felt bound to it, that would make no sense at all, would it? Just like when you use a satnav, you want to be able to flex, to find a way round, to accommodate things you haven't predicted. Because you can almost guarantee the budget will have started to diverge from reality before the ink is even dry.

Although most frequently your charity will have information from past activities to give a good guide or starting point for what the figures might look like, life is always surrounded by a degree of uncertainty, volatility and change. Sometimes you will need to start completely from scratch, with a totally blank sheet, because you are seeking to provide a new activity or service (known as zero-based budgeting).

However accurate your charity's budgeting becomes – however closely what was planned matches reality – remember that it should always be your charitable objects that drive your actions, not trying to deliver what's in the budget. Don't let that budget tail wag the charity dog! Act or refrain from acting because it is the right thing to do strategically, not because your budget dictates it.

Increasing the accuracy of your budget
Although I have told you your budget will, almost certainly, be wrong, it is of course helpful to try to be as accurate in your planning as possible! There is a risk of over ambition – of thinking it's easier to generate resources than is actually the case – or conversely of overestimating the costs and holding back on charitable activities unnecessarily as a consequence. There is a risk that

costs might be incurred for one team and income arise with another, which will need to be managed. Ensure that both sides (the income and expenditure) are married up so you know whether something is a cost to your charity or generates income. Recognise timing differences (investment in one year might not generate income in that year), and factor in all the real costs and benefits in terms of staff time, expenditure and income. This will enable you to make better decisions as to whether something is a good use of charitable funds.

I once heard of a charity that had a number of different ways of raising funds: corporate fundraising, legacy fundraising, event fundraising and fundraising from the public. As a result of not marrying up the costs and income in its budget with the costs and income for those different activities, it didn't spot that although fundraising overall brought in more than the charity spent, corporate fundraising specifically was making a massive loss. Once staff made those connections, the picture became clear. The charity concluded that its resources could be used more effectively and stopped corporate fundraising completely. This freed up staff time to focus on more productive fundraising activities and reduced the costs associated with fundraising, with the positive consequence of increasing the overall profitability of the fundraising team.

The importance of people
The accuracy of a budget, but more importantly the likelihood of plans being successful, can be increased by involving the right people across your charity in the process.

But who are the right people, you might ask? Personally, I would include anyone who is involved in deciding what your charity wants to deliver and anyone who has a fundamental impact on whether it can be delivered. For example, CFG's events team decides what events we can realistically put on during a year – their involvement is critical. Those involved in marketing CFG's events also have an impact on whether the events will be successful – in terms of both deciding on the resources necessary to promote the programme of events and assessing the likelihood of generating income – and so are included in the process of budgeting.

Having representation from those operating on the front line or dealing with the trickiest parts of your charity's activities – not just the finance people – is essential to a good process. Budgeting should not be carried out in secret or just by the finance function. The more open and collaborative your charity's process, the more likely it is to be accurate. Consequently, drafting a budget well might take longer than you think, and requires consultation time for drafting, negotiation, renegotiation and approval. For example, your executive might want to start in the third quarter of your financial year and agree what the principles should be (whether they need to produce a break-even budget; what the attitudes to spending, retaining or building reserves might be; whether there are plans to increase headcount; whether a big project is on the horizon; etc.). Getting a first draft of the budget together early in quarter four of your financial year gives you time to make adjustments before the next financial year. Start planning way before your charity's year end and, ideally, finalise your plans before the start of the new financial year.

To get the best out of the process, the role of your finance team (or finance person if your charity doesn't have a team) should be to:
- manage the process;
- provide technical advice and support;
- test assumptions;
- provide checks and balances;
- make sure the budget is complete (i.e. includes all income and expenditure).

In terms of the first two points in this list, it is not the job of a finance team to sit in a darkened room making the numbers stack up and then present the budget as a done deal. And it's not a great idea for a finance team to receive a set of figures generated by different departments of your charity, only to go to work on the figures with a red pen and a healthy dose of cynicism.

When it comes to testing assumptions and providing checks and balances (the third and fourth points), your charity's finance team should be looking for whether there are new activities and for any major differences from previous budgets. If something is new, there will be no track record against which to assess assumptions about resources needed. However, there may be other similar activities, products or services that can act as guides. These can help your finance team determine how much confidence or certainty there is, and therefore how reliable the assumptions on which the figures are based might be. Perhaps there are other charities that could provide benchmarks for your assumptions. Further questions for your finance team to consider are how much income has been secured or expenditure committed (because these are less moveable than purely speculative or planned numbers), and what contingency or 'plan B' your charity has in place in case plans don't play out as anticipated. This will help decide how much confidence or certainty exists for your plans as well as understanding what the consequences of a back-up plan might be if actions need to be adjusted. Finally, when it comes to ensuring the budget is complete, your finance team, or whoever is responsible for bringing together the various contributions (sometimes the CEO), should check that all costs are provided for in the budget, which costs are variable and which will stay the same, which costs will increase your charity's commitments for future years, and how quickly might a commitment to incur a cost (for example, a contract) be ended or new income be brought in. When it comes to support costs, the team or person bringing together the budget makes sure everything is included: staff, pensions, office, utilities, IT, rates and taxes.

Once a first draft of the budget has been created, the executive (usually the most senior team – the CEO and directors if you have them) should interrogate the evidence supporting the assumptions relating to both income and expenditure:

- How robust are the assumptions?
- Do the assumptions have a spread of different levels of certainty, or is everything either a sure thing or a complete unknown?
- If everything is certain, is there more that could be done (i.e. is the team playing it a bit too safe)? Or, conversely, if everything is completely unknown, is there too much uncertainty, suggesting that your charity is not being realistic?

Consideration should also be given to whether plans are ongoing. For example, will things that happened last year be repeated in the coming year? Think about the impact of future years too. Something may be affordable this year, but if the cost is ongoing and the income is not, how will the gap be managed?

If the budget does not stack up, now is the time to make adjustments. Remember the cycle shown in the figure on page 25? If the budget doesn't appear to show the outcome staff and trustees would be happy to have at the year end, revisit the decisions being taken and whether different choices would be more appropriate.

Whatever the process you follow in your charity, I can't stress this enough: give it plenty of time.

The importance of communication
We've talked about the contents of the budget, who should be involved in developing it and that it can take a lot of time to get right. There is a further element in making a budget work for your charity and that is communication. Ensuring that the information is clear and understandable to the different audiences who need to use it – general staff, 'budget holders' (people who have

authority to spend money), executive team members, trustees and so on – can play a huge part in the successful financial management of your charity.

Think about how you might share the information, both to the staff and to the trustees (whether or not you are part of one of these groups). Will it be divided up by team, by project, by funder, by theme (for example, people, property and services) or by charitable activity? Think about the headings you use in your budget to describe what the income or expenditure consists of, and how these relate to the format that will be shown in your charity's management information and year-end trustees' annual report and accounts. Aligning the budget with these other documents can save work later on. If income and expenditure appear under the same headings across all of your documents, you won't confuse people by making them think they are comparing apples and oranges!

Think about how different stakeholders might use the information. Would a chart or table be easier to understand than a long list of numbers? Make space for commentary or explanatory narrative or images that might indicate if something is new or different from a previous year, or perhaps has a higher level of uncertainty or risk. Where relevant consider putting current performance of activities against the budget for context.

Let's look at the budget of our fictitious charity, the Society of Oneirocritics, as a table of numbers showing this year's budget, last year's actuals and last year's budget. The commentary gives a little insight into levels of confidence and where the numbers come from. I would expect a fuller explanation in the underlying supporting papers.

The Society of Oneirocritics budget

	This year's budget	Last year's actuals	Last year's budget	Commentary
Income				
Grants				
Moon Foundation	30,000	25,000	22,500	Grant secured but ending next year
Dreams Trust	20,000	18,000	18,000	Commitment given over phone to carry on supporting 'as long as we need'
Donations	14,500	15,000	16,000	Expected drop in donations
Online courses and guides				
Introduction to Dreams	24,500	23,000	22,500	Bookings ahead of budget in current financial year; high confidence

3. The building blocks of financial management

Advanced Dream Interpretation	16,000	15,000	15,000	Increased fee but anticipate reduction in number of bookings
Guide 2 Dreams	20,000	19,000	17,000	Increased sales
TOTAL INCOME	**125,000**	**115,000**	**111,000**	
Expenditure				
Staff costs*	(100,000)	(96,000)	(95,000)	2% cost-of-living award proposed but not reflected in these figures
Premises	(12,500)	(12,500)	(12,500)	Closing office is likely to give rise to costs in current year but expect savings in subsequent years (as not yet certain, such impact is not reflected in these figures)
IT**	(4,000)	(3,800)	(2,500)	Investment in IT needed for remote work: estimate included
Other	(1,500)	(1,000)	(1,000)	Materials require refresh and costs reflected in these figures
TOTAL EXPENDITURE	**(118,000)**	**(113,300)**	**(111,000)**	
Surplus/(deficit)	**7,000**	**1,700**	**0**	

* For simplicity I have ignored pensions, National Insurance, etc. but a real budget would need to include these costs.

** For simplicity I have assumed these figures include any depreciation (the reduction of the recorded cost of a fixed asset year on year, over its useful lifetime, until it reaches zero value) of tangible assets.

On the income side, if you were looking at a budget for last year of £22,500 against a figure for this year of £30,000 for the Moon Foundation line, you might wonder whether it was realistic. The commentary informs you that the £30,000 is already secured. However, it is worth noting that this funding will come to an end in the next financial year. The Dreams Trust income looks pretty secure and stable. Looking at the Society's fundraising (donations) aspirations, following a year-on-year decline, the budget for this year is lower than that for last year. However, this might be one area that is revisited if the resources required don't match the aspirations. Can a new campaign be put together to drive greater income for example?

When looking at the planned courses and events it is clear that adjustments have been made in setting the prices of the courses, but the team think that this might result in fewer bookings for the advanced course. It may be that greater effort is focused on the introductory course because it is more cost effective and less price sensitive.

It's a Nightmare with the Numbers

On the costs the first thing to notice is the expenditure is shown in brackets. This is a common way of showing the negative number – but sometimes these are shown as a positive figure and/or in red. You might be familiar with people talking about 'being in the red' or 'in the black', meaning they are in overdraft or in credit. This is a good way to remember this approach if the numbers for your charity are displayed using colour. Looking at the figures, this charity, like many others, is terminating its office lease. As the commentary shows, in the short term, there are likely to be charges and costs of closing down the office, but in future years there will likely be a drop. There is not enough information yet to include any new figures in the budget, so those looking at the figures need to be on their guard that this is an area of high uncertainty where the numbers will be subject to change. Finally, the charity anticipates modest investments in technology and refreshing materials. It has been possible to put figures on these expenses, and the detail is included in the budget.

Now let's look at some examples of different ways to display the same information so you can consider what might work best in your charity and what you prefer.

Example 1

A bar chart like the one below can help you to show lots of information at once, including a breakdown of the total income and expenditure, and the major types of costs or income. This approach can help you to spot changes between different years when you include data relating to other years.

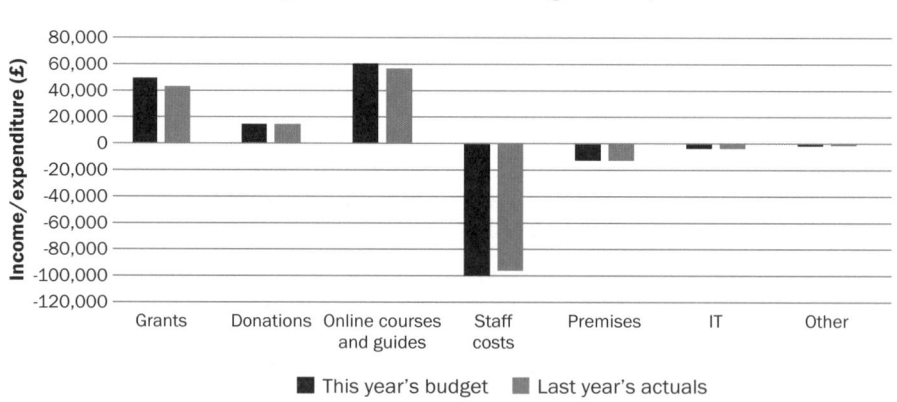

The visual display shows you very easily that income and expenditure are growing, that grants remain a significant part of income), and that it is important for the online courses to do well. It also shows that the staff costs continue to be the biggest outlay for the Society.

3. The building blocks of financial management

Example 2

The same information can be displayed in a table. A simple table can summarise the top-level income and expenditure and highlight your charity's overall anticipated position against the previous year's performance if breakdowns of each line aren't needed. Also think about combining different ways of displaying data – both charts and tables used together could help stakeholders to understand your charity's financial status.

The Society of Oneirocritics budget comparison

	This year's budget	Last year's actuals
Income		
Grants	50,000	43,000
Donations	14,500	15,000
Online courses and guides	60,500	57,000
Total income	125,000	115,000
Expenditure		
Staff costs	100,000	96,000
Premises	12,500	12,500
IT	4,000	3,800
Other	1,500	1,000
Total expenditure	118,000	113,300
Surplus/(deficit)	7,000	1,700

It's a Nightmare with the Numbers

Example 3
Combining income and expenditure in the same bar chart can help you to identify whether your charity is seeking to grow or is reducing its activities. Showing more than one year together (rather than just the budgeted position for the present year) can highlight trends.

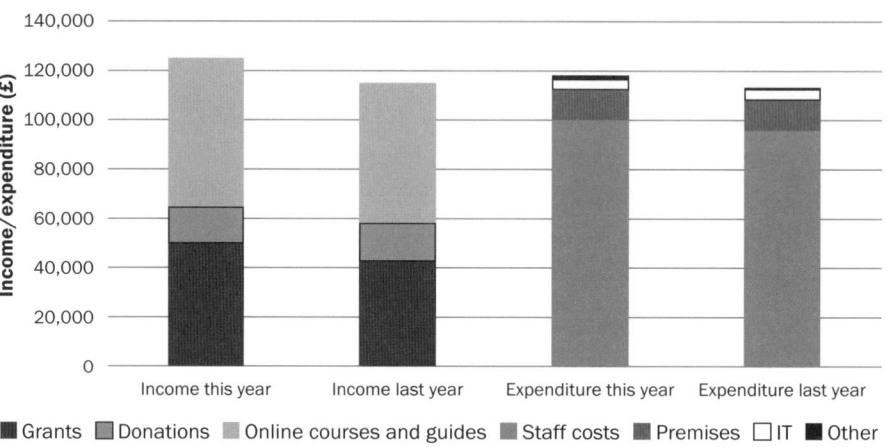

Management information must-haves

You may use or be familiar with the phrase 'management accounts' and be expecting me to use it here. However, it means different things to different people, so it isn't always very useful. In some charities, the term sweeps up the full range of information – from forecasts and cash flows to wider key performance indicators (KPIs). For the purposes of this book, I am referring to the financial reports produced by management, often on a monthly or quarterly basis, that provide accounting and financial information to assist your charity in determining how it is performing and how it should be managed. Therefore, in this book, I have adopted the term 'management information'.

Management information usually goes into much more detail than the statutory accounts your charity is required to submit to your regulator and/or Companies House (the sole registrar of UK companies; see www.gov.uk/government/organisations/companies-house). They are also produced for a different purpose. Management information is not required to follow the Charities Statement of Recommended Practice (SORP) (see chapter 1) – there is no fixed format your charity must observe when producing them.

It is important that what you produce is useful and drives decision-making, so that if you need to adjust your plans, you can take action. Those adjustments might be to ensure that your charity remains viable or they might be about seizing opportunities to really soar. Much of the information included will, like in your statutory accounts, be historical and tell you about past performance. However, imagine driving a car. As you drive down the road, you check the rear-view mirrors. Now think about trying to drive that car only looking behind you. You would soon crash, wouldn't you? So

3. The building blocks of financial management

management information is like rear-view mirrors – it provides detail that helps you process driving conditions, but you must always remain focused on the road ahead.

Who uses management information?
If management information is produced and circulated but then just gathers dust, effort is wasted. Make sure that it is discussed and debated, and that it enables staff (and, where relevant, trustees) to draw conclusions on what's going on and why.

For your finance people, management information is a key part of their role and helps them to get a detailed picture of the state of your charity's finances so that they can highlight areas for decisions or action.

For your directors, managers and those delivering projects, management information is vital to understanding the overall finances of your charity, including resourcing and capacity within your teams, and influencing, informing and supporting decision makers. For these people, management information is an opportunity to see a financial expression of what is playing out in their areas of responsibility, in the context of the charity's wider performance.

Trustees don't always see complete management information. They may receive a different pack of information to the executive that includes a simple summary of financial data, with the detailed figures being made available to them on request if they want to ask questions. What is included varies from charity to charity. I have sat on boards that saw little detail from month to month and boards that wanted to see everything, all the time – such as cash-flow forecasts (projections telling you how much cash is going to be paid into and paid out of your bank account in any given period), a draft balance sheet (a snapshot of how funds are held at a particular point in time) and a draft of the charity's statement of financial activities (a table in the accounts which sets out the income and expenditure in various areas). (For more detailed explanations of these terms, do refer to the glossary.)

In many charities, instead of (or in addition to) the trustees receiving a summary, detailed management information may be provided to an individual (potentially the treasurer or the chair of the finance committee) or members of a sub-committee charged with keeping a closer eye on financial performance. Using a sub-committee in this way can promote a good understanding of the overall finances among the members and it can help the staff to work through operational decisions with a trusted group, usually including experts. But always remember that all trustees are responsible for the decisions taken (see chapter 1) so the use of a sub-committee should not be an excuse for the rest of the board to disengage from the finances.

Who management information is circulated to is also entirely within your charity's gift. Do all teams need to see the information or just a few? What level of staff will usefully be able to engage with the information? My advice is to include anyone who is responsible for delivering the work that brings in and spends the money. They need to understand the context in which your charity is operating.

Whatever your charity's approach, have clarity of purpose when sharing information. It should be clear who is being asked to do what, and what they are required to do with the information they receive. Be clear on whether the recipient is being asked to make a specific decision, debate options, offer advice or perhaps approve a proposal.

Good management information enables you to spot trends, identify one-off changes and get ahead of problems. In other words, it allows you to predict problems so you can avoid them and spot opportunities so you can seize them.

Marvellous management information
What's in the best management information? As mentioned earlier when discussing the importance of communication, good management information will mirror the structure and content of the budget (which the staff and trustees should be familiar with). This structure is then populated with the figures known at the point of producing the information (known as actuals). It compares the real income and expenditure against budget, identifying any differences (known as variances), and provides a narrative that puts the information into context. This narrative should include the information's relationships to relevant data, such as the trends in a previous financial year, or other information which could help stakeholders to understand what is really going on.

For example, consider this scenario: the plan is to carry out 12 training courses at a delivery cost of £2,000 each, so the budget is set at £24,000. The management information shows that expenditure currently stands at £23,000 so there is a variance of £1,000 (less spent). This may seem like a success. But if it actually cost £23,000 to deliver only seven courses (versus the twelve planned), the position may be very different. This could be a positive or negative thing – those seven courses might have accommodated more delegates and generated greater income. It is important to use the information to understand what is happening and not to track performance against the budgeted figures.

Good management information is accurate and up to date. It strikes a balance between accuracy and timeliness. Greater accuracy can take longer to achieve, and that may undermine the usefulness and purpose of the information. For instance, if it takes the finance team most of the month to produce accurate information, thereby reducing the time available to bring in necessary changes, has the right balance been struck? Don't let the best be the enemy of the good: strike a balance so you have good-enough information.

Finance professionals and other staff – as well as the trustees or committee members who see your management information – should be able to identify which key areas require their focus. And your management information should meet the needs of the people using it, delivering what they want and need to know. Your charity should determine the most helpful presentation of information, to give maximum accessibility to the widest audience. Just like with budgets, charts or colours can help staff and trustees to identify areas that are performing outside expectations. Some charities like to use emojis to communicate visually whether something is great, terrible, worrying or puzzling. They won't be everyone's cup of tea, but traffic lights, arrows and colour-coding are all frequently used and can prove very illuminating. Also bear in mind how the users of this information might access it – will they be viewing it on screen or in print? Are the font sizes, styles or colours going to impede access? Have you considered providing 'alt text' explanations of figures (i.e. descriptions for people who are blind or have limited vision)? Expressing numbers as percentages of the budget with any implications – such as '£100,000 is 85% of the budgeted income (and we're only in the second quarter of the financial year)' – might bring out the information and aid understanding.

Experiment with different ways of sharing the information. Ask users what is more or less helpful. Remember the key word here is 'management'. If management information doesn't help staff (and, where relevant, trustees) to manage, it is just a waste of time.

Similarly, the numbers are not enough. Your rule of thumb should be 'no numbers without the narrative'. I've looked at figures as a trustee where no comments, explanations or context were provided on why a figure was the way it was. This is really unhelpful! Something may look positive taking the raw numbers at face value, but there may be underlying information the management team or staff know which identifies a worrying trend. Think back to the Society's budget – the £30,000 grant from the Moon Foundation looks good when plotted against the previous year's grant of £25,000, but we know that it will stop the next year. In your management information, you might consider including commentary about discussions with new possible sources of grants, or whether the Dreams Trust (the Society's other grant funder) might be happy to extend its support to fill that future hole. Unless such information is shared, it can be nigh on impossible to spot a problem or get comfort from the numbers. Conversely, there may be figures that strike horror into the reader at first sight that are actually far less concerning once the commentary is added!

I can give examples of both from my day job. A few years ago, at CFG we were showing a decent surplus by midway through the year. If they had just been given the top line, the trustees might have concluded this was positive news. However, when you looked at the commentary, there was a potential problem. Marketing was underspent and the lion's share of the surplus had arisen from vacancies across the charity. Both these facts pointed to a risk that we would be unable to secure income from events and membership. This prompted a discussion about ways to bring in additional resources. In the other direction, I have seen management information that showed income from grants was significantly down year to date. This would have caused alarm without additional context from the staff. The executive were able to share with the trustees that agreement in principle had been given from a grant maker for financial support and that this was likely to be confirmed in the near future – thus making the picture a positive one.

Making sense of management information

When looking at a set of management information, you may find the following questions useful. They are lifted from *It's a Battle on the Board* by Debra Allcock Tyler:

- Is there a big gap between budgeted income and actual income? Is that gap positive or negative? If so, you will want to understand why the gap is there.
- Is there a big gap between the budgeted expenditure and the actual expenditure? Is that gap positive or negative? Again, you will want to understand why the gap is there.
- Is there anything that looks odd? For example, has there been a drop in income in one area but not a drop in expenditure related to that same area?
- Are there patterns? For example, are the same income lines down each month or do they vary? If the lines are the same, what is the reason for that?
- Are the forecasts against budget positive or negative?
- Overall, does income exceed expenditure? If it doesn't, was that budgeted?
- Are there any areas of particular risk in the forecast?
- What plans does the executive have to manage the situation going forward?

Forecasting foundations

Forecasting can be an integral part of management information or it can stand alone. You can also do it for your whole charity or a specific project. When I think of forecasting, I think about someone gesticulating in front of a map of the British Isles covered in images of clouds, wind and pollen counts! Much like the weather forecast, financial forecasting is about predicting what will happen within a specific period of time – perhaps a month, a quarter, a year or the duration of a specific project – based on what is already known. Forecasting is a tool which helps you understand how something is performing and whether you need to make changes to ensure successful delivery (whether of a specific project or your charity's overall plans) or to make sure your charity has enough cash to meet its needs.

When I talked about budgeting, I explained the importance of understanding when things are likely to happen, what levels of certainty exist, and whether activities are continuations from a previous year or entirely new. So, if the budget is what the team thought might happen, a forecast updates that to show what did happen and what you now think the future holds.

Therefore, typically, a forecast will start from the actuals (what you have spent or generated) and be compared to the original budget. What went before may help you to predict what will come, but this is more an art than a science! As a result, when you (or anyone else) are looking at a forecast, you need to think about how accurate it is before making decisions. The credibility of forecasting can be built over time. For example, if a past forecast was pretty accurate compared to what happened, this may provide a level of comfort that the person doing the forecasting took into account the right factors in their predictions. The converse can be true – if past forecasts have been way off (perhaps being too optimistic), this could undermine confidence in future forecasts. There may be areas of activity for which confidence is greater because, for example, your charity has been given a commitment to support or a strong indication a contract will be extended. Other areas may have more uncertainties or be based on more assumptions.

As part of budgeting, your charity might have modelled a range of scenarios – for example, you might have invested in a new fundraising campaign with a different tone of voice and approach, believing that it will generate far better returns this year. In such a case, you might have mapped out the possible outcomes of your investment as part of the budgeting process. You might then have used this modelling to underpin assumptions in a forecast (as well as helping the executive and staff track how those plans are performing). It is important that the same level of curiosity and challenge that accompanies the creation of a budget is present when considering or creating a forecast. Ask questions of the numbers and the explanations given for them.

When looking at your charity's financial performance as a whole, a forecast will ordinarily extend to the financial year end. However, how frequently the executive and/or the trustees want forecasts to be created should be dictated by what is useful to your charity. Some charities will forecast a year ahead from wherever they are (taking information over the financial year end if they are already part way through the financial year) in order to give them a better understanding of the health and performance of their charity on a rolling basis. There are no rules on when or for what period your charity should forecast, but the certainty available to you (or lack of it) can act as a guide to help you decide what will be of greatest practical use. Just like with producing management information, do your forecasts too frequently and lots of time will be spent trying to make predictions – time that could be spent on your charity's activities. Do them too infrequently and there may not be enough time to implement the changes. This is what forecasting is all about.

Let's go back to the Society – what might its mid-year forecast (and the end of the second quarter) look like?

The Society of Oneirocritics second quarter forecast

	Last year's actuals	Year-to-date Sep actuals	This year's budget	Forecast to year end	Commentary
Income					
Grants					
Moon Foundation	25,000	15,000	30,000	30,000	Second Moon Foundation grant due shortly so on track
Dreams Trust	18,000	20,000	20,000	20,000	
Donations	15,000	12,000	14,500	15,000	Expected drop in donations looks unlikely
Online courses and guides					
Introduction to Dreams	23,000	23,000	24,500	25,500	Bookings ahead of anticipated numbers
Advanced Dream Interpretation	15,000	14,250	16,000	15,000	Increased fee appears to have led to a reduction in bookings compared to same period last year
Guide 2 Dreams	19,000	11,000	20,000	25,000	Increased sales compared to same period last year
TOTAL INCOME	115,000	95,250	125,000	130,500	
Expenditure					
Staff costs	(96,000)	(51,000)	(100,000)	(102,000)	Additional 2% cost-of-living award applied from 1 April
Premises	(12,500)	(10,500)	(12,500)	(14,500)	Costs of closing office; expect savings in subsequent years
IT	(3,800)	(4,000)	(4,000)	(6,000)	Investment in IT for remote work
Other	(1,000)	(900)	(1,500)	(2,000)	Materials require refresh
TOTAL EXPENDITURE	(113,300)	(66,400)	(118,000)	(124,500)	
TOTAL	1,700	28,850	7,000	6,000	

Looking at different lines of the forecast in isolation can tell very different stories. For example, the income on its own implies the year-end position is forecast to be slightly ahead of the budget (at £130,500 forecast versus £125,000 budgeted). If we just looked at the year-to-date figures, we might assume that the year's performance is well ahead and that the Society is on track for a bumper year: it is only two quarters in but has already brought in 76% of the full year's budget and at this point in the year has a healthy surplus (£28,850 versus £7,000 budgeted). However, looking at the forecast's bigger picture shows that the executive believes things are going to end slightly behind the budget overall (£6,000 forecast versus £7,000 budgeted). The prediction that increasing the fee for the advanced course would decrease the number of bookings appears to have proven correct, but the introductory course is performing better than expected. Unexpectedly, the income from donations has held up. Perhaps the trustees and executive might think about whether there is an opportunity to drive further income to improve the year-end position and/or perhaps reduce the fee for the advanced course (i.e. subsidise it) if the charity concludes it is important to the charity's mission. These are levers that the executive and trustees can pull to attempt to change the outcome.

The expenditure side shows that there will, as predicted, be costs resulting from closing the office and making wider adjustments to the charity's capacity for remote working (increase to £14,500 for office costs and to £6,000 for IT investment for the full year). These are one-off costs and appear to be set to reduce in future years. But the trustees and executive would want to ensure that the expenditure didn't balloon and that there were sufficient funds in reserve (see chapter 5) to cover any shortfalls. Additionally, the costs associated with materials refresh appear to have been underestimated during the budget and are now set to cost an additional £500 bringing the costs to £2,000. Fortunately, at this point the income looks set to adequately cover most of those additional costs.

Although a finance team may include an element of prediction or forecasting every month as part of their management information, an exercise to forecast the year-end position is, in my experience, ideally undertaken quarterly at most. There is an exception – in times of crisis or when significant events that have a financial impact on your charity happen, it can be really informative to take stock. However, generally speaking, quarterly forecasting is sufficient. For example, my organisation, CFG, receives much of its income early in the financial year through membership fees. Therefore, at the end of quarter one, we can have a reasonably good view of the impact of our renewals process on the full year's figures. So quarterly forecasting, particularly following the first quarter, is of most use to us. A charity that has a major fundraising event, like Comic Relief or the Royal British Legion (with its Poppy Appeal), may find the timing of a forecast is less about financial periods and more driven by the specific event. The success of an event or campaign that produces substantial income may well set the tone for the rest of the year or indeed plans for future years.

Much like budgeting, forecasting is a best guess – but based on a bit more fact. As your charity progresses through the year, you will have more and more real knowledge of how different elements of income and expenditure have performed (the actuals) and therefore will be able to reduce the room for error in your forecasting. You will also have information which enables staff and trustees to determine future income and expenditure with a better degree of certainty. For example, talks with a funder may be going well, or conversely training courses might not have been selling. The closer to the end of the financial year you are, the more certainty should, in theory, be contained in your forecasts.

Forecasting is also about being realistic. As with budgeting, there may be a temptation to be overly optimistic – or pessimistic – about how things are performing. In theory, the more forecasting is done, the better the finance team or person should get at it. As with the approach to budgeting, it may help to provide departments with a template. It is sensible to reflect the same titles, headings or groupings that are used in your budget, as people should be familiar with them, making it easier for people to provide the right information. Again, including the relevant people from across your charity is important, but the forecast shouldn't be made into a labour-intensive slog. Make it light touch and keep in mind what level of accuracy is good enough.

One specific type of forecast is a cash-flow forecast.

Cash-flow crucials

When people use the generic term 'cash flow', they typically mean a cash-flow projection or forecast. However, it is worth mentioning that there are two types of cash flow:

- **A cash-flow statement:** This is a statement providing information about how your charity uses cash (required by the SORP).
- **A cash-flow projection or forecast:** This describes how cash flows in and out of your charity, usually by month.

Let's consider these in turn.

SORP statement of cash flows

Some charities will have to produce a cash-flow statement as part of their SORP compliance because they are bigger charities. The 'statement of cash flows' provides information about how your charity uses the cash generated by its activities and about changes in cash and cash equivalents that you hold.

What are cash equivalents? The SORP says they are short-term assets that are easy to convert into cash (otherwise called 'liquid') where it is known how much they will convert to, and where that amount is unlikely to change. It identifies short-term assets as ones which will 'mature' (come to an end) within three months of your charity getting them.

A statement of cash flows can also provide information that is helpful in assessing the financial health of your charity in respect of its liquidity (i.e. the ease with which it can pay its bills or spending commitments, such as grants in the short term) and its underlying solvency (i.e. its ability to meet longer-term obligations as they fall due).

The statement must analyse cash flows using three standard headings: 'Operating Activities' (the things your charity does to produce income), 'Investing Activities' (acquisitions and disposals of investments) and 'Financing Activities' (bank loans, overdrafts, etc.). So, the SORP statement of cash flows is not a cash-flow forecast – it is a more prescriptive layout of certain types of money and reflects your financial year.

A cash-flow forecast
A cash-flow forecast contains more detailed information, plotting expected cash in and cash out for a period that the staff or trustees wish to monitor. It helps you to keep track of whether there is enough cash to pay the bills.

I always urge charities that don't routinely undertake cash-flow forecasting to add it into their toolkit for financial management, because it is so helpful in managing financial risks. This is especially important in times of change, where there is a reasonable degree of risk that your charity will be short of money or where income and/or expenditure is highly variable.

A cash-flow forecast aims to predict how much money your charity will have in the bank at any given point over a number of days, weeks or months. You have complete freedom to determine the frequency of your cash-flow forecasting. When things are incredibly tight – for example, if a funding stream is suddenly lost or your charity suffers an unexpected cost – the executive and trustees may want to monitor your cash flow daily or weekly. In more comfortable times, your charity will probably forecast cash far less often.

Your charity doesn't need to be or have a finance professional at its disposal to create a cash-flow forecast either. The process is simple:
1. Take your budget and split out the receipts and payments you anticipate receiving over the year into a month-by-month scheme. Ignore non-cash items, such as depreciation.
2. Taking your current bank balance, add the money you expect to receive and subtract the money you expect to spend in the first month, to get your expected bank balance at the end of that month.
3. Repeat for each subsequent month to chart your cash flow for the period for which you want to forecast.

You will probably want to split out material items, such as a training course that brings in a lot of money, and/or group together other amounts which don't have such a big impact on your cash flow. Periodically, reforecasts can be done, adjusting the predictions to take account of actual movements in cash. Cash flows can also be used to look ahead beyond the year end – perhaps to the following year – to give a better understanding of the cash flows on a rolling basis.

Let's look at the Society's cash-flow forecast at the end of its second quarter. This illustrative example shows some actual receipts and some projections to the financial year end.

It's a Nightmare with the Numbers

The Society of Oneirocritics cash-flow forecast

	Apr	May	Jun	Jul	Aug	Sep	Oct	Nov	Dec	Jan	Feb	Mar
	Actual	**Actual**	**Actual**	**Actual**	**Actual**	**Actual**	**CFF**	**CFF**	**CFF**	**CFF**	**CFF**	**CFF**
Income												
Grants	20,000	15,000					15,000					
Donations	750	2,250	2,250	500	5,250	1,000	500	500	500	500	500	500
Online courses and guides	12,175	2,200	11,325	12,575	3,000	6,975	3,650	3,300	2,150	2,600	3,350	2,200
Total income	32,925	19,450	13,575	13,075	8,250	7,975	19,150	3,800	2,650	3,100	3,850	2,700
Expenditure												
Staff costs	(8,500)	(8,500)	(8,500)	(8,500)	(8,500)	(8,500)	(8,500)	(8,500)	(8,500)	(8,500)	(8,500)	(8,500)
Premises	(1,040)	(1,040)	(4,900)	(1,440)	(1,040)	(1,040)	(1,040)	(1,040)	(1,040)	(880)		

3. The building blocks of financial management

IT	(1,500)			(1,000)	(1,500)			(1,000)	(1,000)			
Other			(900)					(1,100)				
Total outgoings	(11,040)	(9,540)	(14,300)	(10,940)	(11,040)	(9,540)	(9,540)	(11,640)	(10,540)	(9,380)	(8,500)	(8,500)
Net in/out per month	21,885	9,910	(725)	2,135	(2,790)	(1,565)	9,610	(7,840)	(7,890)	(6,280)	(4,650)	(5,800)
Opening balance	46,990	68,875	78,785	78,060	80,195	77,405	75,840	85,450	77,610	69,720	63,440	58,790
Balance at month end	68,875	78,785	78,060	80,195	77,405	75,840	85,450	77,610	69,720	63,440	58,790	52,990

To this opening balance the 'net' (the figure arrived at by deducting outgoing cash from incoming cash) is added.

The resulting balance is then carried forward to become the opening balance for the next month.

CFF = cash-flow forecast.

Examining your cash-flow forecast can help you identify pinch points and potential actions to address them. For example, if there is a point at which a balance is uncomfortably low in one month but your charity is expecting a grant to start the next, would the funder be open to bringing the first payment forward? Similarly, can expenditure be delayed to a point where your bank account is looking healthier? In our example, the Society has several months where income is exceeded by withdrawals. However, the balance remains comfortable throughout the year, dropping to a low point by the year end.

There are various ways to display information too: as for your budget and management information, you can use charts and tables as visual aids to help stakeholders understand the ebbs and flows of your charity's financial situation, and to help improve the accessibility and usefulness of the information for those who rely on it. Combining information can help people to identify where decisions may need to be made or actions taken. For example, a bar chart of your budgeted income and expenditure with a line graph of your actual cash flow could be the best way to show what's happening. I said earlier that there is a temptation to be overly optimistic or pessimistic when forecasting. However, when it comes to cash-flow forecasting, your charity can afford to be a bit more of a pessimist with its income assumptions! This is because in times of financial constraint, cash is king, so assuming the worst and planning for the best can safeguard against running out of money.

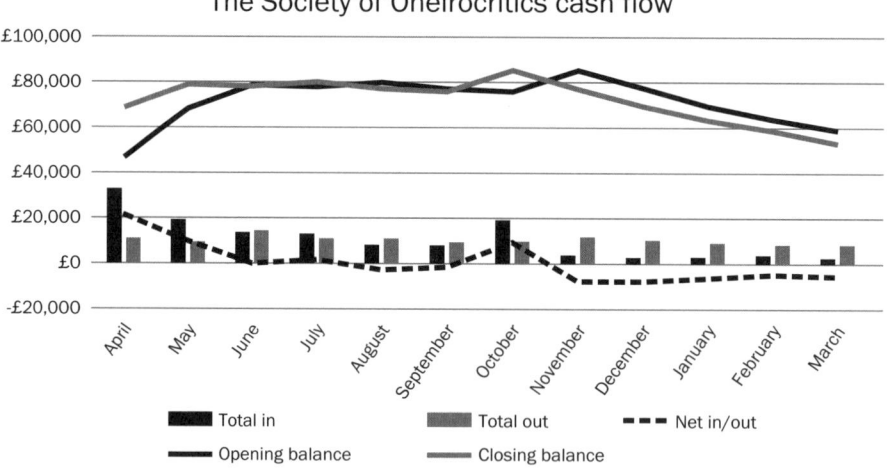

Reporting to the board

There are two forms of reporting that typically happen: internal reporting by the executive to the trustees, and external reporting to your charity's stakeholders. In this chapter I am only going to cover internal reporting *to* the board as it is arguably a tool that trustees use to manage their charity's finances. In chapters 6 and 7, I will focus on the external reporting (reporting *by* the board) your charity may be required (or may choose) to do.

Boards have both the advantage and the disadvantage of being able to dip into the day-to-day running of their charity. Think about that young distant relative you only see periodically. Unlike their parents, you see the step changes brought about as time passes. Although their parents know they are growing and changing, the big differences won't be as noticeable to them. With trustees it's the same. Things that will be less noticeable to staff will jump out to the board. This is a huge advantage.

On the other side, going back to my analogy of your young distant relative, there may be behaviours or things about them that puzzle, worry or surprise someone who has not seen them for a while. Perhaps the meek, quiet child has suddenly dyed their hair pink! However, a short conversation with the parent who lives with the child, day in, day out, will give context and help you to understand what's going on – whether it's a passing phase or a trend and whether, in context, there is cause for concern. You might see that your initial judgement was based on surface information and influenced by your own fears, prejudices and baggage, which can be dispelled by a quick explanation. If trustees are going to understand the situation and give useful input, they need the context from those who have the relevant knowledge and are closest to the reality.

Most trustees will only look at their charity's numbers in any depth once a quarter, so it is important that the information paints a clear picture for them. The suggestions I made earlier in this chapter about increasing accessibility and making information easier to engage with are all equally relevant to reporting. Using images or symbols (like emojis, traffic lights, etc.), charts, tables and additional information can help trustees to understand and interpret your charity's financial reports more easily. Think about:

- What does the board need to be able to quickly form an accurate picture?
- How can the board members be given the relevant history and context in a simple way?
- How can the information be made more accessible?

Be prepared to experiment with different approaches until you can settle upon an approach that works for all.

In 2013, CFG ran a competition – on innovation in the field of charity finance – which was designed to carry on the work of our founder trustee, Adrian Randall. In her work *More of the Wood, Less of the Trees*, the inaugural prize winner, Hilary Seaward, tackled the ongoing challenge of the nightmare with numbers experienced by many trustees. She explored how financial information can be presented to boards alongside commentary and performance data in a way that can increase understanding and aid useful debate. Although things have changed markedly over the past decade, the principles have stood the test of time. I won't reproduce the detail contained in Hilary's work but will rather pull out some lessons and ideas which really landed with me.

What Hilary found, particularly with trustees, was that pages of figures were less likely to drive positive engagement between trustees and staff. They could even cause trustees to switch off when it comes to the numbers. She asked trustees why good financial governance was difficult to achieve and what inhibited their engagement with financial information. The phrase that kept coming up was that trustees couldn't 'see the wood for the trees'. So, at the heart of Hilary's work was a desire to find a simple way of striking the right balance – producing enough information to be able to see the big picture but not so much that the reader got bogged down in detail and ultimately put off. I hope this thinking will provoke you to consider what might work with your charity's internal reporting.

Hilary observed:

- Figures in and of themselves don't pose concerns for trustees, provided they are put in context.
- The length of a document can make or break understanding, with trustees more likely to read a report containing management information if it is shorter.
- Jargon switches people off and could exclude – simple words are more helpful.
- Management information should be part of a dialogue and not a broadcast.
- Financial items should be discussed midway through the board meeting. Include them too early and the trustees won't have warmed up; too late and they might be worn out!

Hilary's work suggested a condensed format for management information over three pages: short enough to be concise but detailed enough to contain relevant data on which understanding can be built and decisions taken. It may not be possible to get your content onto three physical pages, and in any case information is now more frequently reviewed as a digital document rather than printed out. However, the principle is clear – make it as concise as possible.

Hilary's condensed format is made up of the following:
1. the context;
2. the headlines;
3. the detail.

Let's consider these sections in turn.

Setting the context
This section establishes the context and provides narrative without numbers. It highlights high and low points, perhaps including a quote or some inspiring feedback from a beneficiary relating to the reporting period. The purpose is to remind the trustees that the figures are a means to an end and to focus their thinking on the charity's objects. In this section, the executive can ask a few simple questions of the board to guide or stimulate conversation on the

3. The building blocks of financial management

relevant issues for the reporting period. These could be questions to provoke thought or specific questions that require the board to provide an answer.

What would be your executive's questions? For example, maybe the executive could benefit from the trustees confirming your charity's financial priorities or that a tentative conclusion they have reached resonates with the board?

Headline figures

Headline figures produced in an engaging and visual way – together with a brief reminder of discussions in the most relevant recent meetings – can help to refresh the trustees' memories of what has been discussed before. In turn, this can help them get to grips with the big picture. Which figures are considered to be important will vary between charities, but they could include information about the financial viability of different charity activities, a cash flow, reserves at a glance, progress towards a major project, progress against benchmarks, or trends relevant to your charity's work.

The detail

Key to sharing the detail successfully is understanding what works best for your trustees:

- Do the trustees favour visual over written information?
- Is it clear at a glance whether something is positive or negative? (Use of colours, emojis, arrows, etc. can bring information to life.)
- Does the information help the trustees to identify questions or concerns they have during their preparation for the board meeting, perhaps through prompts?
- Is it clear how certain income and expenditure are? For example, are they guaranteed or just wishful thinking? (You can consider adopting a sliding scale of probability.)

Inspired by Hilary's key proposals back in 2013, I've created a checklist for you to use when thinking about your internal reporting.

No.	Item	Action for the charity to take (what/who)	Completed
1	**Clutter:** Do all the elements aid understanding? If any don't, cut them out.		
2	**Presentation:** Is it readable on the average laptop screen? If it's printed, can it be read without super-human vision?		

No.	Item	Action for the charity to take (what/who)	Completed
3	**Length:** How long is your report? Keep it as short as possible. Can detail, if required, be provided in appendices?		
4	**Engagement:** Have the executive asked questions they'd like the trustees to consider? Would you personally find reading what has been produced useful, interesting and helpful?		
5	**Charity's objects:** Is there a reminder of what your charity is there to do to keep the trustees focused?		
6	**Proximity:** Does the reader have to flick through pages to marry up commentary and numbers? Can the proximity of numbers and narrative be improved?		
7	**Placement:** Where in the board meeting agenda does the financial report come? Avoid putting it at the beginning or end of the agenda.		
8	**Simplicity:** Are you liberally using jargon or acronyms that the trustees may be unfamiliar with? If so, opt for simpler text and set out what acronyms stand for.		
9	**Playfulness:** Is there any lightness, humour or quirkiness in the report that might work well with the audience and make it more memorable?		
10	**Review:** Have you reviewed and included what is of most importance to your charity right now? Are there benchmarks that your charity's performance can be compared against that might assist in providing context for your trustees? What other information would the trustees find useful?		

Miscellaneous tool titbits

The tools you introduce and the frequency with which they are deployed are entirely down to your charity. Take time to think about what is useful for your trustees, your executive, and the wider staff and volunteers who play a role in delivering your charity's activities. Ask them what works best for them and think about how and whether you can accommodate their views.

Be brave and willing to experiment with different approaches. If you are a finance professional, you will know you are as committed to and driven by the cause as everyone else, wanting your charity's impact to be as great as it can be. If you're a trustee or a member of staff, you should remember that too, and be open to the surprising possibility that finance professionals will be enthusiastic about making their discipline more engaging to a wider audience. Don't assume there is only one way of presenting financial information. It will make everyone's lives easier if nobody finds numbers to be a nightmare!

Great financial management can increase your charity's bang for its buck, so working out how your charity engages with and deploys the various elements is time well spent.

Main chapter takeaways

- If you're tasked with governance responsibilities, don't be afraid to ask for information to be made more accessible or to use less accounting jargon. Be clear on what you want to see, when you want to see it and why. Stay at the strategic level and avoid being sucked into the weeds.
- Focus on the 'so what' and why – don't be falsely reassured things are matching the budget, and conversely don't get spooked if the finances don't match the expectations. Remain focused on your beneficiaries and don't blindly deliver to a budget.
- Be open about what you know and don't know – what is assumption and what is fact.
- Involve yourself (and others across your charity) in planning and monitoring finances: don't leave this to someone else.

4 Risky business

If you can meet with Triumph and Disaster
And treat those two impostors just the same
Rudyard Kipling

When Rudyard Kipling wrote the words in the epigraph to this chapter in his poem 'If', I am pretty sure he didn't have running a charity in mind! But this quote always makes me think 'ooh, that's great risk management' whenever I come across it.

This chapter is not only interested in the risks simply labelled 'financial'. Other risks can lead to problems with your charity's numbers. Reputational risk can lead to an exodus of donors, bringing financial ruin. When a key member of staff is lost, your charity's ability to bring in income might suffer. Risk considerations will have knock-on impacts on trustees' decisions about the quantity of reserves they wish to maintain (which we'll cover in chapter 5). However, risks can also be positive – as this chapter will explore. For example, that same loss of a key member of staff could also mean you benefit from not needing to pay their salary or have the opportunity to rethink a role and bring in new talent.

If you're having a nightmare with numbers, it won't be eased simply by being able to make sense of the spreadsheets you receive. In addition, you will need to understand your operating environment, attempt to predict the future and make the most of the resources available to your charity – all of which are inextricably linked to risk management.

Those responsible for the numbers (your finance person or team) frequently also have responsibility for risk and are the source of information within your charity. It's likely you will communicate your charity's approach to risk to the outside world through your trustees' annual report and accounts, and therefore how your finance person or team approach risk is likely to shape what's reported. If your charity is big enough to have a risk professional or department dedicated to risk management, the people responsible for checking whether your risk management activities are working are likely to be from finance (such as internal auditors, who are tasked with providing assurance on internal processes and systems). From the governance perspective, you may have a sub-committee to consider finance and risk together, or your board may look at these topics as a whole.

In this chapter we will explore some of the established mechanisms used in risk management. This should help you understand what your charity is required to do, and it will hopefully also challenge your thinking about which bits of your charity's current systems and processes are helping you to maximise impact and not just minimise harm. I hope this chapter will help you meet with triumph and disaster and treat those impostors the same!

> **Outcomes**
> After reading this chapter you will:
> - Understand the terminology and risk management tools commonly used in the charity sector
> - Be familiar with the compliance requirements relating to risk management when it comes to charities
> - Be able to assess what is working for your charity and what changes you may need to consider in its risk management framework

Risk is life
What is risk?

I have a slide I use when talking about risk and risk management that simply reads 'risk is life'. Risks are encountered in all walks of life, in everything you do or choose not to do. Life is inherently risky and nothing we do is risk free. I don't say this to turn you into a quivering wreck but to give you the perspective that nothing we do (or choose not to do) is risk free. As with everything, there are trade-offs. This is where management of risks comes in.

What is risk management?

The Charity Commission for England and Wales's guidance *Charities and Risk Management* (CC26) says that identifying and managing things that might or are likely to happen to a charity over its lifetime is a key part of effective governance – whatever your size or however simple or complex you might be. It goes on to say that by managing risk effectively, trustees:
- can help to ensure that significant risks are known and kept under review;
- are enabled to make informed decisions and act in good time;
- can ensure their charity makes the most of opportunities;
- can improve strategic planning for the future;
- can ensure their charity achieves its aims.

In other words, you need to engage in risk management so that your charity can get the most out of the resources it has.

For most of you, in practice, risk management will feel like it's focused entirely on stopping bad stuff from happening or preparing your charity for the eventuality of the proverbial hitting the fan. But risk management should be about making decisions well and about effective use of resources, not just avoiding the negative stuff. It is about your charity trying to get the most out of life for your beneficiaries. It's about doing everything you can with what you've got. It's not about the numbers in a risk register or other tools you might have in place, and it's not only about transferring, mitigating or avoiding risk, or preparing to respond to it. It is also about knowing when to go for something, to invest or to lean into a risk because the possible upside is worth it.

Let me take the simple example of crossing the road. The risk is that you might get run over and injured. But you still want or need to cross the road despite the risk because, for instance, there is an amazing cake shop on the other side that's giving away free samples! Risk management means putting things in place to help you cross safely, but they won't necessarily take the risk away entirely.

For example, there are risk management tools, which prevent you being run over when you cross, in place on some roads but not on others. Pelican crossings (which control the flow of road users and pedestrians using traffic lights) exist to reduce the risk of a person being struck by a vehicle when moving from one side of the road to the other. However, as with the risk management tools you will use in the charity context, the presence or absence of a specific risk mitigation tool (the crossing) will not guarantee the road is safe to cross at the precise moment you set foot on it. Risk mitigation tools are not always universally effective – however similar two situations might look on the surface.

Let's continue to think about the basic need to cross the road. The principle is the same whatever the road you want to cross, but the circumstances can be very different. For example, motorways are completely unsuitable for a pedestrian to cross on foot so they have absolute rules – no pedestrians allowed! Other roads – say, country lanes – may not deploy such measures to reduce risk because there is simply insufficient space, or perhaps the local council has inadequate resources available for such measures to be installed. The road may nonetheless be precarious for walkers! Alternative tools might be more suitable to a specific road or situation, such as a temporary crossing. They might operate only at specific times, like a school crossing guard, or be there permanently as a fundamental way to safeguard pedestrians, such as a footbridge.

Some of the controls for reducing the risk inherent in crossing the road may increase the risk in other ways (for example, a footbridge might offer safe passage on foot but increase the risk of something dropping onto the road from above). Pedestrians interact with other road users – they don't exist in a bubble. Increasing safety for pedestrians may reduce it for others. There is no single solution!

Then we throw the huge variable of humans into the mix. Imagine you are walking up to a pelican crossing. It's a road you know well. The light is red for pedestrians but, being familiar with the flow of traffic, you can easily see that the danger of being struck by a car is minimal, so you take the opportunity to 'beat the lights' and cross. Conversely, the green light for pedestrians may be displayed, indicating it's safe to cross, but you can hear sirens from an emergency vehicle approaching. Putting your entire faith in the signal to go – ignoring the sirens and striding across anyway – would not be sensible.

Risk management is the same. Over-reliance on the controls you put in place to reduce risks can, perversely, increase risk. There are always multiple ways to approach any risk. And opportunities may sometimes require us to step outside our standard actions, be flexible, and assess benefit and harm rather than sticking to an established way of operating. (There will, of course, be some risks, such as specific health and safety requirements in our motorway example, where the controls we must use are dictated and we have little individual choice.)

It's about being clear about what you want to do (cross the road) and what the inherent risks are (getting run over), and then considering whether there are things you can do to help minimise the risks (controls, like using a pedestrian crossing).

The nature of the risks you face as a charity will relate to:

- **Governance:** Perhaps your board isn't functioning well and is failing to make decisions.
- **Operational matters:** Maybe your management information is erratic and unclear, your policies are incomplete, or your procedures are out of date.
- **Finances:** Perhaps you have a lack of money, or so much money that your donors might think you're unfairly hoarding it.
- **Law:** Maybe an ex-employee is planning to take you to an employment tribunal.
- **Other compliance matters:** Perhaps you haven't been filing your accounts on time.
- **Things specific to the environment in which you operate:** Maybe public interest is focused on an issue which demands greater attention than before, such as mould in a housing setting.

These risks may hit your reputation or your bank balance (and often both). Risks invariably interact and it is therefore important to think about them in clusters rather than individually. This is particularly important in times of uncertainty. Some risks are obvious, and you can see where they will have a direct and often immediate impact. Others may be less obvious, with indirect impacts or impacts which might arise after some time goes by. One example is uncertainty affecting your funders, supporters, suppliers, delivery partners or others that your charity relies upon to do its work.

Risks may undermine your charity's ability to deliver its charitable objects – or, dealt with effectively, they may enable your charity to seize opportunities, accelerating you towards your goals. Whatever the nature of the risks being considered, and however they are categorised and organised, the most important thing is not the resulting documents – it's understanding your charity. Templates, guides and lists of different risk types are helpful to aid your thinking (CC26 contains a really helpful run-down of things that you might consider in Annex 2). However, ultimately the nature of the risks your charity encounters and what you do in response will be specific to you.

Furthermore, with echoes of Donald Rumsfeld in his 'known knowns, known unknowns and unknown unknowns' speech in 2002 at a Pentagon press conference just prior to the Iraq War, there are risks that you know your charity will or is likely to encounter, risks that you know about but don't think will be relevant to your charity (or where you know you can mitigate the impact), and risks you simply don't know about that may jump up and bite your charity unexpectedly. For example, I doubt that many organisations had a global pandemic on their risk register, or the 2010 eruption of a volcano in Iceland, which forced planes to stay grounded for a prolonged period, causing a huge impact across sectors.

In conclusion, when you think about 'risk management', it's important to understand that this means not only the processes and documents which support how you approach risk but also the mindset and behaviour of the people involved in delivering your charity's activities.

Some common risk management tools

A confession and a caveat: I'm a risk management enthusiast but a real sceptic about whether the plethora of toolkits and frameworks that have been built within the risk industry actually manage risk well. In my view, those managing risk have become caught up with calculating, weighting, identifying and recording risks, tying themselves up in knots to identify the handful of most important risks and spending way too little time thinking about managing them.

There is a danger of charities getting hooked on an illusion of an environment in which it is possible to predict, measure, monitor and eradicate the majority of risks. Increasingly detailed and complicated mechanisms are often deployed, and calculations are undertaken to quantify (or score) the extent, likelihood and impact of 'inherent' (naturally existing) and 'mitigated' (after actions have been taken to address them) risks. Jargon is often used, making information inaccessible. An excessive pursuit of control can lead to wasted time and resources.

The most commonly used tools can confuse what is achievable with what is desirable, leading to a perpetual sense that if the risk comes home to roost, someone or something has failed, when the reality may be that the situation was unavoidable. False comfort can be placed in *War and Peace*-length risk registers and scoring mechanisms, on the faulty assumption that if the document is complete, then the risks must be managed. There is also a danger of us overestimating the effectiveness of the actions we would take to reduce the fallout if things went wrong. I fear many have lost sight of the critical power of the discussion and focus instead entirely on the documents.

Because here is the thing: not all 'good' conclusions lead to success, and sometimes great outcomes come from pretty rubbish decisions. In the end, triumph is sometimes a product of good fortune, and disaster sometimes flows from making bold decisions to encounter risks that were worth taking but just didn't pay off.

So where does that leave us? I do not believe we are destined to throw up our hands and cry 'what will be will be'. As a pragmatist, I recognise the futility of angling for every reader to chuck out their existing models. Indeed, that would probably, as the saying goes, be 'chucking the baby out with the bathwater'! I am very happy to admit that authoritative support in managing risk can give you great comfort – for example, depending on the size of your charity, you may employ risk professionals or members of specialist organisations (like the Institute of Risk Management), or you may engage internal auditors. So the mechanisms of risk management are not all bad – there are steps that we can take to break free of the constraints established risk management frameworks may shackle us with, and we can make improvements in the way we use traditional models.

I do not intend for this section to be comprehensive in covering all of the very many models available. Instead, I'm going to pick out a few of the more frequently used tools in the charity sector, explain them and, where possible, give you some suggestions on how you might get the best out of them if they are relevant to your charity.

Broadly speaking, all risk management models cover:
- understanding your charity and coming to an agreement within and with the board on your charity's willingness to accept, take or avoid risk (your charity's 'risk appetite');
- identifying what risks your charity faces;
- assessing the risks and determining what actions can be taken in response;
- monitoring the effectiveness of your charity's approach.

Let's look at some of the specific tools which intend to support those aims.

The risk register
The most commonly used tool in the risk management armoury is the risk register, illustrated in the table below. Typically, it will be a table jam-packed with figures, with columns providing:
1. a number to identify each risk;
2. descriptions of each risk;
3. numbers to represent how inherently risky each risk is (its impact and how likely it is to happen);
4. actions that will be or have been taken to mitigate the risk;
5. a score representing the impact of the actions taken to reduce the risk (called the 'mitigated' or 'net risk' score);
6. a summary of the actions or further steps to be taken or relevant commentary;
7. the person responsible operationally for managing the risk (often called the 'owner').

I cover how to calculate the scores later in this section.

4. Risky business

The Society of Oneirocritics extract from risk register

1	2	3	4	5	6	7
No.	Risk description	Inherent score (0–25)	Actions	Net score (0–25)	Commentary	Owner
1	Trustees hot-foot it off to the Bahamas with the reserves	15	Dual signatories on the bank, one of which must be executive; due diligence on prospective trustees	11	New process in place to screen out trustees with an unhealthy interest in the Caribbean; willing to accept the residual risk because confiscating trustees' passports may be disproportionate	CEO
2	Inexperienced dream interpreter becomes traumatised after reading our materials	6	Clear disclaimer on materials; insurance; crisis communications plan	4	Reduced likelihood of risk to reasonable level and prepare to manage bad press if necessary	CEO

Other information included (not shown in this fictitious extract) might be:
- traffic lights – so-called RAG (red, amber, green) reports – to help you identify different levels of concern;
- a numerical representation of a target level of risk your charity wants to reach for each risk;
- a number or colour to identify the appetite your charity has for each risk;
- a trend indicator (whether the risk has improved or worsened);
- methods to link to your charity's strategic goals (e.g. by showing how a specific risk might impact a particular strategic priority).

Many charities will have separate registers for strategic risks (those which are likely to advance or prevent their strategy being delivered) and operational risks (those things that happen day to day but which on their own are not likely to impact the big picture). They may share only the more strategically important stuff with the board, keeping the operational bits on a more detailed level to be discussed by senior staff. If there is a sub-committee charged with looking at risk, they tend to sit somewhere between the executive and board, reducing the amount of information the board needs to see and accessing operational details as required. Some charities seek to further limit the number of risks considered at board level to a manageable number – say, the biggest five strategic risks – or use their organisational priorities to order the risks and cross-reference them to their activities. For example, they might number the risks and say, 'Risks 3, 5 and 6 relate to our organisational priority to increase beneficiary satisfaction.' I think it can be helpful to provide this explicit link back to your charity's strategy.

Setting a specific number of risks for the board to consider can have the consequence of missing out areas that could have a great impact on your charity or lead to you talking about things that don't really need to be discussed (just because they're in your top risks). I prefer a dynamic approach that enables your charity to consider the active risks – however few or many that might be. But there is a balance to be struck.

When risk registers were mostly physical papers, I joked that a hefty lever-arch file containing a massive document would be opened once a year, as the external auditor was due to start work, and the dust blown off it – the document being updated in order to satisfy scrutiny requirements and not to drive performance. Of course, most charities keep such documents digitally now, and many will be too small to worry about auditors, but the metaphor of the dusty file still works. The document can become a compliance exercise rather than an active way of keeping risks in view. Another weakness of a register is that, however well devised and complete it is, it can only capture what is known – not things which hit your charity from left field (your unknown unknowns). My final bugbear is that it drives people towards a mindset of avoiding harm, not maximising impact. I'll give you some tips on trying to shift into that positive way of thinking later in the chapter.

Whatever the downsides, it is highly likely that you will use a risk register within your charity, so you will need to consider and act on the information contained in it. To help you get the most out of your charity's risk register and to make it a living document, ask yourself the following questions (cross-referenced to the illustrative risk register, on page 59, to help you):

1. Does the description of the risk tell you enough about what it is and what you can do about it? (columns 2, 4 and 6)
    a. Avoid generic descriptions like 'loss of key member of staff', because the steps your charity might be able to take and the risks arising from staff departures will differ depending on so many factors. Instead, be specific – for example, 'unexpected loss of CEO' or 'unplanned resignation of lead on [key project]'.
    b. Be clear on what you are trying to achieve – the 'risk objective' (columns 4 and 6): is your charity setting out to reduce the possibility of something happening or the impact of it (or perhaps both)? Perhaps the board and staff are happy to accept the risk and instead concentrate resources on making sure that your charity can resume business as usual quickly if the risk occurs?
2. Does the scoring system make sense to everyone who needs to use it and help them understand the impacts of the actions taken – whether something is getting better or worse? (columns 3 and 5)
    a. Don't spend too much time debating a score because it is only representative of the level of risk and has an element of subjectivity. (columns 3 and 5)
    b. Be clear about whose thinking the scores represent (that of senior staff, the board or both?). This will enable you to understand the perspective the score represents. (columns 3, 5 and 7)
    c. Explore whether in practice the actions taken have reduced the risk, and how (i.e. have the actions taken reduced the likelihood and/or impact of a risk?). If relevant, consider over what timescale the actions should take effect. (columns 4, 5 and 6)
    d. Ask yourself whether your charity should accept (also referred to as 'tolerating') the level of risk after the actions have been taken. If not, what more can be done? This question can be asked of individual trustees or staff, or of the executive and board collectively. (columns 4, 5 and 6)
3. Is the register driving action? (all columns)
    a. Think about change and movement between reviews – has the risk got worse or better since last time?
    b. Think about what is not included as well as what is, ensuring that anything you spot that is missing is considered and documented appropriately.
    c. Spend time talking about the strategically important things (things that can advance or hold back your progress towards your charitable objects) rather than sweating over every line in the risk register.

4. Are you thinking beyond the obvious risks? (all columns)
   a. Look for connections between risks – can you cross-reference between risks within the register, make connections with your charity's strategic priorities, or otherwise make the connections between different risks explicit so that it's more obvious when risks might occur together, causing greater impact?
   b. Look for trends – are there patterns based on time, conditions or other factors which will enable your charity to carry forward lessons from one situation to another?
5. What is your charity's mechanism for ensuring action is taken in a timely fashion?
   a. Is there a regular fixed meeting to talk about risk?
   b. Is risk embedded in all conversations?
   c. Does your charity have a way of tracking risks that are currently impacting it?

The most important function of a risk register, in my view, is to facilitate discussion. If it takes too long for trustees and staff to get through every entry in one sitting, the register is unlikely to be helping. You are likely to be spending little time on each risk or potentially focusing on one or two individuals' pet issues. Can the register be slimmed down? Can discussions be focused on things that the staff or the board are most worried about – the things keeping them up at night? Alternatively, if the consensus is that the register cannot be shortened in length, can the staff and trustees deep-dive into topics on the register periodically or alternatively look at areas that have changed or things that have been static for a while (to ensure nothing is being missed)?

It's up to your charity to determine how frequently and in what depth it reviews the risk register. Things not going to plan may present you with a good point for reflection on whether your charity's processes are effective and whether you feel risks are well managed.

Calculating a score for a risk register
This section won't teach you how to do the calculations, just show you some common approaches (there are various methods of estimating level of risk). If you understand these approaches, then you should be better equipped to make sense of the numbers you will see contained in a risk register. Charities that use scoring methods tend to first look at the inherent risk in a situation (before taking any action) – this is the inherent score (column 3) in the example on page 59. Then, they recalculate the score based on the difference the planned actions might make in terms of reducing the likelihood (L), impact (I) or both – this is the net score (column 5) in the example. The Charity Commission guidance CC26 (the key word here being 'guidance', which means your charity is not required to do it this way) uses scales from 1 to 5 to express these elements and offers suggested definitions of each score (set out below). It is important that there is agreement on what your scales mean for your charity.

Don't assume everyone has a shared understanding of the numbers – check in and use a key for reference. You're also free to adopt whatever words for each number mean the most to those involved.

Here is CC26's scoring system for likelihood:

1	2	3	4	5
Remote	Unlikely	Possible	Probable	Highly probable
May only occur in exceptional circumstances	Expected to occur in a few circumstances	Expected to occur in some circumstances	Expected to occur in many circumstances	Expected to occur frequently and in most circumstances

And here is CC26's scoring system for impact:

1	2	3	4	5
Insignificant	Minor	Moderate	Major	Extreme/ catastrophic
■ No impact on service ■ No impact on reputation ■ Complaint unlikely ■ Litigation risk remote	■ Slight impact on service ■ Slight impact on reputation ■ Complaint possible ■ Litigation possible	■ Some service disruption ■ Potential for adverse publicity – avoidable with careful handling ■ Complaint probable ■ Litigation probable	■ Service disrupted ■ Adverse publicity not avoidable (local media) ■ Complaint probable ■ Litigation probable	■ Service interrupted for significant time ■ Major adverse publicity not avoidable (national media) ■ Major litigation expected ■ Resignation of senior management and board ■ Loss of beneficiary confidence

The numbers for each risk are calculated from the risk's likelihood and impact scores. You may be familiar with a methodology whereby likelihood and impact are given equal importance (i.e. $L \times I = risk\ score$), with the highest-scoring risks being those that the trustees should consider to be major risks. However, methodologies have evolved to accommodate events that are rare or unprecedented, where the circumstances are not known or rapidly change, and there may be situations or factors beyond a charity's control. Such risks, like the global COVID-19 pandemic, can have a huge impact even if the chances of them happening seem remote. So instead of straight multiplication, the formula might be $(L \times I) + I = risk\ score$, to place more emphasis on the impact element.

In my view, the methodology your charity uses (i.e. $L \times I$ or $(L \times I) + I$) is less important than ensuring that everyone discussing risk understands the methodology you're using. Try to avoid lengthy debates on what a score should be. I have sat in multiple meetings where differences of opinion on whether something should be a 3 or 4 generated more debate than whether the actions taken to manage the risk were effective! The scoring process can end up consuming more time than the benefit it delivers.

A downside of using a scoring methodology is that it can make you focus on the big scores to the exclusion of the small ones. So, it is important that lower-impact risks are recognised as having the potential to come together with other risks in a cumulative way, become high-impact risks in their own right (escalate in seriousness), or trigger a domino effect on a series of risks, causing them to materialise in quick succession and causing major problems. CC26 says, 'Many studies have shown that most business failures are the result of a series of small, linked events having too great a cumulative impact to deal with rather than a single large event.' It's important to keep this in mind.

An alternative to scoring

The process of understanding how likely something is, what its impact might be and its connectedness to other risks is incredibly important. But it doesn't require a figure to be assigned. If your charity wishes to approach risk differently, an alternative method could be to apply a simple two-by-two matrix looking at likelihood and impact as shown in the chart below. In this approach, the position of each risk on the axes is agreed through discussion, capturing the feelings of individuals as to how likely or impactful a risk might be.

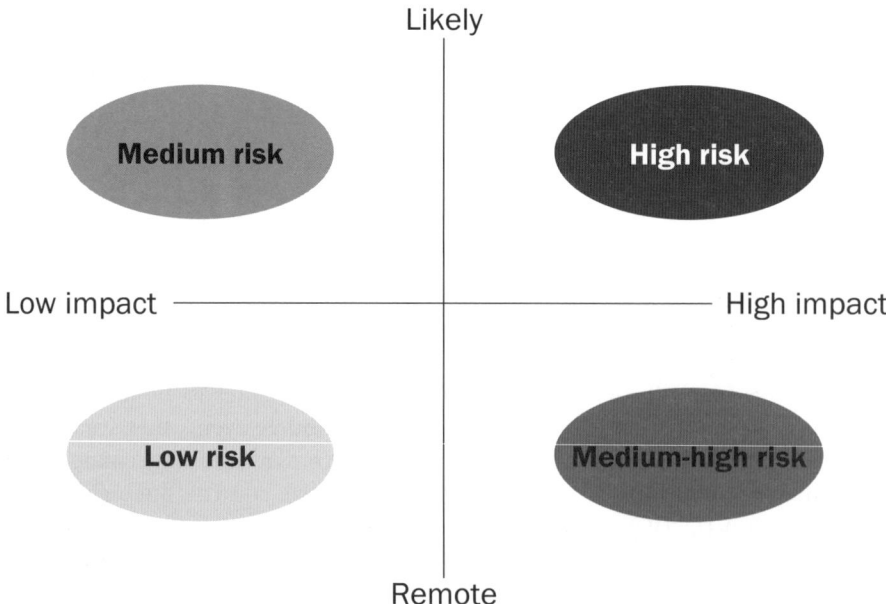

This next chart shows how this system could be applied to the Society of Oneirocritics. Here, the four risks are:
1. Higher levels of staff illness create a capacity squeeze.
2. A contract to deliver services worth 25% of income is not renewed.
3. The project manager leaves before the project is complete.
4. A beneficiary is traumatised by applying dream interpretation materials.

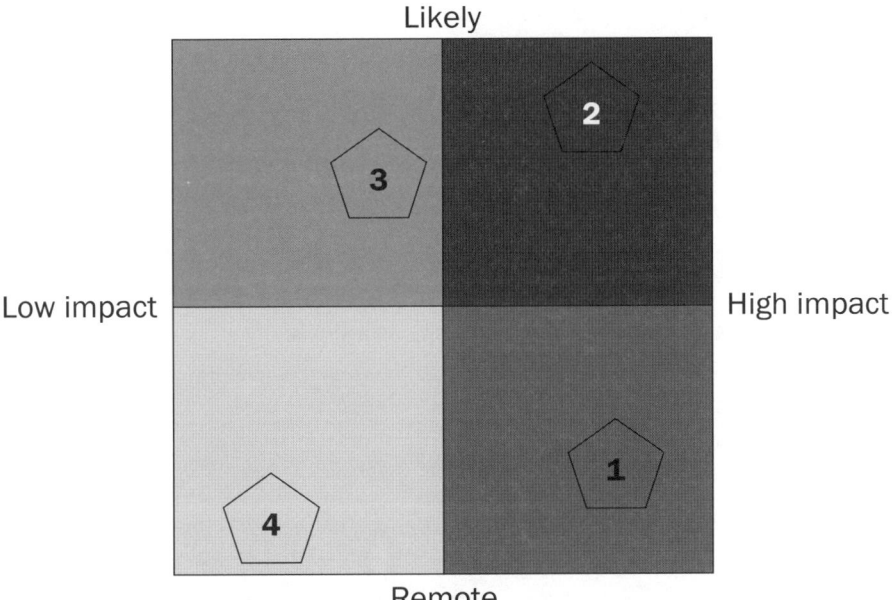

By plotting all the risks on this matrix, trustees and staff can also get an indication of the combined risk exposure. The matrix acts as a visual aid which shows you whether your charity is dealing with a few high risks, multiple small risks, or a combination of risks with different levels of likelihood and impact. The matrix can help you to determine your charity's resilience and the adequacy of the resources at its disposal. It can highlight the trade-offs that may be required as well as your charity's capacity to seize opportunities. I'll say more on this point in the subsection below on heat maps.

Remember that any methodology for scoring or rating risk involves a degree of judgement or subjectivity because different people will come to different conclusions about the likelihood or probable impact of a risk (perhaps as a result of their own experiences). The methodology can be informed with data and information arising from experience and/or trends, but it is not a scientific or fixed outcome.

Heat maps
When you have plotted all your risks onto it, the matrix just considered operates like a simplified heat map. The more typical heat map tool explored

in this subsection gives you a visual distribution of risks that have been scored. Heat maps can be deployed to show the inherent risk and, if desired, the movement after you have decided on mitigating actions (net risk). Alternatively, you can use them to only plot net risk. Heat maps tend to be used in addition to a risk register, with the numbers of the risks corresponding between the two tools.

In the example given in CC26, the heat map assesses risk by increasing the weighting of impact. The scoring used is $(L \times I) + I$, which as explained above puts extra emphasis on the assessment of impact. Applying this to the four Society's risks above looks as follows:

1. Higher levels of staff illness create a capacity squeeze: $(2 \times 4) + 4 = 12$
2. A contract to deliver services worth 25% of income is not renewed: $(4 \times 4) + 4 = 20$
3. The project manager leaves before the project is complete: $(5 \times 2) + 2 = 12$
4. A user is traumatised by applying dream interpretation materials: $(2 \times 2) + 2 = 6$

The above risks plotted on a heat map look as follows:

Impact		1 Remote	2 Unlikely	3 Possible	4 Probable	5 Highly probable
Extreme/ catastrophic 5		10	15	20	25	30
Major 4		8	12 **(1)**	16	20 **(2)**	24
Moderate 3		6	9	12	15	18
Minor 2		4	6 **(4)**	8	10	12 **(3)**
Insignificant 1		2	6	4	5	6

Likelihood

My advice to anyone using a heat map is to remember that there is no perfect distribution of risks across the map. One charity's ability to live with multiple high-scoring risks may be greater than another's ability to deal with far fewer and/or lower-scoring risks. The tool is there to prompt discussion, debate and decision-making, not to dictate a particular approach.

Tools for determining your risk appetite

There are three tools I'm going to cover for determining your risk appetite: adopting a scale, codifying your appetite in a written policy and using an appetite tracker.

Adopting a risk scale

There are going to be certain things that you just *cannot* afford to get wrong, or the sky will fall in. Some of these red lines will be obvious – such as safeguarding in a children's charity – but others might take a bit more thought. Adopting a scale to express different levels of organisational risk appetite can provide a framework for conversations to help you identify these red lines. It can also help you to establish your collective view on areas such as the risks of non-compliance with regulations, your board and executive's desire to grow through mergers, and your board and executive's willingness to borrow. This is because a risk scale gives you a shared language for discussing the discomfort people might feel in each area.

To express your appetite for risk (and its often-forgotten bedfellow, opportunity), your charity may wish to adopt a sliding scale with risk aversion on one end, high tolerance for risk (or hunger to undertake an activity despite the level of risk) on the other, and moderate tolerance in the middle. You should also agree a description for each point on the scale. For example:

- **Risk averse:** This might be described as including those matters for which your charity has zero tolerance (such as the safeguarding example above).
- **Moderate tolerance:** This might be described as including those matters where there is a chance that things will not go to plan but, on balance, the chance of success is greater than failure. For example, for an educational charity, this could mean investing in the delivery of a new course that may or may not be successful (in the event of failure, leading to less income or wasted development costs).
- **High tolerance:** This might be described as including those matters where your charity is keen to innovate or take on a high risk of failure because the level of potential reward is also high. For example, for an animal welfare charity, this could mean investing in an initiative to make slaughter more humane. This could land poorly with some stakeholders, but the charity could decide the improvements in animal welfare are worth the risk.

Putting your charity's risk appetite down in writing

You will, no doubt, have heard someone moan at some point about their trustees being too risk averse, or hear someone who has spectacularly failed being judged as a reckless risk taker. A certain behaviour may be bold in one person's view but, on exactly the same facts, appear reckless to someone else! Appetite for risk can be perceived as too little or too great and, unlike in the story of Goldilocks and the three bears, rarely 'just right'. Sadly, there is no perfect equation that can tell you where, in any given scenario, your appetite for risk should sit.

Appetites will also change as a result of individual and collective experiences. The board of a charity that I once advised had taken a relatively big risk in acquiring another organisation. They'd done their risk assessments and, on paper, it had been a risk worth taking. Unfortunately, it didn't work out and the acquired organisation eventually was put into administration. Despite doing all the things it should have, the charity lost a significant amount for them – around £85,000 – plus they had committed a lot of time and energy which hadn't paid off. And they lost some valued staff, which was also painful.

Later on, when an opportunity to acquire another organisation came up, the board absolutely refused to even consider it because of the previous failure. The risk was minimal, it was strategically a good fit and the staff believed the acquisition would hugely benefit the charity. However, the scars of the previous experience overshadowed the balance of risk and benefit. In the end, another charity took the opportunity presented by the merger and benefitted greatly. The board had allowed its experience of failure to colour its judgement. It did not judge the acquisition on its own merits but based on their emotions (and, to be honest, embarrassment) about the venture that had failed. That is a really poor approach to risk-taking. Each opportunity needs to be judged on its own merits.

Similarly, your own personal experiences outside your charity can affect your decision-making. Let's say you invested in a high-risk and high-return scheme only to lose your savings. It would be unsurprising if this made you less likely to support your charity's investment in schemes that felt similar (using the jargon of risk, your 'risk tolerance' would have been reduced).

You might also see things happening around you that markedly shift your previous assessments and appetite for risk more broadly. Think about how social housing providers consider fire safety risk in their buildings in the aftermath of the terrible Grenfell Tower disaster. Their understanding of the nature and impact of the risk itself has radically altered as a result of witnessing the horrors endured by those involved in the tragedy. Consequently, these providers have a better understanding of existing – and in some cases previously unknown – risks.

Sometimes our assessment of, and therefore appetite for, risk can become counterproductive. There is a great TEDx Talk called 'Risk Literacy', delivered by a German psychologist, Gerd Gigerenzer. In a nutshell, he says that emotions can make people respond illogically to risk – undertaking activities that are, ironically, riskier in the pursuit of safety. The example he gives is of the American public's response to internal flights shortly after 9/11 (the terrorist attacks of 11 September 2001). Many perceived the risk of dying in a plane crash to be so great that they took to driving long haul as an alternative. In the 12 months following 9/11, an estimated 1,600 extra people died in collisions on America's highways as a result of long-haul journeys. No life was lost in an internal plane crash during the same period. People's zero appetite for flying – instead opting for a travel method they perceived to be a lesser risk – had a disastrous consequence.

An organisation's appetite for risk is made up of the combined thoughts and feelings of a collection of individuals. It will always therefore be a mash-up of:
- the willingness of the staff, usually the executive, and/or board to accept (or not) the potential downsides of opportunities;
- their assessment of the effort required to balance avoiding harm with the costs associated with doing so.

Your risk appetite is influenced by the culture within the staff and the culture at board level (which may not be the same). It is shaped by individuals' personal experiences, tolerances for risk and desire to drive forward in their own lives. However scientifically an organisation claims to have pinned down assessment of its risk appetite, this will always be subjective to a degree. You will also need to make trade-offs: more risk might mean the chance of greater reward. Conversely, less risk might deliver fewer positive outcomes for your beneficiaries.

A tool you can use to capture this thinking (i.e. to codify your risk appetite) is the risk appetite statement. You might alternatively call it your 'risk policy' or something else. Whatever you call this document, it should codify your charity's risk appetite and how decisions will be made, and it can help to guide staff and trustees through key decisions requiring a balance between risk and reward. It won't give you all the answers, but it may get you more quickly to an answer by giving you a shared language for debate.

Within your charity, you might use a scale that recognises the numerical value of a risk or opportunity as well as the chances of success or failure. This could factor in scores from your risk assessments and/or be tied to the different authorities delegated by the board. Such approaches can help staff make decisions that are aligned with the appetite and expectations of your board by setting out:
- how much risk can be managed;
- at what levels;
- when to escalate risk management decisions to more senior individuals within the executive and staff or the board.

The most important thing is to be clear what the words on the scale mean for your charity.

Here are some more points to consider when working together as a charity to codify your risk appetite:
- Does everyone (executive and trustees) understand the motivations, experiences and approaches to risk of individual members of the board? (This means some people on the board may need to get to know their *own* predispositions a bit better!)
- Rather than just consolidating all views or going with the majority appetite for tolerating a particular risk, take particular note of the outliers. Those individuals could have a more accurate risk perception

It's a Nightmare with the Numbers

but be in the minority, or they could have a particular bugbear about an issue that could derail a decision if not handled well.
- Are there differences between the board and the executive (CEO and senior staff)? Perhaps one group is made up of people more comfortable with higher levels of risk and the other of individuals who tend to lean more towards caution. These differences matter not only when it comes to making decisions but also in terms of your charity's ability to deal with triumph and disaster.
- Get to know what makes your charity's people tick if you wish to have positive conversations about learning, and avoid the blame game when things go belly up. We rarely examine how well we manage risks when things go well – we tend to do so with a great dose of hindsight and in the cold light of failure.

Appetite trackers

Of the various risk committees on which I have served, quite a few of the larger ones have developed trackers to show the current level of a risk versus the organisation's agreed risk appetite for an issue. Such trackers are designed to enable those reviewing the management of risk – usually the executive, trustees or risk committees – to determine whether the severity of a risk being experienced matches the stated appetite for it.

In the example shown, the risk appetites' descriptions and numerical risk scores from the risk register are plotted on the y-axis and the different risks being tracked along the x-axis. The hatched areas show the range the board or executive has agreed is appropriate to each risk. For risk 1, for example, the risk appetite lies between a moderate and high tolerance for risk, whereas for risk 3, the charity is more risk averse. The current score attributed to each risk is then plotted on the tracker as a solid line to show how the risk measures up to the stated appetite.

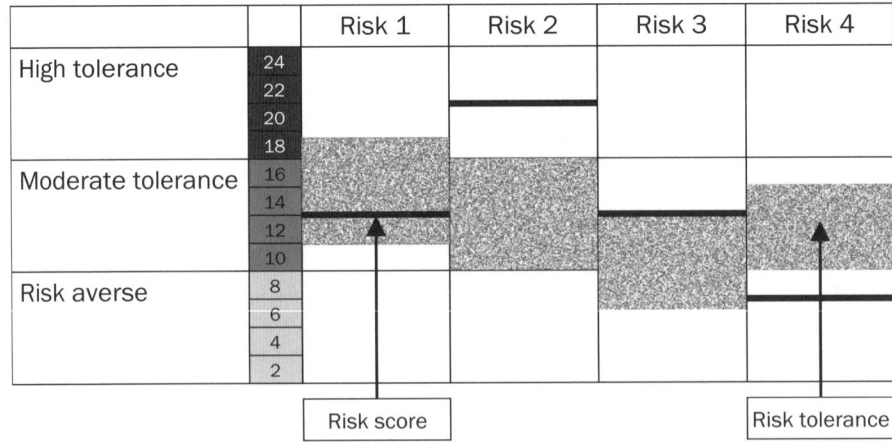

From this example, we can conclude that risks 1 and 3 are currently within the appetite of the board, with risks 2 and 4 being outside the stated appetite. We can further conclude that, in the case of risk 4, there is flexibility to take greater risk if the return appears appropriate. In contrast, perhaps the charity hasn't struck the right balance for risk 2 and more actions should be taken to manage the risk.

Reluctant tolerance of greater risk?
There is something inherently difficult about managing risks which are outside our stated appetite. In my experience, this often occurs as a result of matters that are beyond your control. Sometimes things happen, such as inflation suddenly increasing or a change in the law, which make the circumstances your charity faces more inherently risky without the executive and trustees having a realistic way to enhance the measures in place to deal with these greater risks.

I've found that boards and risk committees can perform mental acrobatics at times like this, trying to reflect the greater risk in their register while failing to recognise that they can do practically nothing more about it. It is almost unavoidable that they will have to accept greater risk than they anticipated or than is desirable, yet this is rarely reflected in their risk appetite score, which almost always remains at the same level as before the thing happened. This results in the charity increasingly operating outside its stated appetite – a very uncomfortable position for all. Whether this is because boards confuse reluctant tolerance of increased risk with appearing to be blasé or less bothered about it, I can only speculate.

Scoring and amending scores to reflect changed circumstances can help you understand the risks your charity is currently living with and debate whether further actions to reduce risks are possible. But if those scores don't change behaviour or lead to new actions because there is little more you can do, by default, your charity's tolerance for living with greater risk has increased. You may need to give more thought to crisis communications, regulatory consequences, insurance and other measures to prepare for the risk coming home to roost. In my view, this is a more productive use of energy!

Required risk rubrics
So far, this chapter has outlined various options for how to manage risk within your charity. It's obvious, of course, but worth saying: your charity cannot operate on blind luck and hope to meet its obligations to the people and causes it serves under charity law (such as delivering a public benefit). But you may be wondering which – if any – of the risk management tools are required by law.

The short answer is that there is no dictated way of approaching risk management. The law does not require a charity to keep a risk register, for example. All charities, whatever their size and area of activity, must manage risk regardless of any formal disclosures they may need to make to comply with the Charities Statement of Recommended Practice (SORP) or regulations. But beyond that, the decision on which tools your charity adopts is down to you. I would encourage you to assess what you use not on whether it replicates standard practice but on whether it genuinely helps. Weigh up how much work goes into maintaining tools and whether they add value. There is a danger that a lot of work goes into applying these tools and populating the corresponding documents, with little value being extracted from the time spent.

The structure and formality of your charity's model for managing risk will need to be greater if yours is a larger charity (with an annual income of over £500,000) and/or a limited company, because there are requirements, set out in the following paragraphs, that you will otherwise find it difficult to meet.

For charities that are required to follow the SORP (see appendix 1), the generic requirement on risk states that a financial review report must include a description of the 'principal risks and uncertainties facing the charity and its subsidiary undertakings' that the trustees have identified together with a summary of what they intend to do to manage those risks.

There is no constraint as to the number of risks and uncertainties that should be included, although 'principal' would suggest your annual report and accounts don't have to include every risk you have identified. Remember, too, that the responsibility rests with the trustees, not with the staff (see chapter 1). It is commonplace for the majority of the risk management work to have been carried out and documented by the staff. However, while the administration and implementation of actions can be delegated, the responsibility for risk management and any required disclosures remains with the board.

The Charities (Accounts and Reports) Regulations 2008 for England and Wales further require charities that are subjected to an audit to make a risk management statement in their trustees' annual report confirming that 'the charity trustees have given consideration to the major risks to which the charity is exposed and satisfied themselves that systems or procedures are established in order to manage those risks'.

Charities that are incorporated under company law and are not within the definition of a small company must include a business review in their directors' report, which must contain a description of the principal risks and uncertainties they face. (A small company will be an entity with any two of the following: an annual turnover of £10.2 million or less, £5.11 million or less on the balance sheet or, on average, 50 employees or less in a year.) It is common practice for the directors' report to be subsumed within the trustees' annual report as part and parcel of the reporting charities need to undertake, even though charities that are also companies have to report to both Companies House and their charity regulator.

Let's take a look at what is required in a risk management statement for those charities required to produce one. And, even if your charity is not in that category, the discipline of producing an annual statement may be a useful addition to your risk management monitoring.

Risk management statement

This table sets out which entities (charities or companies) are required to produce a risk management statement:

Charity not required to follow the SORP	No statement required
Charity required to follow the SORP but not large and not a company	Content in annual report on the principal risks and management of them
Charitable company **Large entity required to follow the SORP**	Risk statement in annual report and a business review in the directors' report (can be combined into one statement)

Your charity's risk management statement, required by the SORP and published in your trustees' annual report and accounts, is intended to provide insights into your charity's management and the major risks and hazards you have encountered. But it is also an opportunity to share learning, signpost to changes made or indicate how your charity intends to tackle challenges going forward. In other words, it is an opportunity to demonstrate good governance.

How you put your risk management statement together will reflect the nature, size and complexity of your charity's structure and activities. There is no template or boilerplate approach that you have to follow, and your charity can decide to simply tell its story as a narrative rather than providing data, charts or statistics.

Whatever the format your executive and trustees choose, use this checklist of requirements for your charity's statement.

Requirement	*Present? (yes or no)*
Have you acknowledged the trustees' responsibilities in relation to risk?	
Have you provided an overview of your charity's processes in relation to risk management?	
Have you identified the major risks, and can you confirm they have been reviewed or assessed?	
Does your charity's risk management statement confirm that controls are in place to manage the major risks?	

Many charities, particularly bigger ones and those with more complex activities, will go further than the points shown in the checklist to give more detailed descriptions of the major risks they face (linking them to their operational and strategic objectives). They may also describe their procedures and which risks they have considered: financial, operational, compliance and other categories of identifiable risk. They may detail the impact and effectiveness of their chosen approach. They will seek to demonstrate their ability to identify, assess and reduce the likelihood of risks materialising – and their impact, should the events occur. Such charities may be more expansive about their monitoring processes and how the management of risk is embedded in all that they do.

Soberingly serious
A topic related to risk is serious incident reporting. I am not going to cover this in massive detail but you should ensure you understand it as part of your charity's consideration of risk management more broadly. The regimes in England and Wales, Scotland, and Northern Ireland require registered charities to report serious incidents to the relevant regulator.

For the regulators, a serious incident is an adverse event, or an allegation of one, that fulfils one or more of the following:
- gives rise to or risks giving rise to significant harm to a charity's beneficiaries, staff, volunteers or others;
- causes or risks causing financial loss or damage to assets and property;
- causes or risks causing other harm to work or reputation.

'Significant' is taken contextually, looking at your charity's staff, operations, reputation and finances. In other words, a significant risk is one that has caused or is threatening to cause your charity major harm. An example of a serious incident could be theft of charity money by an employee or alleged abuse of a beneficiary by a charity worker.

When such incidents arise, in addition to trying to deal with the actual problem, you must make a report to the relevant regulator. This obligation and responsibility to report in a timely manner rests with your charity's trustees – although, in practice, it may be delegated to someone else within your charity, such as a member of staff or an adviser. It's important that your executive and trustees know what the serious incident reporting requirements are. They should also be aware that if the trustees conclude no report is necessary, they are strongly recommended to document their decision not to report, so they can explain their decision if called upon to do so.

The point of all this is that the regulators are looking to see that the trustees have taken steps to minimise the fallout for the charity and those it serves from a risk which has materialised or threatens to do so. In its guidance on serious incidents, the Charity Commission acknowledges that most situations can be resolved by a charity's trustees. However, the reporting regime is a crucial part of the regulators' own risk management. It gives them a heads up should they wish to undertake steps to protect a charity from further harm or if they might need to take action about a wider problem for other charities that has been highlighted by the reporting charity's experience.

A list of the things which would trigger a serious incident report can be found in the Charity Commission's guidance 'How to Report a Serious Incident in Your Charity'.

Weighing up what works

The most important question I want you to ask yourself, whether you mostly wear a governance hat or an operations hat, is this: do the tools your charity uses work?

In 2013, Charity Finance Group (CFG) experienced some massive challenges as a result of multiple risks coming home to roost all at once. CFG stands for great financial management. During a crunchy and difficult restructure, which through poor luck and a dose of misjudgement on my part didn't go to plan, I found myself with some reputationally damaging headlines – both implied and overt criticisms were levelled about the state of CFG's financial management. Once we had weathered the storm, I reviewed the position with my trustees and concluded that the things which had nearly brought us down were absent from our risk register. In fact, nothing about our risk management process had really helped us navigate the stormy waters! Looking back, like many organisations, we had spent too much time talking about risks which were beyond our control (such as the death of Queen Elizabeth II during a major income-generating event we were holding in Westminster) and not enough time actively discussing the things we could control. Conversations centred more on whether something was a red or an amber, a 4 or a 5, and not enough discussion was focused on driving higher impact rather than just minimising harm. As an organisation, we were ill-prepared for risk coming from unexpected directions. I carry the scars of ineffective risk management, despite having many of the standard tools in place and committed, skilled people involved. Happily, that means I can also share the broad lessons I learned.

After this happened, we threw out our risk register entirely and started from scratch on our approach to risk management! I became very interested in how charities can engage with risk more positively and effectively, watched presentations, read books, and sought out new models and ways of thinking. I cannot share *everything* I learned in this chapter, but I hope the following two observations prompt your thinking. Firstly, culture is massively important to risk management. Secondly, simple tools are more easily embedded in practice than complex ones. I'll say a bit on culture and then I'll share a simple model that I discovered in *Harvard Business Review* and adapted for CFG's use.

Culture

Everyone – all levels of staff, the executive and the board – should own risk and take responsibility for both spotting things going off the rails and flagging opportunities that would otherwise be missed. Assigning a named owner to each risk in your risk register may help to provide focus and leadership, but it can also result in others not taking responsibility. Sharing responsibility requires a positive attitude towards risk and failure. Ask yourself how your charity responds to failure:

- Do the **senior staff** encourage the people they manage to try new ideas and share with their colleagues when things don't go to plan?
- What about the **trustees** – do they support the staff equally in the face of triumph and disaster? Or do they turn a blind eye to poor management if the outcome is great and beat the staff up if a well-thought-through decision ends badly?

Giving permission to fail is an essential part of a positive risk culture, because learning consequentially becomes the norm. When a charity has a culture that allows freedom to act within clear boundaries and encourages open discussion about success and failure, risk management is much improved.

At your charity, is risk embedded in all conversations? Do the staff and trustees discuss risk every time a decision is made, at all levels, throughout your board meetings and in briefings? If not, make this happen! Make risk part of conversations at all levels of your charity – not just something that senior folk talk about. Avoid the jargon of risk management, major on the debate not the documents, and focus on how your charity can minimise harm *and* maximise opportunity.

Consider our fictitious charity, the Society of Oneirocritics. It delivers training at both an introductory and an advanced level for would-be dream interpreters. This is central to the delivery of the Society's charitable activity and is a major income stream as well as meeting beneficiary needs. The team responsible for promoting the training monitors how many people sign up to each course. Let's assume the advanced training is really struggling. A minimising-harm mindset results in more of the Society's resources being pumped into promoting the struggling training to try and generate more sign-ups. However, the flip side might be that the training sessions for the introductory courses are booked out early and potential attendees turned away or placed on a waiting list. Traditional risk management methods might show the popular training as 'green' and the struggling training as 'red', with more focus being given to reducing the red risk.

But let's look at the Society's experience through a positive risk culture lens. If we equip the Society with a more balanced view of risk management – one which embraces opportunity – this scenario plays out differently. What if the staff have autonomy to generate a certain value of income from delivering content which meets beneficiary needs? Instead of marketing resources being thrown at the courses suffering low bookings, attention is turned to the courses booking out quickly. Could the dates currently booked for the advanced courses instead be used to accommodate more dates for the introductory courses, given they are in greater demand? By leaning into what is working and delivering more dates for the popular training, the Society could reduce its risk of financial loss, accommodate those individuals seeking training who would otherwise have been left unsupported, be more effectively led by its beneficiaries' needs, and generate greater returns through higher levels of bookings.

The table below contains some examples of risks along with two perspectives: one focused on minimising harm and an alternative, based on a positive risk culture, that focuses on using questions to maximise opportunities. I stress, you need both!

Minimising harm	*Maximising opportunity*
Loss of a key member of staff	
■ Robust exit strategy ■ Handover process ■ Three months' notice for senior staff	How do we create a positive culture which: ■ minimises reliance on individuals? ■ swiftly attracts and retains talent? ■ identifies the morale and performance of teams?
Major IT failure; server fails	
■ Protocol for recovery from back-ups within 24 hours ■ Service level agreements with outsourced provider, including penalties	Can we: ■ explore a move to cloud-based solutions? ■ develop an IT strategy focusing on organisational need over the next 18 months, and opportunities to drive efficiency and effectiveness?
Adequate control of finances	
■ Controls and processes for budgeting ■ Authorisation levels ■ Regular forecasting ■ Reduction of expenditure to keep within budget	What resources do we need to: ■ deliver maximum impact? ■ achieve the most with what we have? ■ generate more income?

Before leaving the topic of culture behind us, I feel the need to specifically talk about trustee behaviour. While the culture within a charity should encompass staff and trustees alike, it is not unusual for the culture operating in the board room to be quite different from that experienced on the front line. It's understandable that when it comes to risk, particularly when something is blowing up in your face or there is a big decision to be made around risk and reward, trustees may become risk averse. They are not submerged within the day-to-day running of the charity, after all. Their perceptions of risk will be very different from the staff's. They are also the ones responsible – the ones whose necks will be on the line if disaster comes calling!

Sometimes they will feel the need to meddle in management to assuage their fear of doing nothing. In *It's a Battle on the Board*, Debra Allcock Tyler covers trustees' duties and behaviours brilliantly. In her chapter 10, on risk, she includes my story of having twins, which I'll now share in more detail.

I had an unexpected twin pregnancy in my mid-30s, which automatically put me in the high-risk category in the eyes of the medical profession. But this was not my first rodeo (it was my third!), and my husband and I employed independent midwives, specialists in twin births, to manage the risks we faced. The NHS obstetrician was really nervous about our decision to opt out of multiple visits to the hospital but, other than it being usual protocol, could offer us no reasons why we should comply. He was deeply uncomfortable because he would be deprived of the usual measurements and data that following the usual process would deliver. Through discussion, we established that he trusted our midwives but was fearful our babies would not grow. I asked if he could make them grow – he admitted he could not!

He was reaching for action (in this case frequently dragging us into hospital) to address his own understandable discomfort, despite the fact that this would not change the outcome of our pregnancy. Often trustees will do the same – get staff to jump through hoops, asking them to provide more and more information and distracting them from the job of managing the risk – for no tangible change in the outcome. So, before trustees ask for something to be done or produced, they should stop and ask themselves if they can 'make the babies grow'!

By the way, I went to 41 weeks and delivered two healthy girls, at home!

Simplifying your charity's framework

In some regards, it really doesn't matter what mechanism your charity decides to use to monitor and manage risk, provided it is clear and drives behaviour at all levels. But, frequently, people end up doing stuff not because it helps to drive impact and avoids harm but because it is what the established risk framework requires. They end up feeding a risk management monster and producing documents and reports unnecessarily. If you want to think differently and simplify your charity's framework, I recommend starting with a model developed by Robert Kaplan and Anette Mikes, published in *Harvard Business Review* in 2012. In their model, Kaplan and Mikes organise risks into just three categories:

- **External risks:** These are those matters which are beyond your control – such as a pandemic – and for which all you can do is prepare a contingency or disaster recovery plan.
- **Preventable risks:** These are those matters where controls, policies, processes and procedures can prevent things going wrong.

- **Strategic risks:** These are those risks which you choose to engage with in order to pursue your strategy, where you have to think about the balance between risk and reward and where regular dialogue is hugely important.

Preventable risks will cover an awful lot of standard risk register entries which get discussed ad nauseum in the board room unnecessarily. For example, compliance with regulations can be an incredibly serious matter but, once controls are in place and compliance is being monitored, do they really need to be discussed at length routinely? Of course, if a new risk materialises or a threshold is reached, a discussion should be had and, if required, further actions put in place. The same goes for external risks – once the appropriate mechanisms are in place, periodic review and discussion by exception is really all that's required. This frees up time for the last category – strategic risk. You should discuss this final category constantly, embedding the discussions into everything your charity does and all your decision-making.

As Kaplan and Mikes conceived their model thinking specifically about business, I adapted the model for CFG and the charity context more widely. See the image below for my version.

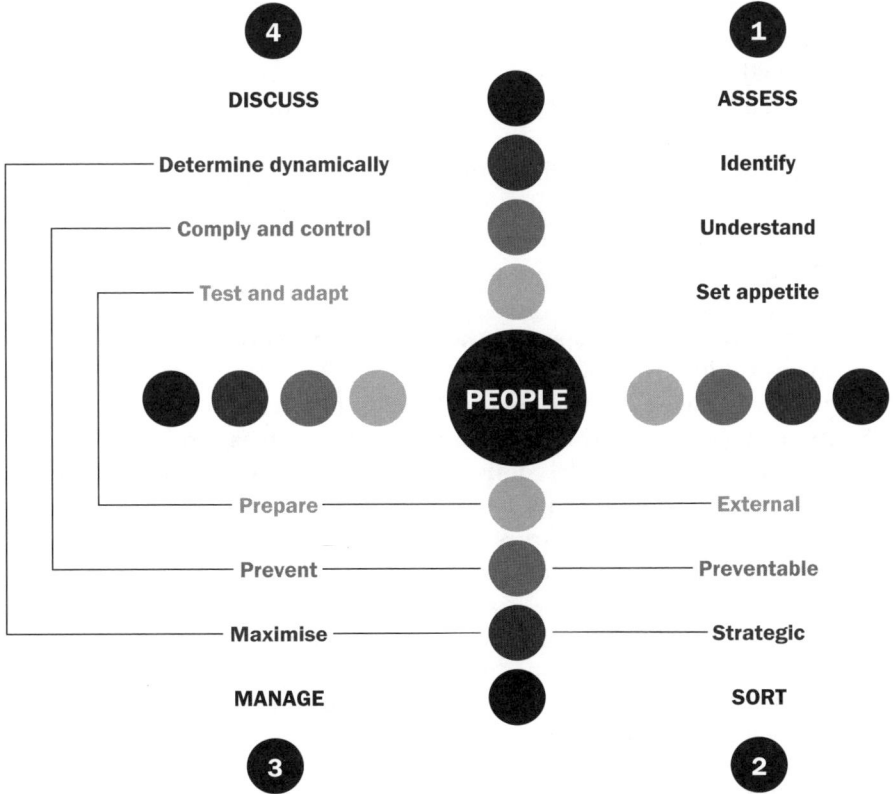

1. ASSESS. Start by **identifying** which areas give rise to risks and opportunities within your organisation and group them together. For example, at CFG we have overarching areas like 'reputation' (ensuring CFG's reputation is maintained and positive), 'people and development' (ensuring we attract, retain and reward staff to maintain an environment where we are not unduly reliant on any single member of staff, reduce unnecessary turnover, improve morale and demonstrate excellence as a social change organisation) and 'systems' (ensuring our systems drive and support CFG's business needs and offer the flexibility to adapt to changes in the operating environment). It's important that you **understand** each area – what might happen that could affect the area and what the impact would be? Are each of the areas related to other aspects of your work? Finally, think about what your **appetite** for risk and opportunity is. What are the things you absolutely cannot allow to go pear-shaped? For example, at CFG this would be financial management, given the nature of our organisation. Where are you happy to be bolder? This could be trying out a new way of managing risk!
2. SORT. Then sort your risks and opportunities into the three categories as set out in the Kaplan and Mikes's approach, i.e. external, preventable or strategic risks.
3. MANAGE. Depending on which of the three categories the risk or opportunity belongs to, its management follows the model to the corresponding option:
   - prepare – aim to prepare for the risk or opportunity materialising and set up controls;
   - prevent – aim to prevent any harm from the risk or opportunity, and monitor how effective your controls are and whether they are being complied with;
   - maximise – aim to maximise the positive impact of the risk or opportunity.
4. DISCUSS. Having grouped your risks and opportunities into one of the three categories and identified the most suitable management approach for each, follow the model to identify the appropriate level of discussion on each risk or opportunity:
   - External/prepare – this leads to infrequent or by-exception discussions.
   - Preventable/prevent – this leads to, again, infrequent or by-exception discussions.
   - Strategic/maximise – this leads to continuous discussions and decision-making based on a dynamic approach driven by emerging or newly encountered issues. These discussions should be embedded at every level of your organisation and in everything you do.

The overall process should be ongoing and with regular rotation of risks or opportunities around the model to make sure that you're capturing all the relevant ones, anticipating issues and feeding back into your processes, systems and controls any lessons that emerge from the things you encounter and the decisions you make.

Living with risk

There is no single right answer or perfect risk management framework – or at least, if there is, I've not nailed it yet, although I'm committed to making continual improvements to the systems and approach I use. To use a well-worn cliché, it's a journey, not a destination. It may sound heinous in a book on understanding the numbers, but I would encourage you to question whether complicated scoring or boiling things down to a number really helps with your charity's management or whether it adds to your nightmare.

Don't do it the way it's always been done because of habit – make sure your charity is getting value from its precious resources. Step back and reassess. Has your charity dealt with disaster well? Has it spotted and seized opportunities for triumph? Do your executive and trustees learn and adapt, flex and change, according to the environment you're experiencing, whether it is possible to predict what's coming down the road or not?

We cannot live a risk-free life, but we can navigate the risks we encounter more productively and positively. I hope you have been prompted to think about a more positive agenda on risk and have gained a firmer grip on this part of your nightmare with the numbers.

Main chapter takeaways

- Make sure your charity's risk models are clear, jargon free, universally understood and driving change. If they aren't, refresh them.
- Organisational risk appetite is a mash-up of individuals' opinions (make sure you know where each individual trustee or executive team member sits on the risk spectrum!).
- Embed risk (avoiding harm and maximising opportunity) at all levels and focus on culture, not just numbers.

5 'Rainy day' reserves

It's often said that reserves are something kept for a rainy day – a lot of us feel like we're living in a monsoon! Sarah Elliot, CEO NCVO

One of the most misunderstood areas of charity finance is what reserves are and whether charities need to hold them. Urban myths – such as that you have to stash a prescribed number of months of operating costs under the mattress – have taken hold of the sector's financial thinking like ivy clinging to the bricks of an old wall: harmful and difficult to budge.

Typically, people have tended to think of reserves as 'rainy day' funds for when things aren't going well. In anticipation of difficulties or disasters , we've been encouraged to hold onto cash. If reserves were ever purely funds for a rainy day, we have to be alive to of the fact, as Sarah puts it, we've been living in monsoon conditions for some time. You could be forgiven for wondering whether it will stop raining long enough to even consider replenishing the pot or whether we are doomed to remain soaked to the skin by the relentless onslaught for all time!

But, of course, not all charities are in the same boat. Some, out of choice, don't retain reserves. Others prefer to think more in terms of liquidity (i.e. the ease with which they can turn assets into cash) than reserves – relying on using assets to respond to crisis, risk or opportunity rather than keeping a cash reserve to one side. Reserves aren't always put away for a rainy day. Sometimes they are gathered in anticipation of a piece of work, to acquire an asset in the future, or to permit a significant change of strategy or direction.

In this chapter we will look at what the law and best practice really require of your charity in relation to reserves, explore a basic model your charity can use or adapt for its own circumstances, and look into some alternative thinking that could help you reframe what reserves are to your charity.

> **Outcomes**
> **After reading this chapter you will:**
> - **Understand the legal position and best practice in terms of reserves**
> - **Have a model to draw on when putting together your charity's reserves policy**
> - **Have information against which to test your charity's thinking on reserves**

What are reserves?

At a very basic level, reserves are the funds your charity has left over that it sets aside, either to spend in the coming year or to save for difficult periods: you probably think of them as savings or a rainy day fund (as discussed above). There are lots of words people use when talking about reserves. They may be thinking about the technical meaning (what has to be included in your charity's accounts) or they might be thinking more generally ('What have we got in reserve?'). In many board rooms and in conversations with charity executives, I have heard words such as 'general', 'free' and 'cash' reserves used interchangeably. But when people use these terms, they don't always mean the same thing. Money your charity has not spent might be restricted or unrestricted, and it can also be designated (see the glossary for explanations of these terms). I have frequently heard people talk of funds held in 'reserve', including different types of fund. But not all funds can be freely spent on everything your charity does, and trustees could come up against problems if they did. The whole topic is a source of confusion. That's why this book has a whole chapter on it!

Let's take the technical bit first. For the purposes of your charity's accounts, reserves exclude endowments, restricted funds and any unrestricted funds your charity can't easily spend (for example, if you would need to sell an asset to get your hands on the cash). The following figure neatly summarises these different categories. It comes from *Beyond Reserves*, produced by Charity Finance Group (CFG) and partners to provide an in-depth exploration of the considerations around keeping reserves. It is what I would describe as an 'oldie but a goodie'. It includes a lot of thinking which can help your executive and trustees to decide what they are holding – and for what purpose – and to form a policy to reflect those decisions.

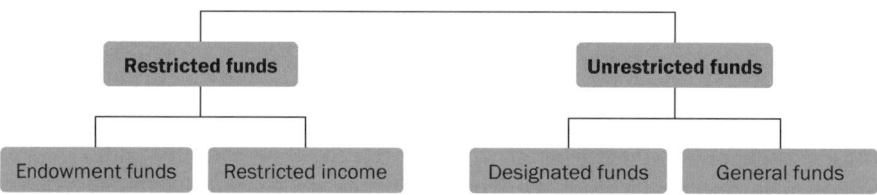

The official guidance issued by the Charity Commission for England and Wales in relation to reserves, *Charity Reserves: Building resilience* (CC19), is really only concerned with the funds that fall into the right-hand side of the above diagram – unrestricted money. (The Office of the Scottish Charity Regulator and the Charity Commission for Northern Ireland have produced separate guidance on reserves.) When reserves are discussed, the Charity Commission also does not include tangible fixed assets, such as land and buildings, or investments held solely to further your charitable objects. However, these are important to bear in mind when thinking about your charity's policy on reserves. They are also important to those looking at an alternative to holding cash reserves – such as a liquidity policy, where investments and other assets are assessed on the basis of the ability to turn them into cash.

In this chapter I am going to talk about all types of fund, because I believe that in order to understand what your charity can spend, it also needs to understand what it cannot.

The legal requirements and guidance around reserves
What does the law require?
The first thing to say is that your charity does not have to have reserves. There is no requirement in law to do so. In fact, virtually the opposite is true: charity law dictates that charity trustees should spend income within a reasonable time of being given it and should only keep it back for good reasons. However, before you hot-foot it back to your charity to say, 'Ha, see, we don't need to hold any reserves!', I hasten to add that there is a balance to be struck between the various legal duties that trustees have relating to financial stewardship. Specifically, these duties are to:
- act in the best interests of your charity;
- manage your charity's resources responsibly;
- act with reasonable care and skill.

While the law does not require you to keep reserves, the bottom line is that your charity *should* if your trustees consider it in the best interests of your charity and it helps them manage resources responsibly. Sometimes this implicit power is also explicitly enshrined in a charity's governing document. For example, your governing document might say something like, 'In furtherance of the objects but not otherwise the charity may ... accumulate and set aside funds for special purposes or as reserves'.

Whether the power to hold reserves is explicit or implicit, trustees need to use it appropriately. If they use it without justification, then by holding income in reserve they might not be fulfilling their legal obligations and could be criticised by your charity's regulator or challenged by a stakeholder.

What do the regulators require?
As I said in chapter 1, your charity may not be required to follow the Charities Statement of Recommended Practice (SORP), depending on its size and whether it is constituted as a company. Irrespective of the specific requirements of the SORP, which we will come on to later in this chapter, all charities ought to develop a reserves policy that justifies and explains the decision to hold (or not) reserves. Such a policy should be published in your trustees' annual report, and some charities also publish it in annual reviews and on their websites. It should explain how and when money held back will be used, and if your trustees don't feel holding reserves is necessary, that fact and their reasoning should be set out clearly.

In the aftermath of some high-profile charity failures, the Charity Commission included in its guidance that, when thinking about their reserves, trustees should consider the impact of unplanned closures as well as their spending commitments, potential liabilities and financial forecasts. Since this change, there have been many who have interpreted this as keeping back sufficient money to manage financial collapse. I personally do not encourage trustees to think about unplanned closure unduly. After all, the financial position of a charity facing closure is not just determined by its free reserves but also by its assets, staff numbers and so on. If your charity is confident it can keep operating into the foreseeable future, increasing its reserves to deal with all the associated costs of winding up could unnecessarily tie up money that could be delivering charitable activities. I would encourage executives and trustees to prioritise thinking about beneficiaries, the risks identified through your charity's risk management procedures (covered in the previous chapter), and delivering impact instead of overly focusing on avoiding *unplanned* closure.

Of course, if your charity's financial position leads your executive and trustees to consider that closure may be necessary, this is a serious issue and you should get appropriate legal advice. However, reserves policies are not, in my view, the place to be prioritising the payment of creditors.

What must you do if you are subject to the SORP?
For those reporting under the SORP, your charity must explain any policy it has for holding reserves, state the amount of those reserves and clarify why they are held. If your trustees decide keeping money in reserve is unnecessary, they are required to disclose this and provide their reasons. The SORP also says that the review of reserves in your trustees' annual report should:
- state the total amount held;
- identify what's restricted and explain material sums designated or otherwise committed;
- give an indication of the time within which the funds will be spent;
- identify amounts that your charity can only spend by disposing of an asset or investment;
- compare the stated amounts to your policy;
- if you are holding more or less than your charity's policy says is needed, set out what you will do about this.

There are also more detailed requirements within the SORP on how these figures are shown in the accounts, but these requirements are beyond the scope of this book.

Larger charities have more onerous requirements and expectations. Those with an annual income over £500,000 are encouraged to include additional information in their review of their charity's reserves, particularly around risks and how reserves may be used to manage them.

You'd be forgiven for thinking your charity's reserves policy should therefore be a complicated and extensive published report. But the reality is that the requirement to have a position on whether or not to retain reserves is satisfied by the inclusion of brief information in your trustees' annual report: your charity is not required to publish a tome! For example, the following would be perfectly adequate:

> As part of our annual budget-setting, the trustees consider what the appropriate level of reserves to maintain should be. The trustees retain funds to provide working capital, manage unexpected drops in income, handle

5. 'Rainy day' reserves

unexpected increases in expenditure and provide cover against a range of risks. The trustees consider reserves of between £120,000 and £175,000 to be appropriate.

The six months myth

There is an urban myth that at some point the regulators stated that the minimum quantity of reserves to be held was six months' worth of operating costs. Nowhere in the SORP or the regulators' guidance are reserves ever expressed in number of months of expenditure. So why is this way of thinking about reserves still a benchmark for many? I can only presume it is an easy shorthand. Trustees may also feel more comfortable thinking in terms of having a certain number of months before insolvency if the income tap is turned off entirely. The NCVO's *UK Civil Society Almanac*, for example, talks about average number of months' worth of operating costs held in reserve. While thinking this way can be helpful to get a sense of the resilience of the sector as a whole (as part of the wider data set the *Almanac* contains), I think it is really unhelpful at an individual charity level when thinking about reserves – even in times of crisis.

For a start, what are operating costs? What would you include and what would you leave out? And how would trustees know whether six months is sufficient or not to get your charity out of crisis or to bring about necessary change? It's debatable whether all income sources are likely to be switched off at the same time; in reality, such dips are more likely to be phased. If your charity is really up the creek without a paddle, it's likely that things will also be happening which lower its overall spending, such as staff exiting stage left to find greater security.

As a rule of thumb, I believe people think of this six months figure in terms of buying sufficient time to do something major: get new funding, lay off staff, find a new office and so on. But the reality is that applying such an arbitrary calculation will mean some charities hold way too little for their circumstances and others hold way too much.

So, before you begin to think about putting together a reserves policy for your charity, forget the idea of holding six months' operating costs.

Putting together a reserves policy

The starting point for putting together a reserves policy is to establish a level of understanding across your trustees and executive as to the resources available to your charity, the robustness or predictability of your income, your business model, your committed expenditure, and the speed with which each service or activity can be paused or stopped (or, conversely, the extent to which you need to be able to move quickly and invest resources in new activities). For example:

- Is your charity guaranteed grant income or is some of it speculative?
- How much of your charity's costs are fixed?
- What expenditure is flexible (i.e. where the executive or trustees can choose not to spend)?

If your charity's income is guaranteed, or if you have loads of flexibility on how much you spend if there is a shortfall of income, then your reserves may be less important. If, however, your income is a bit more shaky or your charity lacks flexibility in what is spent, then your executive and trustees will need to think about when they might need to dip into reserves to help your charity survive or do important work.

Your charity is not more successful if it has large reserves. Your charity is successful if it is achieving its objectives, which are *not* to build up reserves but to do your charitable work. Reserves are a tool to help your charity remain financially resilient from year to year.

Take a strategic view when thinking about reserves and build them into your charity's overall financial and strategic planning. Huge flexibility can be built into budgets and plans, and this may negate the need to hold money back in reserve in specific areas. For example, at CFG we include contingencies in events' budgets, particularly for new events, because we know they might not deliver an immediate return. This means we don't need to keep a sum in reserve against the potential under-performance of those events, because the budget has already allowed for the risk. You might also only include figures that are certain within your financial planning, knowing that a proportion of the less certain income items (which you have not included) will materialise. This too could reduce your need to keep money in reserve to cover the risk of receiving less income.

5. 'Rainy day' reserves

Getting started

Here are some simple questions to consider as your charity gets started on creating its reserves policy or reviewing an existing one:

- Why do your trustees want to hold back funds in reserve? This may be to satisfy one or more of the following needs:
  - to safeguard against the loss of income;
  - to save up to buy a future asset or developing a future project;
  - to respond to increased costs;
  - to pay for a reduction or increase in staff headcount;
  - to bridge a gap between grants or contracts.
- Has a funder imposed restrictions on sums held?
  - What is the extent of the requirements for the restricted fund?
  - Do the restricted funds cover the entire activities to which they relate or is there a shortfall, such as core costs, to which they do not extend? (This means your charity will have to have other income to supplement the restricted fund or hold reserves.)
- How predictable is your charity's income and how committed is its expenditure?
  - How much of your charity's income is secured before the financial year starts? For how long?
  - Is there lots of expenditure that your charity is bound to, such as staff salaries, the cost of premises, and costs associated with the delivery of grants or contracts?
  - What are the links between income and expenditure (i.e. how easily do they match up, and will stopping expenditure undermine corresponding income)?
- How quickly can your executive and trustees change the way your charity operates?
  - Can assets be easily turned into cash?
  - Are your spending commitments hard to flex?
  - Can alternative funds be raised easily?
  - Can your charity stop doing things quickly?
  - Do you hold insurance that would mitigate loss and/or increased costs?

Once you have thought about these fundamentals, how might you go about thinking about the detailed numbers? There are three main areas your charity should think about when pulling a reserves policy together:

1. **Working capital:** This is money that your charity is using every day or month in order to keep running. It includes cash and money owed as well as things your charity is selling or things that could be sold quickly.
2. **Keeping your charity's activities going:** This relates to the balance between how volatile your charity's income is and how easily you can flex your expenditure.
3. **The specific risks your charity faces:** For example, maybe your charity is nearing the end of a two-phase project which has been funded for the first phase but you are yet to secure funding for the second phase.

A reserves policy should be a living document. You should review it when there are major changes in the operation of your charity or its working environment, and as part of your yearly budget cycle. How your charity holds the money it decides to keep in reserve – for example, as investments – is a further consideration (once your trustees have decided how much is needed). We will cover this topic in a light-touch way in chapter 8.

For example, DSC, where I was the chair for a while, reviews its reserves position every quarter as part of its normal board meetings. The trustees discuss what the forecasts are telling them about financial performance and how that may affect the reserves position. They then discuss and decide whether the charity needs to dip into its reserves or whether the executive needs to curtail spending in order to preserve or build the reserves position.

Reserves range
Once you have understood your charity's needs, it is unlikely that your reserves will be a single specific sum. It is more likely that what your trustees decide is needed in reserve will have minimum and maximum levels – a range of amounts that suit your charity. In my view, how you describe your range should avoid less meaningful terms like 'three to six months' operating costs'. Instead, state specific amounts: 'We need between £27,000 and £36,000 in reserve.' Additionally, as covered elsewhere in this book (see particularly chapters 3 and 6), giving numbers without a narrative is not helpful, so it's important to say how this range was settled upon. See 'A worked reserves example' below for how this might look.

CC19 (the Charity Commission's reserves guidance) agrees that there is no single level or even a range of reserves that is right for all charities. It says the level should be set by trustees and reflect the particular circumstances of the charity. Adopting a target range which is appropriate to your charity's circumstances gives you greater flexibility in communications and is more realistic in terms of changing needs. Rarely will there be a single figure that represents what your charity needs, whether for a financial year or any given period.

Restricted funds
Understanding the extent of any restrictions imposed on your funds is helpful in calculating how much you may need to keep in your general reserves. As a reminder, restricted funds consist of money that was given or donated to your charity for a specific piece of work or purpose. Pesh Framjee, a respected accountant and charity finance expert, says in the helpsheet *Reserves Policy: Setting and implementing weather protection* that it is important to understand what a restriction covers. Sometimes restrictions are widely drafted and enable these funds to be used for a variety of fixed and core costs. In other words, in some cases, the restriction isn't that restrictive!

Thus, restricted funds should not automatically be excluded from your thinking around establishing a reserves policy. But be careful not to go beyond what any restrictions permit. For example, if your charity has been given money to buy a therapy rabbit, the money is restricted to buying the animal. It may also be within the restriction to provide for vet bills, food and so on, but the restriction probably doesn't extend to wider costs. However, if the restriction is to fund the service of providing therapy rabbits to people who need them, it probably also includes core costs (such as a contribution to electricity, staff time and similar expenses that are relevant to providing the service). It's also important to be aware of designated funds, which are amounts of reserves that have been deliberately set aside or earmarked for a particular activity, too. You may regard these funds as being like restricted funds because you've already set them aside for something else, but if circumstances change, you can decide to make them available to meet necessary expenditure.

Risk and reserves
In my view, there are two elements to risk and reserves: the macro operating environment (the political, economic, social, technological, legal and environmental conditions that impact how all organisations can operate) and the micro considerations (specific to each charity). Traditionally, risk and reserves are often framed in terms of accommodating those occurrences which, while remote, could be catastrophic to your charity's financial well-being (often called 'black swans'). Such events can be either macro events, which affect everyone, or micro events, which are specific to your charity. You would be forgiven for thinking that in the recent past we've experienced less of a single swan and more of a flock as we faced income from all resources being interrupted, demand spiking, and uncertainty in the wider economy and society.

Whether or not your reserves policy includes black-swan events, once they materialise, you will need to consider reserve calculations. You may conclude that such events are unlikely to reoccur and holding money in reserve in case of a repeat is unnecessary.

Alternatively, particularly if the event took you by surprise or was widespread, such as the COVID-19 pandemic, that experience can lead in the opposite direction: to entirely rethinking your policy and concluding reserves were inadequate and sums ought to be held to allow you to withstand potential future disruptions.

If your charity does determine more is required in the tank to safeguard against future crises, there is a further challenge in the current environment – how do staff go about generating reserves when what was held has been depleted? Maybe you even have fewer staff in total and your charity is facing uncertainty for the foreseeable future.

The reality is you won't know whether your charity's conclusion is right until it is too late. It's a judgement call that must balance your current needs with the risks. However, I would caution against knee-jerk reactions to a higher-risk operating environment, such as cutting expenditure on vital services just to shore up your charity's reserves, or losing fundraising staff. Such measures might help your short-term position but will limit your ability to generate funds for the future. In these turbulent times, it may seem like we need to totally rethink how we decide what we keep in reserve versus what we spend, but things may not have changed as much as we feel they have. Your charity's ability to withstand one black swan is not necessarily a reliable predictor of its ability to face another. Indeed, in the face of increased risk, it might be time to reduce the sums you hold, releasing funds to enable you to adapt to new ways of working or to meet need arising from what has occurred.

Chapter 4, on risk, identified different types of risk your charity might face. Thinking about the risks that are particular to your charity, consider what the financial impact might be of each:

- Can you safeguard against the financial impact through flexibility in your budget (for example, by halting a piece of work so as to reduce the expenditure that you would otherwise commit)?
- Can you safeguard against the financial impact through an insurance policy?
- Might a funder underwrite a particular venture because your charity is treading new ground?

You should always include the potential financial impact of a risk in your charity's considerations of how much you need to keep in reserve. However, your charity does not have to keep in reserve sums which reflect the entire exposure to the risk, because there may be other financial tools and actions that render holding a greater amount unnecessary. Furthermore, a balance needs to be struck between short-term and longer-terms risks, so you can serve your beneficiaries both as soon as possible *and* in the future.

Reputation
The sums your charity holds in reserve can have a reputational impact. If your charity is perceived to be holding too much in the bank, it may open you up to criticism when seeking to raise funds, or demands to use the money from staff, volunteers or other stakeholders. Conversely, if your charity holds little or no cash in reserve, you may appear to your stakeholders as economically unstable or fragile. However, please don't get hung up on maintaining reserves as an end in itself. Reputation shouldn't be your biggest driver – your organisational need should be.

There is a very simple antidote to this potential reputational problem: explain your charity's reserves policy clearly and transparently to your stakeholders, such as in your trustees' annual report, your charity's impact reports or on your website. For example:

- **High reserves matching your policy:** If you hold large sums (ones that others raise an eyebrow at) but they are within your charity's policy, your trustees should explain why so much is needed.

- **High reserves outside your policy:** If your charity has more reserves than your trustees have determined your charity needs as set out in your reserves policy, show how the number will be spent down. For example, 'As a result of a period of major growth, we currently have reserves in excess of our policy. The trustees have agreed to use £70,000 of the funds to reach more people, develop our services in a new location and invest in system improvements to provide easier access for our beneficiaries.'
- **Low reserves matching your policy:** If your charity holds little or no reserves but the trustees are happy with that position, explain why they have come to that conclusion.
- **Low reserves outside your policy:** If your charity has lower reserves than your trustees have determined are necessary in your policy, tell the story of why this is the case and how your charity intends to increase the sums held in due course. For example, 'We were unable to run our major fundraising event and relied on reserves to bridge the gap, reducing the sums we hold to outside our agreed reserves range. The trustees have agreed that investment in digital capacity is necessary to secure future income sufficient to generate surpluses and rebuild our reserves. This decision will, in the short term, keep our reserves below the lower end of the acceptable reserves policy level, but it will provide surpluses next year and thereafter.'
- **Uncertain position:** If your charity has not yet worked out what future calls on its reserves will be but feels volatility could create problems in meeting your expenditure commitments, avoid using reserves to fund permanent costs without knowing how the corresponding income will be generated on an ongoing basis. Always explain any adjustments in your charity's policies arising from the experiences your charity has had.

So, your charity can manage reputational risks by being clear on its policy and plans, but what can you do if the sum of money your trustees think is needed and the actual sum of money that can realistically be generated are poles apart? (This may be as a result of generally tough economic conditions or a situation particular to your charity.) What can you do, practically speaking, and how can you manage the reputational impact in that scenario? Let's explore this topic with a case study.

A charity I know of had a sum of £100,000 in excess of its reserves range (which had been set at between £150,000 and £250,000) and was in the process of a planned spend-down (including operational and strategic investments) when the COVID-19 pandemic hit. Like many others, it went into survival mode – switching its use of reserves to bridge drops in income and invest in technology (enabling it to shift wholesale to online provision). The draw on reserves necessary to survive did not just expend the sums in excess of the charity's policy but resulted in the reserves held dropping to £125,000, which was below the minimum amount stated as desirable in the charity's policy.

Once the charity could shift from survival to something more like business as usual, it reviewed its reserves policy. The charity concluded:
- Its reserves policy was probably inadequate because the charity would not have survived the pandemic if it had not happened to have more in reserves than was set out in its policy. Therefore, it would be prudent to amend the range, increasing the lower figure to £200,000 and the upper figure to £300,000.
- It still needed to spend a sum of £50,000 which it had already designated for investment in organisational development as intended if it was to generate surpluses in future years.
- It was improbable that it would generate surpluses to rebuild its reserves for the foreseeable future.

In this situation, a charity might decide that being so far outside its reserves policy (£125,000 actual versus a range of £200,000–£300,000) is too reputationally damaging and therefore choose not to amend its reserves range (despite concluding that holding more in reserve would be prudent). After all, being £25,000 below your minimum reserves level of £150,000 might look more financially robust than being £75,000 adrift (£125,000 versus a minimum of £200,000)! The charity might alternatively decide to reduce its reserves range, so that the sum held is back in range (say, by making the lower figure £120,000, so that the actual of £125,000 is now £5,000 above the minimum level). The charity might decide to remove the designation and put the £50,000 back into general reserves – bringing the reserves back within range (£175,000 versus a range of £150,000–£250,000). These would be fairly typical approaches to dealing with the situation to avoid the perception of financial instability. However, I think these options all put maintaining a perception (reserves within range) above what may be in the best interests of the charity in reality (investing in the change necessary to generate future income and setting a policy that reflects the real risks and needs).

This dilemma – whether to prioritise the perception or accept the reality – highlights to me two common mistakes that charities can make:
- The ideal range of reserves reflects trustees' judgement on managing risk and it does not necessarily reflect what is achievable in terms of cold, hard cash.
- Focusing on being within an ideal range of reserves can be a false economy and perversely undermine your charity's resilience rather than strengthen it.

In this situation I would be advising the charity to:
- amend its reserves range to reflect what it believes to be the right range of reserves for its risk profile (i.e. to £200,000–£300,000);
- spend the designated fund as intended (not to invest in change, equipment, staff, fundraising and so on that the charity deems necessary to generate future surpluses would risk long-term losses for the sake of short-term gains);

- clearly set out its policy and the current reserves level in relation to it;
- clearly set out that the plan to rebuild its reserve includes spending the designated fund.

My message is that reserves are not there to be protected and preserved, but to protect and preserve the delivery of charitable impact.

Liquidity policies

A liquidity policy is separate from a reserves policy, but it's important to consider the two together.

As a reminder, liquidity is the term used to describe how easily your charity can access cash. It is the frequency and ease with which assets can be released and cash flow managed, either from cash held in the bank or from stuff your charity can sell to convert into cash in the bank. Some charities choose to focus on liquidity instead of, or as a complement to, a reserves policy. A liquidity policy includes consideration of the opportunity costs (the impact of the loss of the chance to do something else) of only holding money in reserve versus holding less money and borrowing against assets if required. For example, a charity may choose to hold less in reserve because a building it owns can be borrowed against at short notice and on good rates. The alternative of holding funds in reserve might mean resources are tied up, preventing you from using them for your charitable objects and potentially preventing them from contributing to income generation.

A worked reserves example

There are three main elements that should feature in both your calculations and the resulting reserves policy: why, what and how.
- **Why?** The purpose for which your charity wants to hold reserves.
- **What?** The amount (range) your charity wants to hold in reserve.
- **How?** The methodology your charity has used where you have calculated a specific figure or range of reserves.

The principles behind the following methodology are helpful, whatever your charity's business model. Understand the purpose of holding reserves, how much your charity needs and how the sum in the policy was arrived at. I would suggest undertaking this work alongside your budget preparation.

This worked example is based on our fictitious charity, the Society of Oneirocritics. The figures, percentage assumptions and data used are consistent with the Society's numbers and risk considerations. It is essential that you determine the right numbers for your charity. Don't just plug your numbers into this worked example and assume they will be spot on for your needs!

You may recall that it is a small charity (annual income under £1 million, as defined by the Charity Commission) carrying out work which spans education and training, a nightmare counselling service, and policy work. Its salary bill runs to £100,000. The CEO, who also acts as the charity's policy voice, earns £40,000 per year. Two full-time staff members earn £30,000 and £20,000 respectively, and a part-time staff member earns £10,000. (For ease I'm using round numbers and not worrying about pensions, tax, etc.). The Society currently operates from premises that cost it around £12,500 per year (but it is looking to go fully remote) and its IT costs run to a total of £4,000 a year. In terms of income, the charity receives grants (£50,000 per year) for educational work and providing nightmare counselling work, and these are pretty stable. Donations given just because people like to read about what dreams mean are pretty predictable and steady each year (around £15,000). The Society additionally is budgeted to raise funds of around £60,500 each year through selling online courses on dream interpretation and providing information packs. This income is a little more variable, but most bookings are taken early in the year so the Society has a reasonable idea of how the year will go by the end of the first six months.

The Society of Oneirocritics reserves policy

Why? The purpose for which our charity wants to hold reserves

The Society holds reserves to:
- provide a sustainable and appropriate level of working capital;
- allow for periods of unexpected drops in planned income;
- cope with sudden short-term increases in planned expenditure;
- provide cover for other risks, contingencies or unforeseen events (low likelihood of events occurring but, if they did, they would have a significant effect).

What? The range we want to hold in reserve

The Society's current policy is to maintain free reserves within the range of £24,000 to £34,000. This range was calculated by taking into account our risks (a risk-based approach).

How? The methodology we have used to calculate a specific range of reserves.

We calculate this range based on working capital, continuity of services (income and expenditure) and other specific risks as follows:

Working capital

Our business model means the vast majority of our income is received by the end of the second quarter in each year in advance of delivering services. The majority of our costs are paid in arrears and processes are in place to ensure that payments are not made prior to the due dates. There is not a significant difference between our assets and our liabilities, and our cash-flow position is strong. Consequently, we do not require much working capital. Looking at our cash-flow forecast, our maximum exposure to working capital in any one month is just below £8,000. To enable us to withstand any sudden changes to our working capital needs, a sum of £8,000 to £12,000 is deemed to be a reasonable level, representing between approximately 100% and 150% of working capital needs.

5. 'Rainy day' reserves

Income

Income for the budget year is summarised below with indications of the risk levels associated with each type:

Income stream	Draft budget for year	Estimated percentage of budget at risk	Risk value to date
Grants	£50,000	20% (one five-year grant secured; second grant ends next year)	£10,000
Donations	£14,500	15% (expected drop)	£2,175
Sales of dream interpretation courses	£40,500	10% (possible under-performance of advanced course)	£4,050
Sales of information packs	£20,000	10% (reflecting cost-of-living pressures)	£2,000
		Value at risk	**£18,225***

*We have built flexibility into the budget to accommodate these anticipated drops. Thus, we conclude reserves should be retained for between 25% and 50% of the value of income at risk (£4,560–£9,110).

Expenditure

A summarised analysis of expenditure is shown below with indications of the risk levels associated with each type:

Area of expenditure	Draft budget for year	Estimated percentage of budget at risk	Risk value to date
Staff costs	£100,000	8%	£8,000
Premises	£12,500	8%	£1,000
IT	£4,000	8%	£320
		Value at risk	**£9,320***

*Given the high-inflationary environment in which we are currently operating, we are reflecting the entire risk value in our reserves policy.

Other risks, contingencies, opportunities and unforeseen events
We are well insured but conclude that we still need to provide cover for other risks, contingencies, opportunities and unforeseen events, such as a future office move or expansion, possible mergers, potential adverse employment tribunal decisions, an urgent IT issue or opportunities that we may need to invest in outside the flexibility of the budget.

We have estimated the cost of office relocation or paying for the repair of dilapidation in the current office (should we move to home-based working) to be between £5,000 and £10,000. However, based on past experience of moving offices, we anticipate the reduced rent cost will largely offset this liability. Therefore, a further contingency of between £2,000 and £3,000 has been set aside.

Reserves range summary
On the basis of the calculations, the reserves range should be between £24,000 and £34,000 (the rounded figures from the below calculations).

Purpose	Minimum level	Maximum level
Working capital	£8,000	£12,000
Income	£4,560	£9,110
Expenditure	£9,320	£9,320
Other risks, contingencies, opportunities and unforeseen events	£2,000	£3,000
Total	**£23,880**	**£33,430**

Any rounding can be done for ease of reference – you have complete flexibility to do so. You will note that if the 'six months' operating costs' principle were applied, the figure held in reserve might be significantly higher (i.e. approximately £50,000). The impact of this is that you would be holding more in reserve and have less available to be spent on present beneficiary needs.

Hopefully, this extended example has prompted you to consider what reserves might be necessary to safeguard against your charity's risks. You don't need to publish your calculation, but recording the process will help your trustees in the future – who may not all have been in post when the policy was set. Furthermore, it will enable adjustments to be made in the model without going back to the drawing board every time something changes. For example, the tentative decision to close the office might prompt expenditure in other areas, such as republishing materials or investing in digital content. These expenses will impact the assumptions that go into the calculation. However, if you have the calculation on file, you can target such conversations at the relevant areas without having to go back to the drawing board on your reserves completely.

Beyond reserves

We are living in volatile times. Holding excess reserves may be a luxury that few charities have recently experienced, having spent the past few years living through unprecedented squeezes on income sources and soaring demand. However, charities can be quite conservative, and traditionally boards like to have a high level of cover for risks and unforeseen events. This means that large amounts of funds can be held 'just in case' while worthwhile projects go unfunded.

When CFG and partners produced *Beyond Reserves* (mentioned earlier in this chapter), a number of the finance and fundraising directors spoken to in the research for the publication agreed that charities could be more ambitious and take a more commercial view in their thinking around the money they deliberately don't spend. That is to say, they could invest in activities to generate impact in the future rather than keeping sums in reserve to protect against harm. In the face of reduced reserves, as uncertainty and financial crisis remain the prevailing state, should we be focusing on rebuilding reserves or investing what we have remaining in supporting our beneficiaries and adapting to new ways of working?

Ask yourself if your charity could be more ambitious in how it approaches reserves. Investing in new donor recruitment or new ways of working (for example) might lead to greater income in the future and provide a better return than you receive in interest earned on reserves held (or return on monies held as investments).

For a number of the charities that shared their experiences for *Beyond Reserves*, their review of their reserves led them to reduce the level they held by a considerable amount, thus releasing funds to deliver their charitable objects. For many of us, living with lower levels of reserves has been an enforced position, but this is also an opportunity to consider whether we have been over-compensating for risks. For example, you might have provided for risks in your charity's strategy (such as by diversifying your income) but then also held back funds as reserves – effectively providing double cover for the same risk.

As charities, we have an opportunity to reassess the role and level of reserves we need as we navigate choppy waters, so as to take a more strategic approach to managing our reserves. Your charity doesn't need to just hoard cash in anticipation of rain. There are several other reasons why you may need to keep reserves, such as responding to change and investing in new services for your beneficiaries. And you might even decide you don't need an umbrella at all.

Finally, you need to consider how your charity can present its case for holding reserves well – to all external stakeholders. Those who support your charity, those who rely on it and those who provide funds will want to feel confident that you are holding funds back for good reason and not simply to make your trustees and executives feel more comfortable in their beds at night.

Main chapter takeaways
- Be clear on why your charity holds reserves and build consideration of them into your financial management processes.
- Be ambitious about what your charity's resources can achieve. Focus on current and future beneficiaries, and avoid a solely 'rainy day' approach.
- Make sure the board of trustees is clear and transparent about how your charity is performing against its reserves policy.

6 Narrative reporting

Good stories surprise us. They make us think and feel. They stick in our minds and help us remember ideas and concepts in a way that a PowerPoint crammed with bar graphs never can. Joe Lazauskas and Shane Snow

For many years I have been trying to encourage charities to view their trustees' annual report and accounts as an opportunity to tell their stories and inspire their readers. Instead, many see this simply as a bureaucratic compliance burden to be tolerated and endured, rather like the dull PowerPoints described by Joe Lazauskas and Shane Snow above. In this chapter, we're going to concentrate on making the best of this opportunity to connect with your charity's stakeholders via your trustees' annual report. We're going to focus on what needs to go into a trustees' annual report, how your charity might better tell its story and talk effectively about impact, and why it's important to ensure that your charity's narrative connects with its numbers. The purpose of this chapter is to cover this annual event, but I would encourage you to use any lessons picked up in reading this chapter to tell your charity's story more effectively more regularly. Engage with those with a stake in your charity's work and highlight the difference you make whenever you have the opportunity to do so. In this sector we're not producing widgets – we're seeking to change lives.

Numbers without a good narrative are as meaningless as a good narrative without the corresponding numbers when it comes to addressing how resources have been used. This is particularly important in our sector. It can be difficult to pin down the links between the inputs (the money and resources we receive), the outputs (the things we do), the outcomes (the short-term effects of what we do) and the impacts (the long-term differences we bring about). Additionally, when charities deliver more, they don't necessarily secure greater income even if they incur additional costs.

In the next chapter, we will explore the related topic of numbers and notes (the accounting bit of your trustees' annual report and accounts). Of course, the use of a good graph, chart or table to display data can make numbers more accessible, but in this chapter we will concentrate on the power in using words which resonate with your charity's stakeholders and convey more than just the financial performance of your charity.

Can you turn that annual compliance requirement into a way to inspire, connect with and inform your charity's stakeholders, encouraging them to help your staff and trustees deliver the change you all want to see? I think so. Let's try to tell a story which makes your readers think, feel and be pleasantly surprised, lodging your charity's achievements and plans for the future firmly in their minds!

> **Outcomes**
> After reading this chapter you will:
> - Have been challenged to view your trustees' annual report as a chance to tell your charity's story and to connect its narrative with the numbers
> - Understand the basic SORP requirements for the trustees' annual report
> - Be able to recognise the various elements in a performance chain (inputs, outputs, outcomes and impact)

What is narrative reporting?

Although there are multiple ways your charity can (and sometimes must) sell itself to the wider world, through the digital space as well as in more traditional methods, every year charities are required to produce a trustees' annual report and accounts. The Charities Statement of Recommended Practice (SORP) sets out that good reporting provides a context that helps readers of accounts to interpret them.

Good reporting links your charity's activities and achievements to the sources of income used to fund them and the money spent on them. Your accounts will focus on your charity's financial position and financial performance, but without the narrative the people reading your charity accounts won't get a rounded view.

Many charities will not be making the most of the opportunity to provide a narrative for their numbers. Appendix 1 shows which charities are required to produce a trustees' annual report and accounts. Depending on your charity's size and whether you are a company, you may be required to lodge these with the relevant regulator. But, beyond you ticking that regulatory compliance box, your charity's stakeholders (beneficiaries, staff, future staff and volunteers, not to forget donors and funders) will all be interested in what your charity has to say each year. Not using this annual opportunity to really connect is frankly a waste! Even if your charity is so small it's not required to file a trustees' annual report and accounts, think about how to tell those you engage with what your charity has got up to.

6. Narrative reporting

The SORP says that the objective of the trustees' annual report is to provide information about how a charity has performed financially and its financial position at the end of the accounting period, which will be 'useful to a wide range of stakeholders in assessing the trustees' stewardship and management of charitable funds, and to assist the user of the accounts to make economic decisions in relation to the charity'.

If the figures in your trustees' annual report and accounts tell you what happened in the reporting period, the narrative tells readers why it was done, what you learned and what you are planning. Think of the narrative as the 'so what'. It is essential to be accountable to those who have already given your charity funds and transparent about your staff's and trustees' management of the resources given to you to bring about positive social change. Done well, your trustees' annual report can drive future donations and engagement with your charity's cause. It might also be the point of reference for people looking to join your charity as a trustee or member of staff, and potential volunteers may review it before deciding to get involved.

Publishing a separate impact report or annual review

Your trustees' annual report provides an essential link between your legal charitable objects, your wider purposes, your aims and the activities you undertake to achieve them. Charities differ in terms of the legal vehicles they use, the business models under which they operate, whether they have volunteers, whether they employ staff, whether they sell stuff, and whether they rely on grants, donated goods or contracts with the local authority (for example). These variations will make a difference to how your charity's numbers appear and, without a decent narrative, can lead to erroneous conclusions being drawn about your charity. For charities in England and Wales, and those lodging accounts with Companies House, the annual report and accounts is one of the only publicly available documents that anyone can pick up. Stakeholders, including journalists, will draw their own conclusions as to what your charity's figures mean if you have not explained them adequately. So, if nothing else, ensuring your charity tells its story well alongside the figures will give you greater control over the interpretation of your charity's numbers.

There has been a trend for many years of reducing what's included in the official trustees' annual report to the bare minimum required to meet the regulators' demands, and instead lavishing time and resources on a review or impact statement which stands alone from the statutory stuff. But I can't shrug off the feeling that the annual report is seen as 'what we *have* to say', whereas the impact report or review is seen as 'what we *want* to say'.

You may think the official documents give you less freedom to say what your charity wants to say in an accessible and interesting way. Think again – there is massive flexibility in the narrative reporting allowed under the SORP. Your charity is able to tell its story alongside the hard numbers, and having a document that is both rigorous and informative surely must be in your interests. So why not save time and combine the two? Why not do something like my organisation, Charity Finance Group (CFG), and produce a report with interviews, videos and digital content that is interesting, interactive and engaging and from which a compliance document can later be drawn?

Things you have to include in a trustees' annual report

For all charities required to submit an annual report, irrespective of whether it has to comply with the SORP, the following information should be included:
- objectives and activities;
- achievements and performance;
- financial review;
- structure, governance and management;
- reference and administrative details;
- exemptions from disclosure;
- funds held as custodian trustee on behalf of others.

Further aspects that must be reported by charities following the SORP are:
- how what the charity has done delivers a public benefit;
- a policy for holding reserves;
- methods for recruiting and inducting trustees.

Then there are additional requirements if the charity is classified as large (i.e. income over £500,000). If this applies to your charity, you will be expected to state your plans for the future and your strategies for achieving them, together with any significant risks your charity is facing and what you are doing to manage them.

Although the responsibility for compiling the trustees' annual report rests with the trustees, it is likely that the heavy lifting on drafting will be undertaken by charity staff. There are many checklists produced by accountancy firms and others (including CFG) covering the numbers and the narrative in detail that you can freely access. It is worthwhile to work through one of these to ensure your charity has picked up all the relevant elements.

Note that there are small but important differences between operating jurisdictions and different legal forms of charity. These are summarised in appendix 1. I'm also not going to tackle the scrutiny requirements in any detail in this chapter (this is covered in chapter 9).

Linking the narrative and the numbers

An obvious way to link your annual report (the narrative) and your accounts (the numbers) is to use the same headings in both. For example, if your income and expenditure are shown under specific descriptive headings, such as 'Listening Ear Service', in your accounts, then using those same words in the narrative part of the report will aid readers in connecting the context and numbers. It will also better enable your charity to pull out, and explain nuances that may be buried or not obvious when readers are looking at the numbers. In addition, give thought at the outset to what your trustees and staff want stakeholders to understand about your charity's successes as well as what didn't go to plan in the relevant reporting period. See the words and the numbers as two sides of the same coin.

Use testimonials and case studies to illustrate what sits behind your income and expenditure, to help readers relate, connect with and remember what your charity did. Be honest, transparent and forward-looking. Use the narrative to smooth the bumps between accounting periods and explain where investment in one year didn't offer financial return in the same period. Show your charity's commitment to your present and future beneficiaries. For example, a legacy fundraising campaign may take several years to bear fruit. Without a clear narrative about your expenditure, and its importance in the bigger picture, such investments can skew the conclusions people draw from the numbers alone. For example, your charity's fundraising costs may look high relative to the money you're bringing in and raise questions about how well you are spending money to raise money.

Bad costs and good costs

I have a bugbear I must share. The sector has an unhealthy habit about which, if it reflects practices at your charity, I want to urge you to think again.

You will no doubt have seen negative headlines about certain charity costs (such as senior staff pay) or heard fundraising claims about the amount of each £1 that is spent on the cause. The distinction between direct delivery and support costs has, in my view, led to a damaging belief that some charity expenditure is good and the rest is bad. Such thinking leads to false economy, reducing the appetite to spend on essential support, and this in turn undermines your charity's ability to deliver what beneficiaries need. This doesn't deliver efficiency – it delivers inadequate support functions and increases the risk of failure in critical areas such as IT, HR and accounting.

Think of it like building a house. Everyone wants the money to be spent on the bit you see above ground. However, if you don't have solid foundations, however wonderful the brickwork might be, in time cracks will appear. Similarly, you might want to get away with spending as little as possible on the infrastructure of your house (sewerage, electrics, insulation, etc.), but in the long run you would regret not properly investing in and maintaining the structural stuff. The legal reality is that everything your charity spends must be in pursuit of its charitable objects – in other words, it must all be spent 'on the cause'. The IT people, HR personnel and accountants who support the work of your front- line staff providing support direct to the people you serve are just as vital a in delivering your cause – as indeed is the role your CEO plays keeping your charity on track and perhaps attracting supporters.

So please: if your charity is guilty of messages that talk about pence in the pound, percentages spent or the 'golden pound' (guaranteeing everything donated will be spent on front-line activities), stop it! You are not helpfully enabling your charity's stakeholders to see your efficiency – instead you are undermining it. While your charity might play to the assumption that front-line spending is good and back-office spending is bad to encourage supporters to keep giving in the short term, at some point this approach may bite you on the bottom. And even if it doesn't bite *your* bottom, it's definitely not helping other charities!

Inputs, outputs, outcomes and impact

Your trustees' annual report offers an opportunity to explain how what your charity receives as resources in terms of time, talent and money (inputs) is used to do stuff (outputs), what this achieves (outcomes) and the difference it makes (impact). Irrespective of whether your charity reports under the SORP, this approach to thinking about using resources and the relationship to performance is helpful.

If you had unlimited resources as inputs, you could potentially achieve everything you need to help the cause or causes your charity serves. But life isn't like that – you will rarely be free of limitations. Thus, we have to make choices about how we use the precious and limited resources we have. How we communicate those choices not only helps to demonstrate our accountability to our stakeholders but can also inspire further support. This is where your annual report can come in. A good report will show that a charity is open about whether its choices are making the difference it hoped for. It will reveal when the charity knows its activities have not had the desired impact (not just when it has had success). It can be as powerful to share your lessons from things that didn't go to plan as to celebrate the things that did.

In my experience, many charities focus heavily on outputs and outcomes in their narrative reporting – ironically, because they are easier to measure. You can count how many people attended a course (for example, 'we provided ten places at a training event'). You can also count whether the attendees acquired knowledge, perhaps by testing them (for example, 'nine out of ten attendees passed an exam, which demonstrates that they understood more about the topic after the course'). More difficult, however, is showing that the impact of that new knowledge is greater confidence or personal growth.

For example, there is a youth charity I know of that works with socially isolated young people to help them reintegrate into society and reconnect with their families. Its success cannot be measured in the short term, nor indeed numerically. For instance, a real success story for the charity is a young man who, after support and counselling from the charity, reached out to his estranged mother. He spent time with her without it resulting in a vicious argument and the encounter opened the possibility of a stronger relationship. But the history is such that their relationship will take a long time and a lot of work to recover. So, what's the measure? They met for lunch? That in ten years' time they are the best of friends? That he attended a counselling session??

In our efforts to look 'productive' and to tell a compelling story about what we did, we sometimes fall into the trap of reporting or measuring the wrong things. And when we do that, we are in danger of ending up *doing* the wrong things. For example, we focus on the numbers of people in our counselling sessions rather than the longer-term impact of our work. We can sacrifice quality for quantity unintentionally.

It is also important to recognise that impacts can be positive and negative. Your charity may set out to bring about a positive change but, in reality, the impact may not be what you wanted or may even actively work against your goal. Looking at the training course example, let's assume the aim is to build people's confidence and encourage personal growth through teaching them new skills and new ways of thinking that are then used to strengthen a whole community. What if, as a result of their newfound confidence and personal growth, the individuals rapidly leave the community for pastures new, rather than sticking around and contributing on an ongoing basis? Has the impact been positive? Has it achieved the end in mind?

Sometimes the positive impact we achieve through our work has a negative impact on someone else. For example, there's a charity that runs training to help develop leaders. Its work is so good that often the individuals who undertake the training leave where they currently work and go on to more senior roles elsewhere. The organisation that paid for them to attend might see that as a problem, as it has lost a member of staff. However, the charity running the programme probably sees this as a success.

Including such reflections can be really helpful for readers of your annual report, helping them to understand what your charity is doing and how it is using its resources in pursuit of its objectives. If you were reporting on my example of a training course aiming to build confidence in individuals for the benefit of the community, perhaps you would look at the drivers for those individuals leaving and reframe or adjust your programme of training so that the community you intended to impact benefits positively over a longer period of time.

Sometimes sharing the things that are going wrong can actually attract more support. For example, in 2018, Young Lives vs Cancer (formerly known as CLIC Sergent) was widely praised for openly admitting failure. Shortly afterwards, it received a multi-million-pound sponsorship deal from Morrisons. Telling the truth often doesn't put folk off – in fact quite the opposite.

The SORP encourages charities to include a narrative in their trustees' annual report that addresses these questions of inputs, outputs, outcomes and impact. How this is done is down to your staff and trustees. Put simply, impact reporting is about telling people how what your charity did changed something. For example, a charity might have invested in a volunteer engagement manager and now have significantly more volunteers. There is, of course, a danger of tying yourself up in knots trying to prove that what your charity did brought about the change you have observed. There are no one-size-fits-all solutions for expressing your charity's impact, and a lot of time and resources can be spent trying to prove things that are intangible or difficult to measure.

My strong advice would be to work with what your charity has. What quantitative (facts and figures) and qualitative (feelings and observations) data is already there? What can you link together to paint a picture? Be pragmatic about when good enough is good enough. Keep it as simple as possible. Talk to similar charities that appear to be telling their stories well, or read their reports – how do they do it? Recognise the limitations in the data your charity keeps and what it can tell you. You won't be able to prove cause and effect for everything your charity does, so think about proxies that might illustrate how you're doing.

I love the example of an opera company that measured the length of its standing ovations to determine how satisfied audiences were with the performances. By all means, use experts in impact measurement, but only if your charity has the resources to do so and it will meaningfully advance executive and trustee thinking or provide really engaging information or benefit to your beneficiaries or wider stakeholders. Don't just do it because you think you have to prove your charity's impact.

I used to be a trustee of a charity that wanted every child to hold treasured memories of theatre. It wasn't possible to, within any given year, prove this was the impact the charity had achieved. But alongside measuring how many people the charity was reaching and the number of shows it was putting on, we were able to engage with families, teachers and children. We were able to ask children to share their stories of their experiences of a performance and drawings of what they had heard and seen. We could also track the numbers of recordings of soundtracks purchased and the times the charity was asked to do further work or families returned for more. We could even find proxies for how happy a performance made a child feel through feedback forms and evaluations submitted by parents and teachers. The use of images of participants laughing and smiling (of course with relevant permissions) also helped us to judge the impact of our charitable activities. And from these various touchpoints we could paint a picture of how our work left children with wonderful memories. We didn't have to track the children into adulthood and only report on our achievements when we could categorically confirm memories were treasured!

Of course, your charity can't use these kinds of stories if it doesn't collect them, so make sure staff and trustees are in the habit of picking up and keeping these little nuggets, bits of feedback and anecdotes throughout the year, just as they collect hard data each month. They are gold dust in bringing a story to life and connecting with readers.

Main chapter takeaways

- Use your annual report wisely, considering how you can make your reader think and feel. Keep the headings in the accounts and the narrative consistent, to help readers to link key themes.
- It's the *trustees'* annual report. The work can be delegated but not the responsibility, so your trustees should make sure they're happy with the content. It's helpful to agree themes and key messages early on.
- Use the data your charity has: not everything must be proven. Collect and store lovely stories, images, and anecdotes when staff and trustees come across them – they are great for annual reports.
- Don't be afraid of sharing things that didn't go to plan in your trustees' annual report. Lessons learned are just as important as successes.

7 Numbers and notes

When you have mastered the numbers, you will in fact no longer be reading numbers, any more than you read words when reading a book. You will be reading meanings. Harold Geneen

Dealing with your nightmare with the numbers of course requires you to see more than pages of figures. You need to be able to read a set of accounts or other financial information, and understand what the digits mean and how to put them into context. If you get your understanding right, you will find that reading numbers is like reading sheet music – you will pick up the rhythm and melody rather than each individual note.

The previous chapter looked at the narrative reporting part of your trustees' annual report and accounts. In this chapter, we will walk through the accounts part of that annual reporting requirement and address some of the overarching issues about numbers which flow from the accounting framework introduced in chapter 1. The accounts include the financial statements we will cover in this chapter (also known as the primary financial statements), the supporting accounting policies and notes to the accounts. We will look at the types of accounts that charities are required or can choose to produce. I'll highlight some practical considerations that may be useful in day-to-day financial management, not just reporting. And we'll look at some technical things that, unless you know about them, can warp your overall impression of a charity's financial position. We'll also look at some of the common explanatory notes your charity is required to include in the accounts and specific numbers that readers of accounts, including journalists, may be interested in.

> **Outcomes**
> After reading this chapter you will:
> - Understand the different types of accounts you may encounter
> - Understand the various parts that make up the accounts, including common notes
> - Be alert to areas that may be of interest to users of accounts

Numbers

There is no getting away from it: numbers are important – I've written a whole book about them, after all! They may not be the most thrilling part of your charity's work, and they can be the bit that creates your night terrors. But they are an expression of what you do, and how they are represented (the accounts) can impact readers' understanding of your charity. They are often required by funders and stakeholders, and for compliance with rules and regulations.

Your charity's accounts will look at a single financial year in numbers; however, it's worth remembering that the work of your charity is unlikely to fit neatly into the specific accounting period, so you need to put each financial year in context. For example, money you invest in one year may not produce income until future years or, conversely, money you receive in one year might not be spent until the next. It is entirely possible that you will experience deficits and surpluses (see glossary) year to year. You'd be forgiven for thinking this is erratic or reflects poor financial performance, but it is entirely expected for charities! In chapter 5, we explored reserves – a very important element of numbers to become familiar with. This chapter will explore some other numbers you should know about. Some of them might make a big difference to the overall sums in your charity's accounts but are actually less critical when considering the health of your charity. The way you approach and structure a set of accounts can change the information you will get by looking at those accounts.

When it comes to putting your charity's numbers into a set of accounts, there are different approaches you can take, depending on your income and legal structure, and the jurisdiction in which you operate. How your executives and trustees engage with the numbers can be the difference between a well-run charity and one that is not delivering as much impact as it could.

To be brutally honest, working out how a charity has to report on its numbers can be a bit dull and somewhat confusing, even for the finance people among us. Before now you might not have given much thought to how your charity prepares statutory accounts – it's just done the way it is. But knowing a bit more about the options can help you understand your own and others' accounts.

The basis for your charity's statutory accounts

I now need to properly introduce you to two important terms: the 'accrual' basis of accounting and 'receipts and payments' (R&P) approach (otherwise known as 'cash accounting').

The form of accounting your charity uses depends on its legal form. If, as well as being a charity, it is also a company registered with Companies House (also termed a company limited by guarantee), then the only accounting method your charity is permitted to use is the accrual basis. And it doesn't matter if your charity is tiny – the level of income is irrelevant to this decision.

If your charity is unincorporated (including where your legal form is that of a charitable incorporated organisation), you can choose how to record your numbers (note that it is not possible to set up a charitable incorporated organisation in Northern Ireland at present, as that section of the Charities Act (Northern Ireland) 2008 is not yet in force). This means you can use either the accrual basis or the R&P basis (although the R&P regime differs between jurisdictions), provided that your income doesn't exceed £250,000 per year and your governing document doesn't require you to produce accounts that are 'true and fair' (that is to say, they provide an accurate picture of your charity's financial health). Once you get over £250,000 income per year, you are required to produce accrual accounts and comply with the Charities Statement of Recommended Practice (SORP) (see chapter 1) irrespective of your legal form.

Who decides which format to use when you do have a choice? It's often historical, having been decided on the advice of an accountant, lawyer or auditor when your charity was formed, or when it started bringing in more than £250,000 per year. It's rarely decided as a result of an active choice by the executive or trustees after weighing up the pros and cons. But it matters which approach has been adopted, not only because of the regulatory requirements (see appendix 1) but also, in my view, because the decision impacts financial management and financial transparency with your charity's stakeholders. Let me explain the pros and cons of each choice.

To R&P or not to R&P? That is the question!

If your charity is a company or it has an income above £250,000 per year, then you might want to skip this part of the chapter and go straight to page 116, because R&P accounting is not available to your charity. For those under that threshold, unincorporated or otherwise keen to understand the difference between the methods of accounting, read on.

The most compelling reason for choosing this approach is simplicity. If your charity has limited resources and/or bookkeeping skills at its disposal, using the R&P basis provides a basic method of accounting – one which can relieve small charities (which make up the vast majority of the sector) from complying with the requirements of the SORP.

The R&P method of accounting simply reflects when the money was physically received or spent, and not when the charitable activity took place. It isn't suitable for all charities – for example, the Charity Commission for England and Wales says charities that receive lots of donations of non-cash items shouldn't adopt this method. This is because non-cash items are not included in R&P accounts.

R&P is accounting at its most basic. In theory you don't require sophisticated financial qualifications, skills or software packages. Charities using this method don't have to show a 'true and fair' view of their financial position, the trustees are not formally required to determine and report on whether the charity is a 'going concern' (which means it can continue operating into the foreseeable future without incurring debt it has no ability to pay), and you are not obliged to make disclosures about things like trustee remuneration.

Depending on your perspective, this may be a good thing (because it saves resources) or a bad thing (because it isn't very transparent). I am not a fan, personally, because I think R&P turns accounting into something you do to comply with rules rather than something that helps you manage your finances and be transparent about how you raise and spend money. In my personal experience, the people I have trained and spoken to over the years at many of the smallest charities who produce their statutory accounts on this basis carry the mindset of 'money in/money out' through into their day-to-day management of finances too. I've always felt that when charities blindly stick with the option to report on the R&P basis, they miss the opportunity for financial considerations to be at the heart of decision-making. But clearly, managing finances isn't all about the basis of the year-end accounts! Charities that submit R&P accounts should still be able to effectively manage their finances using good forecasting, and they should understand their business model, cash flow and reserves. So make sure that if your charity uses the R&P basis, it also applies the tools that I set out in chapter 3 in all circumstances, as they are the foundations of good financial management whatever approach you take to your year-end report.

In my day job, I have highly skilled finance people available to me, so you may think my dislike for R&P comes without an understanding of the lot of small charities. However, I have significant experience with smaller charities and, given their often hand-to-mouth nature, I feel that what they gain through using the arguably more complex accrual method compensates for that additional complexity and the additional disclosures you may have to navigate. I think it gives greater credibility to your charity's numbers. But I stress that this is my personal opinion, not a regulator's position.

In summary, then, here are some reasons why your charity might choose *not* to adopt the R&P method even if it is available to you and instead choose to account on the accrual basis:

- You want to be able to give funders and stakeholders a 'true and fair' view of your financial position.
- You owe or are owed money that is significant in amount and/or important in its nature.
- Your funders (or lenders) require you to provide accrual accounts.
- Your charity has a lot of non-cash assets or donations (which the R&P accounting approach doesn't accommodate).
- You find the discipline of having to disclose annually whether your charity is a going concern helpful in prompting thought and debate.
- You find that the accrual basis lets you more clearly demonstrate which areas of your work can be self-funded (e.g. through trading or sales) and which require support.
- You anticipate growing and will be required to adopt accrual accounting soon anyway – so it saves you learning a new approach later on.

I believe that when you know not just what cash has hit or left your charity's bank account but also what you have as a liability to spend, the income you have secured, the activities to which your spending and income relate, and the impacts of the timing of your spending and income, you have a far greater ability to plan and a more accurate picture of the health of your charity. This is good financial management. While the nature of your statutory accounts doesn't dictate how you manage your finances (in other words, you could report on the R&P basis but manage your finances using the accrual method), I'm all for aligning the management and the reporting method for reasons of efficiency and transparency. The rigour that comes with accrual accounting and applying the SORP can help you have a better grip.

If I am right in my view, why is this option still available to small charities? Well, not all charities will grow in income. Indeed, the vast majority of charities are small and will never exceed the threshold which would require them to switch to the accrual basis. In practice, some charities' accounts might look very similar in either format – the difference between R&P and accrual accounts may not be big enough to matter. As a result, they might opt for the simpler accounting method. As I've said, charities may find other ways to keep on top of their finances internally which don't feature in their external statutory accounts.

Choosing the R&P basis is perfectly legitimate. In fact, some people argue that more charities should be encouraged to simplify their accounting, not fewer. However, for those charities that are growing rapidly, starting out using one method and then having to change to another basis can create additional challenges and adjustments for the trustees and staff. This is not the end of the world, I hasten to add, but if you can avoid extra work, why wouldn't you? Many adopt the simpler approach because they don't have accounting knowledge at their disposal – they do accounts because they must – but as a result the wider potential that can come from nailing the numbers remains elusive.

Some charities deliberately look at ways to limit their size so they don't get sucked into accrual accounting and the SORP. I sympathise but fear that limiting your growth because the accounting feels too tough is allowing process to get in the way of impact.

I recall working with one charity that asked me how it could actively avoid growing, as its income was nearing £250,000 per year, because it didn't know how to express its numbers using accrual accounting and didn't want to be caught by the SORP. I was able to help its trustees and staff understand what was involved in adopting accrual accounting and reassure them that growing and delivering more impact was more important than the energy, fear or effort required to switch to a new way of doing its accounts.

I hope, as you are reading this book, you are becoming open to thinking more holistically about the role numbers play in charitable activities. Whichever method of accounting your charity chooses, please remember that your statutory accounts report what has happened. They are not the same as day-to-day management of your charity's finances. They are not the most important bit of good financial management – this topic is covered as a whole in chapter 3 – but they are the bit your charity is required to do. If you agree with me but are currently using R&P, finding ways to understand accrual accounting could afford you greater control over and insight from the numbers in the long run. Conversely, if your charity is accounting on the accrual basis and, having considered the minimum requirements, your executive and trustees feel they can save resources and simplify the approach, then a conversation between them about moving to R&P would be a good idea.

'Natural' classification versus activity-based reporting

I also want to talk about the way your charity categorises or 'names' its numbers. As with my thoughts of R&P versus accrual accounting, this is not a technical exploration or a 'how-to' guide for creating accounts. Rather, I think it is worth considering why different entities treat their information in different ways so you can reflect on how your charity expresses its numbers, what this means, and how there might be differences in the ways the numbers of different charities look.

Smaller charities (defined by the SORP as those with an income under £500,000) will often choose to segment their income and expenditure in their year-end financial statements in more 'natural' forms of classification that describe things such as 'salaries, 'rent' and 'technology'. This is instead of showing income and expenditure on the basis of what the money is achieving – the charitable activities to which each transaction relates.

Your classification choices are not dictated by whether you produce your accounts on the R&P or accrual basis. However, because the natural approach is available to smaller charities only, it is common to see R&P and natural classification used together.

What makes up your charity's accounts?

While there is no prescribed format for R&P accounts, there is guidance available from the Charity Commission, the Office of the Scottish Charity Regulator and the Charity Commission for Northern Ireland which provides templates and helpful pointers on what should be included.

Under the SORP, if you use the accrual basis, there are four elements that make up the accounts you submit to your charity's regulator(s):

- A **statement of financial activities (SoFA)**, which provides an analysis of your charity's income and expenditure, endowments and movements of funds in the reporting period (for charities that are also limited companies, an income and expenditure account may be separate to or combined with the SoFA).
- A **balance sheet**, which sets out your charity's assets and liabilities and retained funds at its reporting date.
- A **statement of cash flows** (see chapter 3).
- **Notes to the accounts**, which explain your accounting policies, provide more detail about how your income and expenditure are made up, and provide extra information about particular assets, liabilities, funds and/or transactions.

Let's now explore the first two and last of these.

The SoFA

In addition to being a squidgy upholstered seat for more than one bum, a SoFA is a charity's statement of financial activities. This is something quite unique to charities and arises from the SORP, not from general accounting rules. Its closest comparable in the corporate world would be the profit and loss account. The SORP states that the SoFA is the single accounting statement that tells you what incoming resources you generated, what you spent it on and what's left over at the end of the financial year.

Charities are required to distinguish between different types of fund – for example, whether they are restricted, unrestricted or designated (see chapter 5). Understanding the differences between these pots enables you to make greater sense of the numbers when looking at a SoFA (and also a balance sheet) because it helps you understand how much cash is actually available to spend and on what.

You will recall from chapter 5 that restricted income is money that can only be spent on specific things because the entity or person has given your charity money for that specific activity. If restricted funds are shown as being overdrawn (in deficit), this could indicate your charity is spending more than it was given on a specific project. Spending more on a specific purpose than the funds you received for that purpose is not in itself a problem. Charities often plan to spend more on a purpose than the amounts that they receive for it. The shortfall will normally have to come from your unrestricted funds, and this should not lead to a deficit on the restricted fund. However, the SORP also explains that you may show a deficit on a restricted fund if you have spent funds on the particular purpose before you have received the funds. For example, if you have appealed for funds but need to start the expenditure before the funds reach you. You should only do this if you have a realistic expectation that you will receive income for that purpose that will cover the amount spent. If, in fact, the extra expenditure is because the project wasn't costed accurately or your charity's liabilities in relation to the restriction exceed the assets you hold, then the expenditure will have to come from your unrestricted funds.

Conversely, unrestricted funds (which might also be listed as general funds) are money your charity can spend on whatever it likes – subject to its charitable objects, of course. As mentioned before, your trustees can deliberately set unrestricted funds aside or earmark them for a particular activity. These are known as 'designated' funds. Unlike a restriction, designation allows your trustees to formally change their mind at any point and either 'undesignate' the funds completely or designate them for something else.

Charities that get a lot of restricted funding have to be careful that their costs are either covered within the restrictions, perhaps with a proportion of their restricted funds having been granted as a contribution to their core costs, or that unrestricted funds are available to meet those costs. A charity may have bags of restricted money, but if it cannot keep the lights on or meet commitments outside the restrictions, then it is at risk of failure.

Some charities have endowments. These might be restricted funds that are held so the capital is preserved, with any resulting income (usually interest) being used to finance charitable activity (a 'permanent endowment'). Alternatively, in some endowments, the capital is spent on charitable activity over a period of time (an 'expendable endowment'). Perhaps the most recognisable of the endowed charities are the grant-making foundations. I'm not going to include much on endowments here, but suffice to say that if a charity is endowed, this should be visible from its SoFA.

The accounting rules require comparative financial information, so your SoFA will also contain the numbers for your previous financial year. Sometimes (perhaps because including the information would make the SoFA hard to read) the information will be in a note. Prior-year comparisons enable you to see, relative to your previous accounting period, how that specific income or expenditure has performed. They can also help you to identify trends or changes in your charity's financial health.

The SoFA may cross-reference to various notes, which we will come on to, that provide further information on the numbers. The format and approach you choose for your SoFA should remain consistent between years unless there is a good reason for change – for example, a major change in activities. Where the headings have changed, the accounts should provide an explanation of why.

The final thing to say on the general information in the SoFA relates to investments and pension schemes. The accounting rules dictate how movements in pension schemes and investments (both of which can be big numbers) appear in accounts, and these standards apply to charities too. Consequently, the SORP requires charity accounts to show net gains and losses (the value of the item after the initial cost of it has been taken into account) for investments and pensions separately on the SoFA.

Within the SoFA, you may see the words 'actuarial gains or losses'. This relates to a defined-benefit pension scheme (you might hear this being referred to as a 'DB scheme' or a 'final-salary scheme'). This is a pension scheme where the benefits for the pensioner are guaranteed and the employer therefore has a legal obligation to make sure there are sufficient funds to meet those guarantees. If your charity has at least one defined-benefit pension scheme, it will appear in your SoFA. This figure will show you whether the value is going up or down in the period in question and thus how much money your charity is liable for. A big change in the pension scheme figures (usually in a negative direction) can make your charity look like it is in trouble. But unless any money will be drawn down from the pension scheme (and the pension debt has to be paid off very soon), the liability can be managed over a period of time.

Similarly, movements in the value of investments are also shown on the SoFA. You've probably seen adverts where the voice in the background says 'the value of your investment can go down as well as up' – these movements can result in big numbers. But just as with the pension scheme, as long as your charity isn't about to sell an investment at a big loss or gain, the number isn't that important to the accounts you're reading. The important bit is to be aware of how your investments are performing and whether values are rising or falling. Chapter 8 has more on investments.

You will find figures for your investments (if you have any) showing their gain or loss after the results for the operating activities. If the charity has a defined-benefit pension scheme that gain or loss will appear before the total for the operating activities. You don't need to understand why for the purpose of this chapter and perhaps even this book. But if you do have significant investments or a defined-benefit pension scheme, you need to understand what's going on, as these figures could have a big impact on your charity's annual numbers. You may need to have a more detailed conversation with your charity's internal or external accountants, auditors, pension advisers or investment advisers as appropriate.

There is a standard approach to the SoFA, as set out in the SORP. It offers a certain amount of flexibility, so you can vary the headings and number of columns to best reflect the circumstances of your charity. Thus, not all SoFAs will look exactly the same, but they will broadly follow the structure shown in the following example.

Let's look at what the SoFA of the Society of Oneirocritics might look like.

The Society of Oneirocritics statement of financial activities

	Notes	This year Unrestricted funds	Restricted funds	Total funds	Prior year Total funds
INCOME FROM					
Donations and legacies		15,000		15,000	15,000
Charitable activities					
Education and training		40,500	30,000	70,500	63,000
Policy and influence		25,000		25,000	19,000
Counselling and support			20,000	20,000	18,000
TOTAL INCOME		**80,500**	**50,000**	**130,500**	**115,000**
EXPENDITURE ON					
Raising funds		(13,500)		(13,500)	(12,500)
Charitable activities	**2***				
Education and training		(26,000)	(30,000)	(56,000)	(50,000)
Policy and influence		(27,000)		(27,000)	(23,000)
Counselling and support		(8,000)	(20,000)	(28,000)	(27,800)
TOTAL EXPENDITURE		**(74,500)**	**(50,000)**	**(124,500)**	**(113,300)**
NET (EXPENDITURE)/ INCOME		6,000	0	6,000	1,700
TOTAL FUNDS BROUGHT FORWARD AT [NEW FINANCIAL YEAR DATE]		50,540	0	50,540	48,840
TOTAL FUNDS CARRIED FORWARD AT [FINANCIAL YEAR END DATE]		56,540	0	56,540	50,540

The note would have corresponding further detail. But for the purposes of this book, I am not providing further detail for every note.

The SoFA won't tell you everything, but there are a few pointers you can take from it. Looking at the Society's SoFA, you can see that the charity has a reasonable level of restricted income, which it spends in the same year on restricted activities. There is no line for a pension gain or loss, so the Society does not have a defined-benefit pension scheme. There are no investment gains or losses shown – so again you can tell that the Society has no investments. In this SoFA, income and expenditure are classified by charitable activity, so salaries and other costs are distributed across the various charitable activities, clearly showing which generate income and which do not.

In the Society's SoFA, there is one note – note 2. Although we'll go onto notes in more detail in the next section, it is worth saying at this point that this number in the SoFA will refer to the analysis behind these top-line expenditure figures.

> **Consolidated figures**
>
> In order to generate income through trading activities (which a charity may not be able to do), charities commonly set up trading subsidiaries. This is beneficial not just because those subsidiaries aren't constrained in what they can do (unlike charities) but because the profits generated can be gifted to the parent charity. This is not a topic to expand on in this book, but I mention it because you may come across accounts that are 'consolidated'. Where you see this word, a trading subsidiary or other subsidiaries are brought together with the charity's numbers to show the total income and expenditure of the entities.

Balance sheet

A balance sheet is a snapshot of your funds at year end, showing both long- and short-term assets and liabilities. If your charity produces R&P accounts, there is no requirement to produce a balance sheet, but instead your trustees must produce a statement of assets and liabilities. If you produce accrual accounts, you must produce a balance sheet, which must be signed by trustees authorised by the board to do so.

According to the SORP, the objective of the balance sheet is to show what resources are available to your charity and whether these can be used for everything your charity does or have to be set against specific things because of legal restrictions.

The headings should be consistent between years, with any changes explained. Additionally, as in the SoFA, comparisons to the previous year will be shown for all amounts on the balance sheet. However, unlike in the SoFA, the balance sheet will also show you whether your trustees have designated funds.

Let's look at the Society's balance sheet.

It's a Nightmare with the Numbers

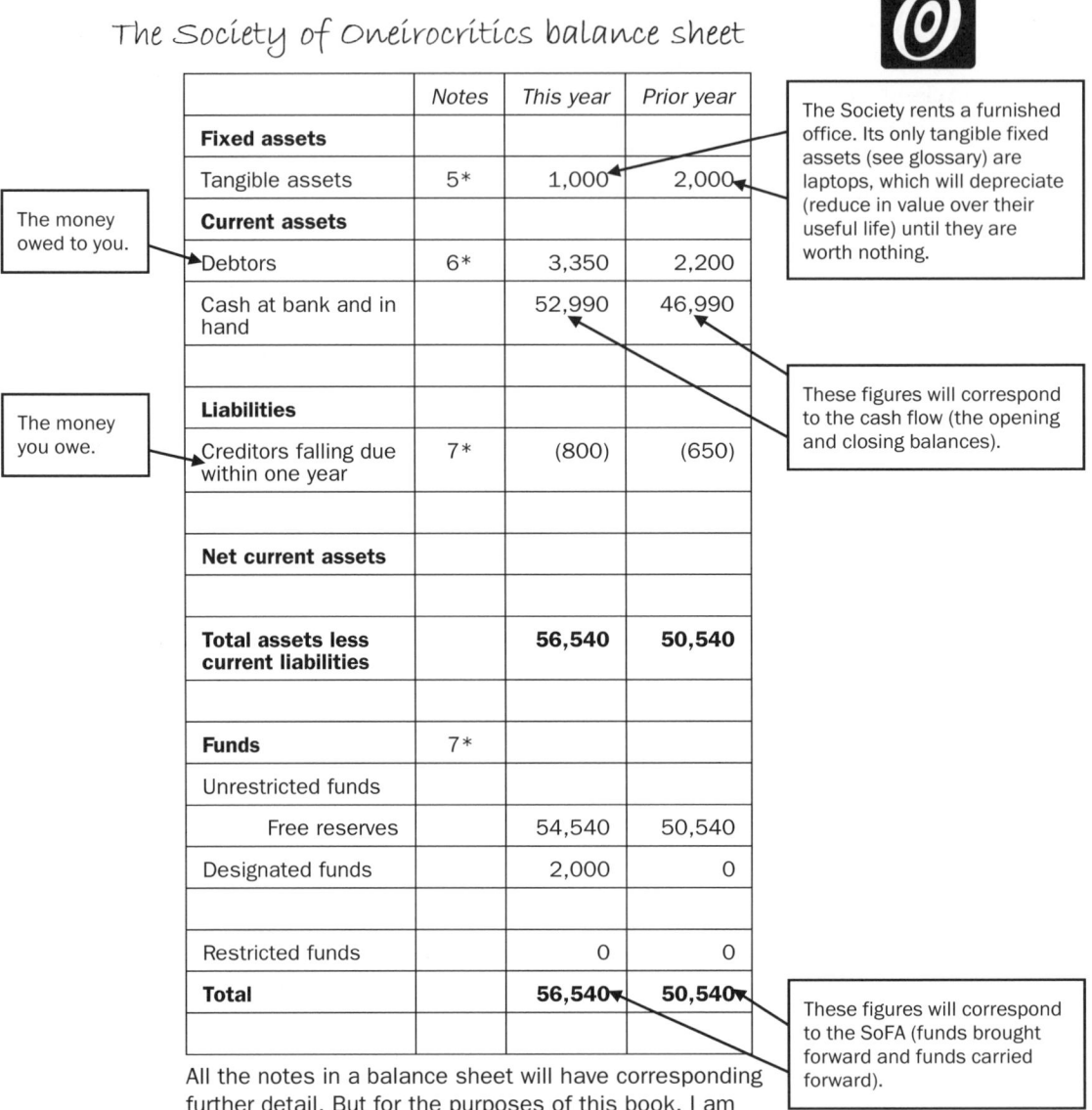

The Society of Oneirocritics balance sheet

	Notes	This year	Prior year
Fixed assets			
Tangible assets	5*	1,000	2,000
Current assets			
Debtors	6*	3,350	2,200
Cash at bank and in hand		52,990	46,990
Liabilities			
Creditors falling due within one year	7*	(800)	(650)
Net current assets			
Total assets less current liabilities		56,540	50,540
Funds	7*		
Unrestricted funds			
Free reserves		54,540	50,540
Designated funds		2,000	0
Restricted funds		0	0
Total		56,540	50,540

- Tangible assets — The money owed to you.
- Debtors — The money owed to you.
- Creditors falling due within one year — The money you owe.
- Tangible assets note: The Society rents a furnished office. Its only tangible fixed assets (see glossary) are laptops, which will depreciate (reduce in value over their useful life) until they are worth nothing.
- Cash at bank and in hand: These figures will correspond to the cash flow (the opening and closing balances).
- Total: These figures will correspond to the SoFA (funds brought forward and funds carried forward).

All the notes in a balance sheet will have corresponding further detail. But for the purposes of this book, I am not providing further detail for every note you might see.

When you read the balance sheet and SoFA together, you start to get a more complete picture and there are useful checks and balances across the documents. For example, the closing fund balances presented in the balance sheet should agree with the equivalent total of unrestricted, restricted and designated funds shown in the 'total funds carried forward' section on the SoFA (£56,540 for the Society). If they don't, you know there is a problem with the numbers you are viewing.

Like the SoFA, the balance sheet is likely to contain references to notes that provide further information on the numbers. In the Society's balance sheet, we have notes for the tangible assets, debtors and creditors, and the breakdown of the movement of funds. Each of these notes will give the reader more detail and help them understand what the top-line numbers are made up of.

When viewing a balance sheet, you can look to see if there are any designations, as these can signpost the trustees' intentions. In the Society's balance sheet, £2,000 has been designated and the detail in the note will explain that this money will go to refresh materials to reflect new ways of working as a result of moving from a physical office and taking a more digital-first approach to content.

More generally, if the balance sheet raises questions, the narrative of your trustees' annual report (see chapter 6) and the notes to the accounts (see page 124) should help you find the answers highlight where you need to ask questions and get further information.

When the accounting treatment changes the result

Within the accounting framework of the SORP, there is flexibility in some areas. The way charities choose to treat certain items, using that permitted flexibility (for example, their accounting policies), can result in two charities that are seemingly the same appearing quite different. This is one of the reasons why the narrative, and not just the numbers, is so important to users of your accounts.

Let's take the example of income recognition of legacies. The SORP sets out the rules around when income of all sorts should be recognised in a set of accounts. The words used are quite legalistic and have specific meanings. For the purposes of this book, I am not going to dive into the detail, so what follows is a fairly non-technical summary of much more technical content. For something to be recognised as income, which obliges you to enter it as income in your accounts, it must satisfy three conditions:

- your charity must establish **entitlement** to the income;
- it must be **probable** (more likely than not) that the economic benefits associated with the transaction or gift will flow to your charity;
- you must be able to reliably **measure** the monetary value with reasonable certainty.

When someone has left your charity money in their will, it may require some interpretation and judgement to determine whether all three income recognition criteria have been met. Imagine the Society and another fictitious charity, the Sleep Well Centre, are left £100,000 each in the will of a beneficiary. Both are yet to receive the money. The Society interprets the criteria as being met and includes the income in its accounts. The Sleep Well Centre, on the other hand, believes the criteria have not been met and therefore does not include the income. The charities are both in the same actual position in the sense that they are both *not* in possession of the money. But the Society, according to its accounts, may look £100,000 better off. So be alert to such areas where judgement is required and be cautious when comparing the position of different organisations.

Notes

Finally, let's look at some notes. In this section I do not cover all the notes you will see in a set of accounts. Those notes will explain your accounting policies, provide more detail on how your income and expenditure are made up, and provide extra information about particular assets and liabilities or about particular funds or transactions. They provide more information, and they explain apparent discrepancies, changes and variances in the numbers.

You might think that note 1 will be the first note you see referenced in the SoFA and wonder why the Society's example of SoFA I shared before starts with note 2. The numbering relates to the disclosure required, wherever it arises in the accounts, and not just to the SoFA or balance sheet. For example, at CFG note 1 might set out our accounting policies and note 2 deal with the fact we have a subsidiary. This would then mean that the first note you see in the SoFA is the note 3. So don't expect to see a complete numerical sequence starting on your SoFA and ending on your balance sheet.

Some will not specifically relate to a line in either document but are nonetheless required (by the SORP or accounting standards) – for example, notes on trustee remuneration and staff salaries.

There is also no standard numbering so that, say, note 7 in one set of accounts will not necessarily cover the same information as note 7 in all sets of accounts.

Notes are required to be numbered in the order that the disclosure or clarification arises. It's important to read the figures with the corresponding notes where they are referenced, because they are designed to give you more information.

The SORP requires that relevant information is explained in the notes to the accounts. However, the SORP doesn't require the accounts to guide the reader by picking up every time information might be helpfully tied back to a particular note. This might not feel very user friendly, but I hope the information in this chapter will help you feel more confident when it comes to the notes contained in the accounts, wherever you find them.

Final warning: not all notes were born equal! Some are very helpful (like the note about movements in funds), some are required by accounting standards but can shed very little light for the average user and swallow acres of space (like pension notes), and some provide details in areas that can generate debate and controversy (such as staff pay). For some notes, the content can be more formulaic and comparable between charities. For other notes, your charity may adopt wording in a way that suits its particular circumstances. Further advice and examples are set out in the SORP. The following is not a comprehensive look at each and every note – I've just picked out a few which I think are likely to be of importance to you.

Helpful notes
Movements in funds

The first one to discuss is the note which unpacks movements in funds. I've highlighted already that funds are shown on both the SoFA and the balance

7. Numbers and notes

sheet and that certain information should tally between the two documents. When viewing these documents, you may be wondering where the final numbers shown come from and how you can tell what's changed since the previous year. This is where the notes come to your aid.

A note on movements in funds will go into more detail, and the SORP gives an example layout for the note in a table form. The headings and layout used in the note should be amended to fit your charity's situation. This note shows you how things have changed in the accounting period and where movements between funds have occurred. It can be very helpful and provides more flesh on the bones of the raw figures.

The Society of Oneirocritics note 7: movement in funds

Fund	Balance as at [financial year start]	Income	Expenditure	Transfer between funds	Balance as at [financial year end]
Unrestricted funds					
Free reserves	50,540	80,500	(74,500)	(2,000)	54,540
Designated funds					
Material refresh	0	0	0	2,000	2,000
Total of unrestricted funds	50,540	80,500	(74,500)	0	56,540
Restricted funds					
Moon Foundation	0	30,000	(30,000)	0	0
Dreams Trust	0	20,000	(20,000)	0	0
Total of restricted funds	0	50,000	(50,000)	0	0
Total all funds	50,540	130,500	(124,500)	0	56,540

Free reserves are those reserves that are wholly at the discretion of our trustees to use for our charitable objects.

The designated fund has been created by the trustees to refresh materials in the light of the decision to close the office and to move content to a digital-first way of working, which is intended to be used over the next 12 months.

The restricted funds from the Moon Foundation (to provide education and training) and the Dreams Trust (to provide counselling and support) were spent entirely on restricted activities during the financial year with no funds carried over.

Expenditure analysis

I was in two minds as to whether to treat this as a helpful note or one that can generate debate – because, in reality, it is both! On the positive side, the note on expenditure will provide much more information on the data you see in the SoFA. It provides a breakdown of your direct, indirect and support costs, along with analysis of figures that might otherwise be shown as natural classifications, such as IT, HR and premises.

On the question of debate, there is an ongoing concern that charities should spend as little on the 'back office' as possible, so if your support cost figures are large, there is a risk that stakeholders will draw negative conclusions. Thus, it is important to make sure you bear in mind the comments and suggestions on this topic in chapter 6 (see page 105) and explain why such expenditure is necessary within the narrative sections of your annual report.

Let's look at the Society's expenditure analysis note to illustrate what you might expect to see.

The Society of Oneirocritics note 2: expenditure analysis

a) Analysis for total expenditure		Staff costs	Support costs	Other direct costs	Total this year	Total prior year
Raising funds		12,000	500	1,000	13,500	12,500
Charitable activities						
Education and training		48,000	2,000	6,000	56,000	50,000
Policy and influence		22,000	1,500	3,500	27,000	23,000
Counselling and support		21,000	1,000	6,000	28,000	27,800
Total expenditure		**103,000**	**5,000**	**16,500**	**124,500**	**113,300**
b) Analysis of support costs	Raising funds	Education and training	Policy and influence	Counselling and support	Total this year	Total prior year
Premises	450	1,250	950	750	3,400	2,950
IT	50	750	300	250	1,350	1,100
Other	0	0	250	0	250	0
	500	**2,000**	**1,500**	**1,000**	**5,000**	**4,050**

Notes that add little but that you probably need to know about
Defined-benefit pension schemes
As mentioned before, not all charities have a defined-benefit pension scheme, but those that do will be familiar with rather lengthy accounting notes that sometimes go on for pages. These are important in that they tell you the technical information about the value of the scheme, but the detail can swamp the important facts you need to know: Is the scheme in deficit? Can you afford the repayment plan? Do you understand the nature of the scheme and the various pros and cons of it? The topic of pensions and decisions to be taken around a defined-benefit scheme is a technical area with which your charity would benefit from expert advice. Make sure you understand the implications for your charity where a defined-benefit pension scheme exists. And get a simple explanation from the finance people which leaves you illuminated, not puzzled!

Other lengthy notes
The accounting standards require prior-year comparisons for every figure in your accounts. In some cases, the resulting volume and/or complexity of the information would make the SoFA difficult to read or carry individual notes across several pages. Some charities deal with this by reproducing their prior year SoFA as a note as an alternative to having multiple columns within the SoFA itself to provide a comparison for each figure.

A note that can cause debate: trustees and employment information
The topic of employment and, in particular, the remuneration of senior staff has periodically popped up on the front pages of the media. Stories of fat-cat salaries and overpaid do-gooders are never far from the headlines (again, go back to page 105 for further context and thoughts). Now I'm not saying this note is the cause – it just provides you with the factual information relating to any staff paid over £60,000 per year in bands of ten thousand. And where a charity is required to disclose the total pay of the key management personnel (which covers charities required to apply the SORP), you will find that information here too.

This note highlights the importance of the narrative you provide, particularly in relation to why trustees set pay at the levels they do. As with the other notes, here is the Society's note, to give you an example.

The Society of Oneirocritics note 3: Trustee and employee information

Trustee and employee information		
a) Trustee information		
No remuneration was paid to or waived by any trustees during the year (prior year: nil). £150 expenses for travel and subsistence were reimbursed to trustees during the year (prior year: £148).		
b) Employee information		
i) employee numbers	*This year*	*Prior year*
Full-time equivalent number of staff employed during the year	3.5	3.5
Average headcount during year	3.5	3.5
ii) employee costs		
Salaries	102,000	96,000
Contractors	Nil	£1,200
Holiday pay accruals	Nil	Nil
Total employee costs	102,000	97,200
iii) No employee earned more than £60,000 during the year (prior year: nil). For the purposes of this note, total salary does not include expenses. Systems are in place for the correct management of expenses.		

Salaries, pensions and benefits: because, for simplicity, I have used round numbers and ignored the costs of National Insurance and pension contributions that might exist under a defined-benefit pension scheme, this detail isn't included in the example, but they would be included in this note in a real situation, setting out any benefits received, the nature of the pension scheme and the contribution levels together with any outstanding contributions at the year end.

Remuneration of key management personnel: larger charities (those with an income of over £500,000) are required to disclose the total cost of the key management personnel of their charity. The Society would not be required to disclose this information given its size. However, for larger charities this figure will include those senior executives deemed to be part of the significant decision-making of the organisation – so probably the CEO and directors.

Some final thoughts

Not all accounts look exactly the same. However, if you become familiar with your charity's accounts and think about the changes between the years, it will help you to ask the questions you need to ask of the numbers and notes in front of you.

Charities which on the surface look like they are the same can have quite different-looking accounts and adopt different accounting policies, so don't make assumptions. Having this questioning mindset is not necessarily about getting your calculator out – it is about being brave enough to ask if the numbers don't look right to you. You'd be surprised at the number of times the non-finance person asks the question which reveals an accounting error or prompts a change of direction.

Don't let the technical stuff put you off. The more you read accounts and ask questions, the more you will feel comfortable with their content and be able to see their meaning.

Main chapter takeaways

- Understand whether how your charity does its accounting (R&P or accrual, and natural classification or by charitable activity) is as a result of an active decision. If not, examine whether your current practice is right for your charity.
- Make it your job to read the numbers and notes that you are given and ask questions if anything looks or feels like it doesn't stack up.
- The numbers and notes may be the output of a technical exercise, but they reflect the activities of your charity, so always keep your beneficiaries in mind.

8 Investments

Money will ruin the life of any man who treats it like anything but a tool with which to work. Henry Ford

If your charity is a small one, you might be thinking that you should skip this chapter, but please don't. The subject of holding investments is not only for large charities, and the contents of this chapter will be useful whatever the size of your charity.

I agree with the sentiment expressed by Henry Ford that money is just a tool. For charities, it is an important resource, but by no means the only resource. This tool can be put to work immediately or it can be invested to contribute to long-term delivery for your charity's beneficiaries. Investments are therefore a means to an end and not an end in themselves.

In chapter 5 I highlighted that trust law requires charities to spend money on delivering their charitable objects and that your charity should only hold back funds for a good reason. Whereas in that chapter we explored why your charity might wish to hold money in reserve, this chapter will look at how it might invest money and what to think about if your trustees choose to do so. But before you think that I am asking you to don the striped suit and braces of the stereotypical investment manager, it's important to be clear that investing doesn't necessarily mean having a flutter on the stock market or owning shares. Investments can be a range of different things over different time horizons, from cash to bricks and mortar.

The Charity Commission for England and Wales, the Office of the Scottish Charity Regulator and the Charity Commission for Northern Ireland all publish various guidance that will be relevant for any trustee or executive team member of a charity holding investments (charity law differs in regard to investment powers between the jurisdictions of the UK). If you want to explore the regulators' guidance in more detail, visit their websites. I won't be exploring the topic of endowments, which is beyond the generic nature of this book. Drawing on the work of Charity Finance Group (CFG), the Charity Investors Group and the guidance of the regulators, I will simply explain what you need to keep in mind when thinking about holding investments and developing investment policies, the types of investment you might hold, and some governance considerations to make sure your charity doesn't end up with investments becoming just another bad dream. If you need a more detailed exploration of charity investments, I recommend *Investing for Charities* by James Brooke Turner.

> **Outcomes**
> After reading this chapter you will:
> - Understand what your charity needs to consider when deciding whether to hold, continue holding or get rid of investments
> - Understand the types of investment charities typically hold
> - Understand governance considerations, including the building blocks for putting together an investment policy

Important things to think about when you're considering investing

You would be forgiven for thinking that investments are held solely to generate money. After all, it's easy to think of investments as just stocks and shares, and indeed, logically, these are aimed at providing a financial return on your charity's investment. However, just as the term 'investments' covers more than just participation in the stock market, what charities try to achieve with their investments can be hugely varied.

There is a range of things charities should consider to be sure they are allowed to hold investments and for those investments to be effective:

- the scope of your charity's investment powers – understand what it is legally permitted to do (for example, your charity's governing document may not allow it to invest in property but will permit it to hold shares);
- what the trustees want to achieve with their investment (their investment objectives);
- the trustees' attitude to risk specifically regarding investments, including any reputational as well as financial considerations that may be relevant;
- how much is available to invest and over what time frame, and any needs your charity has around selling or otherwise disposing of assets;
- the types of investment your trustees might be interested in making;
- who will make the investment decisions (for example, the trustees, the executive or an investment manager) and how the investments will be managed and performance judged;
- the measures required to know how an investment is doing and any reporting requirements your charity needs to put in place;
- any environmental, social or governance considerations relevant to your charity.

What is your charity trying to achieve?

There are four main reasons why your charity might decide to hold investments.

To protect your capital

We are not talking about places like London and Edinburgh here but rather about preserving the value of your assets! Your trustees may decide that if your charity doesn't intend to spend a pot of money for a period of time, investing the funds could protect them from the impact of inflation. This is because inflation can erode the real buying power of your charity's money over time. Of course, deciding to hold an investment doesn't guarantee the capital will be protected. You hear it all the time – the value of your investment can go down as well as up! However, your trustees might decide that the inevitable erosion of the value of cash by not investing it is a bigger risk than the possible reduction in value through an investment that does not perform as expected.

As a way of advancing your charitable aims
Your charity might want to use investments to attempt to alter behaviour in a particular industry. For example, your charity may have health and well-being at the heart of its mission and feel holding shares in, say, a popular food brand enables it to apply pressure to accelerate change by being an activist shareholder. In such circumstances, the investment may be held almost irrespective of financial return.

To generate income
This isn't just a consideration for those charities that hold permanent or expendable endowments (see glossary). It can also be a way for charities to make a lump sum go further for longer. Your trustees might consider that holding investments can generate income that itself can support the delivery of your charitable activities over a long period of time. Perhaps your charity has been given a large legacy or an activity has generated a far greater surplus than planned, or excess reserves have built up over a period and the staff and trustees want to make them work harder. Your trustees might decide that, by investing, your charity can reach more people over a longer period of time and have a greater impact than by spending a lump sum in one go. Income from an investment may also be more predictable than, say, donations and offer more certainty regarding the funds being available over an extended period.

To generate financial and social returns
Sometimes investments are not held to either generate money or to advance your charitable aims, but rather to do both. Your trustees may choose to invest, for example, in buying a building which provides rental income and a premises from which to deliver your charity's services. Or they might invest in activities which are directly aligned to your charity's mission – such as an environmental charity investing in renewable energy initiatives or an employment charity having a loan scheme to support unemployed beneficiaries wanting to start a business. Your trustees will decide whether your charity will place more importance on the finance bit or the social return bit.

Risk and return
It's often said that if you want to get greater returns, you have to take greater risks. However, this is a bit of a lazy way of looking at things. As we explored in

chapter 4, it doesn't always follow that greater risk provides more lucrative or better outcomes. Investing is also not always about generating more money! There are other risks to consider when thinking about your charity's investments. For example, your trustees may decide they simply need to keep the value of their investment from going down (i.e. preserve the asset). Or perhaps they need flexibility so are prepared for an investment to be less likely to generate the maximum financial return so they can release funds quickly if needed.

Sometimes trustees don't need to use the money an investment represents for some time to come, so they can afford to tie the money up for the longer term. But the trade-off could be lower returns or a financial penalty for turning the investment back into cash ('realising' the investment) before the agreed time, should the need occur. For example, if you discover you hold shares in a business that conflicts with your charitable objects, you might be forced to get rid of those shares at short notice, causing you to experience a lower return because you couldn't pick your moment.

In the next section we'll look at some typical investment types (sometimes known as 'asset classes') that charities might hold. It is undoubtedly true that different types of investment are seen as inherently more or less risky, but within the classes of investment other factors can alter the risk profile too. For example, holding shares over a long period of time in an established business might expose your charity to less risk than, say, investing in a start-up and expecting to get your money back in short order. In both cases you're invested in shares, but the risk profiles are different.

Risk can also be affected by the quality of the expert advice and skills available to your charity. You can reduce the risk you face by investing in a range of different investment products offered by an expert investment manager, balancing your short- and longer-term needs under their supervision, and/or drawing on the knowledge and expertise of a committee of experts. In contrast, taking a tip from Bob down the pub who likes to dabble in the markets is probably not such a wise move and might increase your chance of failure!

Some investments can be reputationally damaging too. For example
- shares in entities that work against your charity's objects;
- shares in entities which do not follow good practice in environmental, social and governance areas (so-called ESG, covered in more detail later in this chapter)
- being associated with a third party that becomes embroiled in a scandal.

Questions such as the currency in which an investment is held and the credit rating of the bank into which the funds are deposited can also affect the risk profile of an investment.

These issues all need to be carefully managed. It is beyond the scope of this book to go into depth, but we will look at the mechanisms for getting governance right later in this chapter.

Typical investments charities hold

This section is not intended to cover all types of investment or to offer investment advice to your charity. Rather, by outlining the typical vehicles of investment charities hold, my aim is to help you feel more confident in understanding their nature and characteristics, and thus remove any fear you may have as a member of staff or a trustee about asking the right questions about risk, reputation and return – whether of a sub-committee, the board or someone to whom your charity has delegated investment management. If the investment types your charity holds are not covered here, don't be afraid to ask those managing your investments, whether internal or external, for information.

The nightmare with the numbers doesn't arise just from the figures on a page. It can also emerge, like the cartoon bogeyman from under the bed, simply because you don't have enough information about technical terms in specialist areas and perhaps feel you should. If in doubt – ask!

Equities

In addition to the word 'equities', you may have heard the terms 'stocks' and 'shares'. However, strictly speaking, 'shares' is not completely interchangeable with 'equities'. A 'share' is the individual bit of a company you own (also known as a 'unit'). 'Equity' and 'stocks' means all those individual shares added together – the total stake your charity has in a company. But these distinctions really don't matter that much for the purposes of your discussions regarding investments at a generic level. When we're talking about equities, we're talking about the slice of pie you own (irrespective of whether that slice can feed just you or a family of four). When we're thinking about situations where investment numbers might become a nightmare, basic knowledge will suffice!

When your charity invests in equities, it becomes a part owner of a company that is typically being traded on a stock market. Shares can also be held in companies that are privately owned (not traded on a stock market). The percentage of your ownership is determined by the number of shares (or units) you purchase.

Traditionally, shares are held for a financial return. However, increasingly, they are purchased so charities can have their say at an annual general meeting, to influence behaviour and make representations to the company on the way it works. From the CEO's pay to the treatment of workers to environmental considerations and ethical or moral activism – more investments are being held for more than just financial return. So-called shareholder activism is growing. For instance, the Church of England was very vocal in December 2020 (using its shareholding as a lever) in its support of an ultimately successful campaign to pressurise ExxonMobil to develop a pragmatic way to transition energy production away from fossil fuels to renewables and refresh its board.

Although investments in equities might conjure the image of fast-paced dealing on the trading floors of stock markets, where large sums are won and lost in casino-esque conditions, the reality is that, supported by experts, equities can perform well. Over the long term, they have historically given higher levels of return than other seemingly less risky propositions. Don't assume that 'shares' equals 'high risk'. (Although that is not investment advice, I hasten to add!)

Bonds and gilts
A bond is basically an IOU. Gilts are bonds issued by the UK government. When you invest in a bond, you are effectively lending money to a government or company (or indeed a charity – charities can issue bonds too). You may also have heard the term 'bond' in the context of social investment bonds, social impact bonds or social finance bonds. These are investments where money is lent for a social as well as a financial return, or where return on investment is dependent on achieving social return.

Bonds can be bought and sold and have generally been seen, as a rule of thumb, as less volatile and therefore a lower-risk investment than equities. However, significant uncertainty across economies can upset that apple cart and make bonds feel far less secure. Bonds also historically have tended to offer a higher rate of interest than bank savings accounts. However, volatility, inflation and rising interest rates in the early 2020s brought into question this historical position. I am not convinced that bonds are still seen as quite the solid and steady investment they once were.

Property and land
'Property', 'land', 'real estate' – these are all terms that relate to investments associated with the purchase, management and development of commercial, and sometimes domestic, property. Such property may be held directly – for example, as a building that a charity buys to occupy (saving on rent), use or let out. Or it may be held through products offered by investment managers, where the investment is made either directly or through a fund (i.e. in a underlying portfolio of property). While you might assume that owning bricks and mortar is a less risky proposition, property is not inherently lower risk. Location, condition and the purpose to which property is put can all influence the level of risk.

Collective investment funds (or pooled funds)
Collective investment funds, sometimes known as pooled funds, are investment vehicles where the assets of multiple individual investors are brought together. These investment vehicles can invest in public companies, private companies and other forms of investment. This collective approach to investing means the overall pot is bigger. The thinking behind such funds is that they allow those with smaller amounts to invest to benefit from access to investments in a way they couldn't on their own – either by simply allowing

them to invest at all (due to the reduced cost and administration) or by giving them a greater range of things to invest in. Additionally, in these funds, the risk is shared or spread. Such funds can consist of investors only from a specific sector – such as a pooled fund of only charity assets – or they may include investors from lots of different sectors. You might invest in a collective investment fund as part of a wider portfolio of different types of investment.

Commodities

Put simply, commodities are raw materials and basic resources used to create products that consumers then buy. Mining, iron and steel are all examples of commodities. Given the nature of commodities, you can quickly see some considerations from an ethical point of view. For example, often charities will ask their investment manager not to invest in mining entities for environmental and social reasons. However, commodities can also include agriculture, sugar, wheat and so on. Your charity is not prevented from considering commodities as an investment.

Interest-bearing deposit accounts

You might think that depositing funds in an interest-bearing account is simply 'holding cash'. However, whether cash is an investment or not is about the reason for which your charity is holding it and not necessarily *where* it is held. Your trustees may make an overt and deliberate decision to deposit sums in a specific product or account to which certain conditions are attached in return for higher interest rates. These conditions might relate to access (how quickly funds can be withdrawn) or the proportion of the funds that can be taken out at any one time (perhaps with penalties applied if your charity withdraws over a certain amount), for example. If the reason for holding cash is not for use in the operating activities of the charity, a good argument can be made that it is an investment.

Cash can be an investment even if you don't deliberately select a specific product or bank account for its higher rate of return. Cash held in an instant-access bank account can be considered an investment when it comes to how it is treated in your annual accounts, depending on the purpose for which it is held. If, for example, funds held in cash are clearly not required for ongoing expenditure and working capital, the cash can be treated as an investment.

Be clear, for example within your trustees' annual report or within funding applications, if you are holding cash as an investment, because it can sometimes have an impact on the perception of funders and donors. While these sums wouldn't be added to your reserves total (for accounting purposes), large cash balances may lead some funders, in particular grant-making charities, to query why a charity is seeking funds. Whereas a charity holding other investments may seem more palatable.

Getting governance right

Charities differ in the arrangements they put in place relating to decisions on investments. Arrangements will depend on the internal resources and expertise available, and the importance of investments (relative to your other sources of income) when thinking about how you can achieve your charity's aims. Whatever mechanisms you use, your charity's trustees should be able to show that they are in control of decision-making and have fulfilled the duties of being a trustee. There are also restrictions around who can legally hold investments. For example, an unincorporated association does not have a legal identity, whereas a charity which is also a registered company does. In the case of an unincorporated charity, the trustees would have to hold any investments in the names of the trustees, whereas a charity which is also a registered company can hold them in its own name. It is important to understand the legal restrictions and implications for your charity and trustees before holding investments.

I'll come on to the use of an investment sub-committee, the use of specialist investment managers and investment policies. However, first there are a number of basic questions which you must take into consideration (though the language and underlying legislation may differ between jurisdictions):

1. Do your trustees know what power they have to make investments?
2. If they believe they have the power, is this expressed explicitly within your governing document or are they relying on a generic legal power contained in the relevant legislation?
3. Do your trustees have access to the right expert knowledge, advice and skill? (This is part of their duty to exercise due care and skill – they can, and should, seek specialist advice in areas such as making an investment.)
4. Do your trustees know what risks are involved and how they will be managed (including diversifying the types of investment your charity makes – i.e. not putting all your eggs in one basket – and periodically reviewing your investments)?
5. Do your trustees know what investments would be in the interests of your charity (this can be in a financial sense or in relation to wider non-financial considerations)?
6. Do your trustees have a method for establishing whether investments are consistent with your charity's objects? For example, must they not be in conflict ethically or must they help to achieve your charitable aims?
7. Do your trustees and executive know how to identify and manage conflicts of interest?
8. Do your trustees and executive know how to explain your charity's decisions regarding investments to your stakeholders?

Investment sub-committees

Getting your charity's internal governance structures right is crucial for ensuring that all investment-related risks and returns are managed effectively. It is entirely possible to fulfil the governance requirements relating to investments within the full board of trustees. Your charity doesn't have to set up a separate sub-committee. However, many charities, particularly those with substantial investment portfolios, will choose to convene a sub-committee or working group to ensure the governance considerations around investments are managed well.

Such working groups or sub-committees are usually made up of trustees and executive, often with independent investment-specialist members, to advise the board of trustees on more detailed or technical aspects of investments. They will also usually be responsible for drafting and agreeing an investment policy with the board, appointing any external investment managers or advisers, and analysing any specialist reports received from them.

Your charity should be clear about the remit of any sub-committee, how long individuals can serve on the sub-committee (terms of office), what decisions they can make and how decisions will be reported to the trustees. The full board remains responsible for decisions made by sub-committees, even in specialist areas, so it's important that the full board feels equipped to oversee its sub-committee and understands enough about this specialist topic. However, as stated in the Charity Commission's guidance *Investing Charity Money: A guide for trustees* (CC14), if trustees can demonstrate that they have considered the relevant issues, taken advice where appropriate and reached reasonable decisions, they are unlikely to be criticised for their decisions or for adopting a particular policy.

It is also important to think about who manages investment-related risks that aren't solely to do with financial return. For example, if a scandal emerges about an existing investment or a decision your charity has made to invest in a particular asset, this may have a negative impact on your charity's reputation. Who will take the lead? Such matters of reputation need to be viewed from the full range of angles and carefully balanced. As mentioned, disposing of an asset under stress – because holding the investment has exposed your charity to serious criticism – can reduce the value of the asset.

It's like the proverbial hot potato – dropping it immediately might feel more comfortable for your hands, but you've potentially just dashed your dinner on the floor! Is the risk of getting burned significant enough that you can't tolerate the heat for a bit longer and manage the timing of the disposal carefully? At the end of the day, your trustees' duty is to your charity and those it serves – not to those in the firing line who will be criticised when things get tough. Thinking about these issues and having a communications plan in place will help if the worst happens. And the investment sub-committee may not be the experts in managing these wider risks, so again it's important to make their remit clear.

External investment managers
Often, given the specialist nature of the area, trustees will consider appointing an investment manager or a stockbroker to advise them (such people are known as advisory investment managers) and/or may decide to give

investment managers powers to make limited decisions about the charity's investments on their behalf (such people are called discretionary investment managers). The approach will depend on the extent of expertise internally available to the board of trustees from its members and the charity's staff. Before deciding whether it's appropriate to appoint an advisory or discretionary investment manager, in addition to assessing the skills your charity has at its disposal, it is important to think about the amounts being committed and the costs of appointing such specialists.

Whether you appoint an investment manager or not, trustees are required to take and consider advice from someone experienced in investment matters before they decide to invest or when they are reviewing their investments. Taking independent advice is not always required. Trustees can conclude it isn't necessary, or is inappropriate in the circumstances, if, for example, they have in-house expertise. But it's important to make sure that any advice you receive is impartial. For instance, a trustee with a connection to an entity in which an investment might be made or staff who might benefit – directly or indirectly – from any financial advice provided to your charity present a conflict which must be managed.

Some activities relating to investing and advice around investments are regulated. Again, it is not possible within these pages to give a comprehensive guide covering all bases. A lot of information is available on the Financial Conduct Authority's web pages (www.fca.org.uk) and from other sources, like investment managers, so do make sure your trustees and executive are familiar with the relevant regulated areas and take advice where necessary. I would also again flag James Brooke Turner's book *Investing for Charities*, which goes into way more detail on the subject. There are, however, two types of regulated adviser commonly encountered in relation to investments: independent financial advisers (sometimes referred to as IFAs) and restricted financial advisers (sometimes referred to as 'tied agents'). Independent financial advisers can sell the products of lots of different companies, whereas a restricted adviser, such as one working for a bank or building society, can only give advice on and sell specific products (often their employer's). It's important to know what the specialist your charity engages can do and any limits on the advice or guidance they are permitted to give.

The law requires your charity to have a legal agreement in place if it uses investment managers. This agreement must require the investment managers to invest in line with your charity's investment policy, so it's sensible to include your charity's policy in the legal agreement. Investment managers and other advisers are also very good at helping charities to draw up their policies and many have free resources and templates that can assist you (CFG and the Charity Investors Group have put together a guide, which I'll come on to in the next section). However, trustees cannot delegate the preparation of your charity's policy to an investment manager or another adviser. They must retain overall responsibility, because your policy is your charity's statement of why it is investing and how its investment objectives can be achieved.

Choosing an investment manager, like choosing any other form of professional, requires you to think about your charity's needs. Decide who is going to be involved in the decision and then, to make the right choices, take the following steps:

1. Set your charity's investment objectives.
2. Research investment managers to see which offer services that seem like they would meet these objectives.
3. Create a request for proposals which will be sent to a list of possible investment managers.
4. Shortlist from the responses received.
5. Choose a selection of questions for interviews.
6. Set out a method for determining the likely success or otherwise of the relationship (perhaps based on financial performance, relationships, value of advice or a combination of criteria).
7. Appoint an adviser.
8. Set regular review points – for example, every three to five years – to re-examine your approach and your manager(s).

Investment policies

Whatever the size of your charity, if you have investments, it is important to have a written policy that sets out what you are trying to achieve with them. Such a policy provides a framework for making investment decisions, which will help your trustees (who are ultimately responsible) to manage your charity's resources effectively and to demonstrate good governance.

How will you know whether your investments are achieving what your trustees intended and whether you have made decisions in the interests of your charity's beneficiaries if there isn't a written plan or policy against which you can check your progress? It is important to make sure that your charity's investment policy is consistent with other policies, particularly those relating to risk and reserves. Your board of trustees should own and sign off on the policy – even if the trustees do so on the recommendation of a special sub-committee. Any policy that you adopt should reflect your charity's values, considerations around accountability to stakeholders and governance duties, decision-making, attitude to risk, and ethical policies or stance taken, and be regularly reviewed to make sure it reflects your charity's current needs and objectives. The level of detail needed in your policy will be dependent on the complexity and extent of investments rather than the size of your charity. At the risk of stating the blooming obvious, make sure your investment policy contains your charity's name and registration number, the date on which the policy was adopted, and when it will be reviewed.

Below are the headings that should ideally feature in your charity's policy. These have been drawn from the publication *Writing Your Investment Policy*, co-authored by CFG and the Charity Investors Group, and are included together with some pointers and explanations of the content.

Introduction	This sets the scene and tone of your charity's policy and is important because an investment manager will use the policy as a framework for advice and, where appropriate, decision-making. You want the reader to get a sense of the extent and impact of investments on your charity. Set out the total investment assets you hold or intend to hold, and explain the importance of these to your charity's overall activities. Summarise where the power to invest comes from – your governing document or the law – and any limits or restrictions on this power. Outline how decisions will be made.
Investment objectives	Refer to the four main reasons set out on pages 132–133 as to why charities hold investments. What are your charity's objectives? What are you trying to achieve?
Risk	What is your charity's attitude to risk? What are the trustees' views relating to different classes of asset (see page 135) and how will they make sure risk is managed? This section should also cover any information about the currency your investments will be held in, your preferences regarding the credit ratings of any relevant entities (such as bond issuers or banks) and any other information relevant to risk (such as ESG considerations).
Liquidity requirements	How quickly will your charity need to draw down from the investments and how regularly? Are there any events on the horizon that could impact these considerations?
Time horizon	Is the investment for the long term, medium term or short term? Does this vary between different types of asset? Does your charity have a long-term financial plan or expect any significant changes relating to capital, income or expenditure in the future?
Ethical investment	Is there an ethical investment policy in place? Do your trustees wish to avoid certain investments (negative screening) or target certain investments (positive screening). Does this policy relate to both direct and indirect (via a pooled fund; see page 136) investments? (See also the section on ethical investment below.)

Management, reporting and monitoring	Will your charity use one or more investment managers? What detailed arrangements are you planning, including the remit of your investment manager(s)? What are your charity's reporting requirements (for example, the regularity with which your investment sub-committee meets, if you have one)? Do your trustees have a way of knowing whether your investments are performing as they'd expect?
Approval and review	When was your investment policy approved and how frequently will it be reviewed?

Ethical (or responsible) investment

If you take an ethical investment approach, you might look for investments in companies that actively try to tackle the climate crisis, think about purpose (not just profit), and consider issues around diversity and good governance. You should include any preferences you have around ethical investment in your investment policy. However, there is no fixed method of scoring how responsible or ethical an investment is – or, for that matter, how ethical the E (environmental), S (social) and G (governance) elements are. However, there are many tools and scoring mechanisms that take into account a variety of matters to assess the ESG value of investments. This section is therefore not going to attempt to guide you on what investments will meet your ethical investing criteria.

There was a time when ethical investment was a bit of a minority sport. People thought that if you intended to invest ethically, you would have to compromise on the financial return you received. However, increasingly, this is not the case and, indeed, there is a growing body of evidence from the market that companies which have a greater handle on ESG matters tend to be more stable and provide a greater return over the long term. It is no longer the case that you will compromise your financial returns as a result of taking an ethical stance.

Increasingly, stakeholders are also expecting charities to actively take an ethical position. You might remember the scandal that surrounded Comic Relief in 2013, which had to endure an exposé by *Panorama* regarding investments it held in tobacco, alcohol and arms. In other words, the charity had been found to hold investments, some directly, in funds which invested in areas seen as contrary to its values and objectives. Not only did the negative coverage risk the charity's reputation but also the decision the trustees took to dispose of those investments had a financial impact (selling at pace and not necessarily at the optimal time for achieving a good financial return).

But a word of caution: trustees must consider the ethical implications *for their charity* and not allow their own personal views to colour the agenda. That something may be objectionable to an individual trustee is not the key issue – it is whether it is in the interests of the charity that is important.

It is worth checking your charity's governing document to ensure that your trustees and staff are aware of any ethical (or other) restrictions on the types of asset class your charity is entitled to invest in. An ethical investment policy may help to protect your charity's reputation by demonstrating that you have considered ethical issues. There is no requirement to adopt an ethical policy, but if your charity does, you must explain it in your trustees' annual report.

If your charity holds material (see the glossary) investments, it will need to comment on any ethical considerations your trustees have included in their thinking.

In response to changes in case law, a specially created steering group has developed Charity Investment Governance Principles that will be useful for charities of all sizes. The principles explore best practice in decision-making around charity investments and draw on the experiences of charities across England and Wales. The principles follow the format of the Charity Governance Code (www.charitygovernancecode.org) and are intended to provide additional help and practical support to trustees, staff and investment sub-committee members to tackle the challenges relating specifically to investment governance. The principles complement the Charity Commission's updated guidance *Investing Charity Money: A guide for trustees* (CC14) and the Charity Governance Code.

Finally, it is worth speaking to your investment manager or adviser about their approach to ESG issues. How do they assess ESG, how do they monitor and track progress, and how do they report to you?

Reporting requirements
By now you will be familiar with the fact that not everyone has to report everything, depending on your charity's size and legal constitution. However, assuming your charity does have to complete a trustees' annual report, what do your trustees need to think about when it comes to investments?

The first thing to say is that how you show investments in your accounts can change the overall picture of your charity's finances (as set out in chapter 7), so it's important to make sure that your investments are entered into your accounts properly. If you are in any doubt, seek assurances from your charity's accountant, auditor or independent examiner that they are familiar with the relevant sections of the Charities Statement of Recommended Practice (SORP).

Again, if your charity's investments are material, you must include within your trustees' annual report an outline of any policies your trustees have adopted when choosing financial investments. The report should also contain a statement about the performance of your charity's investments during the reporting period. If an ethical investment policy has been adopted, this must also be explained.

Finally, bear in mind that whatever you say about your investments in your reporting is important, because readers will form a view regarding how your charity retains and uses money from your reports. The words you use to describe what your investments are for, what your trustees are trying to achieve and how those investments performed will be crucial to how readers understand your trustees' annual report and accounts. And don't allow the technical and specialist nature of the topic to prevent your charity's reporting from being clear and informative. Watch out for jargon!

As with all reporting, don't just think about what you must do because of regulations or law – think about how reporting to your stakeholders can be an opportunity to tell your story in a different way – perhaps showing how you are making money work harder not just for your current beneficiaries but for those you will serve in the future.

Invest in good sleep
Holding investments can become the Freddy Krueger-like blood-curdling villain of your dreams, keeping you awake at night and gripped with horror. This is because the topic is a specialist area, packed with jargon, and not the main purpose of a charity. After all, most charities are not set up to invest – they are set up to deliver public benefit, and investments will always be secondary to that. Few charities will have internal resources that are devoted to managing investments, and the work to manage a sub-committee or monitor the performance of investments may form only a small part of the job of the finance professionals among a charity's staff. Becoming familiar with the language, setting up proper governance structures and drawing on expert advice can all help to prevent investments from being a nightmare.

Main chapter takeaways
- Investments can be a way to advance your charity's objectives and aims as well as a method of securing financial return. Explore different ways of using your resources to maximise your charity's impact.
- Assess the skills your charity has available within the staff and board of trustees, and determine whether you need specialist guidance and advice.
- Accounting for investments is a specialist area. Make sure you seek advice from your charity's accountant, auditor or independent examiner.

9 External scrutiny

The path of sound credence is through the thick forest of scepticism.
George Jean Nathan

The mere mention of an audit can strike fear into the very heart of the most resilient of individuals. 'We have the auditors in' uttered by a trustee or charity executive, pale of face and with tremoring voice, is likely to garner the collective support and empathy of the assembled masses: staff and trustees alike. The thought of an accounting professional crawling all over your charity's numbers with a view to issuing an opinion is enough to bring you out in a cold sweat! But it really shouldn't. Far from being horrific and terrifying, the experience of having external or internal scrutiny can, in actual fact, be incredibly useful. The relationship you build with an independent third party who scrutinises and tests your charity's figures can be hugely valuable – even, in my experience, warm!

In this chapter we will look at the various types of scrutiny and the levels of assurance they offer. We'll look at the steps your charity may wish to consider when thinking about appointing an auditor or independent examiner, including the responsibilities of the different parties when it comes to maintaining independence. We'll also briefly look at the concept of 'going concern' and what 'an opinion' might contain.

Far from being a necessary evil to endure, having external or internal scrutiny can make what your charity says more credible, inject a healthy dose of scepticism, and provide you with reassurance that the decisions your trustees and staff are making are grounded in fact. So, I hope that by the end of this chapter your fight through that thick, scary forest will have morphed to become a rewarding walk in nature, under the canopy of protective trees.

> **Outcomes**
> After reading this chapter you will:
> - **Understand the different types of scrutiny (independent examination, external audit and internal audit)**
> - **Be clear on the important considerations for managing your charity's relationship with its external auditor or independent examiner from beginning to end**
> - **Understand the concept of 'going concern' and the different statements that may be made on your charity's scrutinised accounts**

Being assured

Assurance is a bit like 'reassurance': feeling more certain that something is right. That's what scrutiny can give stakeholders when thinking about your charity's numbers – more confidence that what they are looking at is right. I have mentioned in earlier chapters that different charities have different obligations placed upon them, depending on their size and jurisdiction. Scrutiny requirements are frequently dictated in the same way, and once again you can turn to appendix 1 to check the scrutiny requirements for your charity. Basically, if your charity is on the smaller side, you can choose independent examination as the form of scrutiny, whereas larger charities have to have an external audit. Let's start by unpacking what each level of assurance is and on what it is based, beginning with independent examination (the most used form of assurance because the majority of charities are small) and finishing with internal audit (because it is generally only used by larger charities and it is not required by the regulators).

Independent examination

An independent examination is an independent and limited review of your year-end information, and it is a lighter-touch assurance than an audit. It doesn't delve into the underlying information as much as an audit does, and (depending on your charity's size) it doesn't always have to be undertaken by a qualified accountant. If you are under the threshold for needing someone who is qualified to carry out your independent examination (see appendix 1), you will need to assess whether they match your regulator's bar for capability. If your charity's annual income is over £250,000, you will need to appoint an independent examiner who holds a qualification with what is known as a 'qualifying body' (in Scotland it can also be the Auditor General for Scotland or someone appointed by the Accounts Commission for Scotland). A list is set out on page 152 and appendix 1 provides more details.

The key word in the role is 'independent', which means that the individual must not be, or be perceived as being, influenced by their relationship with the charity and its trustees. This rules out trustees of the charity, but it doesn't mean there has to be zero connection with the organisation. An examiner can be one of your charity's supporters – provided the relationship isn't too close. A mum of a child in a charity's pre-school service could probably be the independent examiner (provided she has the right skills), but if she also organises the other volunteers or raises funds, that may be too close a relationship, with too much involvement in the day-to-day administration of the charity. Roles that are highly likely to rule a person out from the role of independent examiner are providing bookkeeping to the charity, being an employee of the charity, serving on a sub-committee overseeing the charity's finances, giving large sums of money to the charity, or having another significant financial or commercial relationship with the charity.

Independent examination provides negative assurance. This means that the independent examiner gives an assurance that they haven't found anything in their consideration of the numbers which would indicate problems ('material uncertainties' – explained on page 163) which need to be brought to the attention of the readers of the accounts. This will include whether they think the charity can carry on for the foreseeable future (its 'going concern' status – considered on page 162).

The audience of an independent examination is not just the trustees but all stakeholders. It could therefore include donors, beneficiaries, regulators, staff and many more.

External audit

Sometimes referred to as 'statutory audit', an external audit is a review of specific matters which provides a higher level of assurance. In terms of your charity, an audit will test:

- whether your accounts are 'true and fair' – that is to say, they provide an accurate picture of the financial health of your charity;
- whether your accounts are drawn up on a 'going concern' basis – which isn't, as a friend in the sector shared with me recently (and which made me laugh out loud), her CEO's suggestion of 'can we just say we're still going and we're still concerned?' – but rather that you can keep running without going bust);
- whether there are any material (see the glossary) uncertainties in your accounting information.

An external audit of accounts has to be carried out by a registered auditor (or in Scotland by the Auditor General for Scotland or an auditor appointed by the Accounts Commission for Scotland; for charities in Northern Ireland, the bodies are set out in the Charities Act). This is the case even if the audit is required by a governing document or a funder rather than because of the size of your charity. An auditor has to be independent of your charity (trustees can get caught up on this issue – it's a little more complicated than for independent examination and I'll expand on this point further later in this chapter; see page 160). While an audit report will be addressed to the trustees, however they are described, the interested audience of an external audit is not just the trustees, finance committee members or staff of a charity but all stakeholders. It will therefore include donors, beneficiaries, regulators and much more.

It's a Nightmare with the Numbers

An audit does not provide a guarantee that all is well within the charity but is a far higher and arguably more robust process of scrutiny than an independent examination. It is important to remember that the auditors are reporting on whether the figures are reliable and truthful. Auditors give 'positive' and 'negative' assurances as part of their work. For example, a positive element might be confirmation that accounts meet with the requirements of the Charities Statement of Recommended Practice (SORP), and a negative element might be that they have found nothing which suggests something is wrong with the accounting records.

Internal audit

An internal audit examines various aspects of a charity's activities to provide assurance to an internal audience (trustees, committee members and/or senior staff, as relevant). The results of this scrutiny are for the charity alone. The audit will often check both the design of processes and compliance with them. So, for example, if an internal auditor is reviewing the effectiveness of financial controls, they will look at the design, nature and extent of those controls and whether staff have followed the measures put in place.

An internal audit is typically undertaken by internal staff, or it can be outsourced to a firm of accountants. Unlike for external auditors, there is no requirement for a qualification or registered auditor status – but it is frequently the case that an internal auditor holds an audit qualification, and they may have a specialist qualification, such as being a member of the Institute of Internal Auditors or another specialist body.

In my experience, internal auditors will grade their findings, giving you clarity on whether your processes and controls are poor, wonderful or somewhere in between. There isn't a standard way of expressing their conclusions, but internal auditors will tell you what their findings mean and will provide recommendations for improving both your processes or systems and, if relevant, ways to ensure your staff are following them. Common terms internal auditors use to express their findings are 'inadequate' (the design and/or execution of the systems and controls are not doing what they should), 'partial' (some bits of the design and/or execution are not working), 'reasonable' (the overall design and execution of the systems and controls are working OK) and 'substantial' (the design and execution of the systems and controls are pretty good). An internal audit may cover financial and non-financial topics. So, for example, an internal auditor might test your compliance with data-governance requirements or health and safety.

Other meanings of audit

Technically, the word 'audit' is not limited to finances. In addition to internal auditors looking at non-financial areas, your charity might be asked by an external stakeholder, such as a funder, or under the terms of a contract or even a regulator, to have an independent audit of its data, IT, safeguarding and so on. In its nature, such non-financial scrutiny will often be similar to an internal audit: the auditor will test your processes and compliance with them to give a level of assurance to the person or entity seeking confidence.

If your charity is asked to carry out an audit, it's important to make sure your staff and trustees know what is being asked for and what is required of them. For example, I once knew of a small charity that was asked for audited accounts as part of some checks a third party, with whom it was contracting, was carrying out. The charity was not required to have an audit but was about to go to the expense of getting one carried out because the contract was a valuable one. First, though, the charity's executive checked with the third party whether their independently examined accounts would do and were pleased to find they were perfectly acceptable. They wouldn't have known if they hadn't asked. Not only will checking audit requirements make sure your charity stays on the right side of the law and regulations, but it can also help you avoid unnecessary extra costs (an audit goes into much more detail and is often more costly than an independent examination).

In addition, independent examination is a relatively modern concept (for example, in England and Wales it was brought in by the Charities Act 1993). Older charities may make reference to audit in their governing documents because that was the only form of external scrutiny available at the time they were set up. If your charity's governing document pre-dates the creation of independent examination, ask your regulator if you can use the term 'audit' to mean the scrutiny required now. Your charity may need to clarify or amend its governing document, or seek permission, before you can have an independent examination carried out instead of an audit.

Finally, the word 'audit' is sometimes used in general parlance as shorthand for all forms of external scrutiny – for example, 'we need an audit of this piece of work' when what is wanted is someone else to check the facts.

Relationships with your charity's scrutineer

The word 'scrutineer' might conjure up a vision of some sort of pirate squinting at a treasure map through a magnifying glass, but all I mean is the person who carries out scrutiny for your charity (whether you have an independent examination or an audit). It's important to think about your relationship with this person from the beginning – whom you select, how you select them, how you maintain the relationship and how you end it – and to ensure they are truly independent. It can be the difference between effective use of time and resources or lots of discomfort and cost.

Starting out: whom to select

As with all relationships, how your charity starts out with its scrutineer can set the tone for the life of the relationship – for good or ill. There is a dizzying array of different qualifications and qualifying bodies with more acronyms than you can shake a stick at. Not all members of all bodies are legally allowed to undertake all forms of scrutiny, even if they appear to have the right letters after their name. For example, not all chartered accountants are also registered auditors.

To help you pick your way through the letter soup, the table below lists some key bodies and the letters they bestow on their members. By all means, use these qualifications and titles to filter a pool of possible candidates – for example, your trustees may feel that it's important that your accountant holds a qualification from one of the main accounting institutes (although if you talk to those who hold the various qualifications, each is of course likely to have their views on which is superior!). However, more importantly, also make sure they have the requisite skills to do the job, and take into account factors such as cost and 'fit' with your charity's team.

Statutory audit professional bodies	*Qualified independent examination bodies (bodies on the left plus)*	*Internal audit bodies*
Institute of Chartered Accountants in England and Wales (ICAEW) Designatory letters: *ACA* or *FCA*	Association of Charity Independent Examiners (ACIE) Designatory letters: *ACIE* or *FCIE*	Chartered Institute of Internal Auditors (IIA) Designatory letters: *CFIIA, CMIIA, PIIA* or *QICA*
Association of Chartered Certified Accountants Designatory letters: *ACCA* or *FCCA*	Association of Accounting Technicians (AAT) Designatory letters: *AAT* or *MAAT*	

9. External scrutiny

Chartered Accountants Ireland (CAI) Designatory letters: *ACA* or *FCA*	Chartered Institute of Management Accountants (CIMA) Designatory letters: *ACMA* or *FCMA*	
Institute of Chartered Accountants of Scotland *(ICAS)* Designatory letters: *CA*	Chartered Institute of Public Finance and Accountancy (CIPFA) Designatory letters: *CPFA* or *FCPFA*	
	Institute of Financial Accountants (IFA) Designatory letters: *IFA AIPA, AFA MIPA* or *FFA FIPA*	

Starting out: how to select

In this section I will refer to 'firms' when talking about audit and 'individuals' when referencing independent examiners, because your charity appoints a firm to conduct an audit, whereas an independent examination is an individual appointment. There are no hard and fast rules that must be applied to the selection. But I would certainly ensure that the firm or individual can satisfy your trustees that they have the right knowledge – charities have their own rules, as this book has frequently pointed out, so your charity's choice of scrutineer needs to be familiar with the rules surrounding charities.

The complexity or simplicity of your charity's process for selecting a scrutineer thereafter really comes down to your staff and trustees. The time frame you need to work to and how much the work is likely to cost may lead to a decision about whether to conduct a competitive process. An independent examination appointment for a few hundred pounds will warrant a less extensive selection process than a complicated audit costing thousands!

You may have heard the term 'beauty parade' in the context of appointing an auditor, internal auditor or independent examiner. This is the term often used to describe a competitive process where you weigh up a range of possible candidates for your role. You may be thinking, 'but how much of our resources do we need to put into the selection process?' It's an important relationship, so I would recommend spending some time thinking about what your charity wants.

If you're conducting a competitive process, the following checklist will be helpful. (And if you don't intend to have a competitive process, you can adapt these prompts to assist you in assessing possible firms and individuals that you approach.)

Appointment planning checklist

This checklist aims to help you decide your approach to making an appointment. Some elements might be deal breakers for your charity, such as the need to work to a fixed time frame, while others might be less important, such as experience with a charity just like yours. Only your charity can decide which things are more or less important.

	Section 1: Determine which factors are important to your charity.			Completed (yes/no)
	Score 1–10 with 1 being not important at all and 10 being essential. A wide variety of factors can be important in any invitation to potential firms/individuals. Some suggestions are given below as to what you can include. You may wish to identify other elements.			
A	Cost: **1 2 3 4 5 6 7 8 9 10** State your ideal budget if there is one: £............................ Value added: **1 2 3 4 5 6 7 8 9 10** Are there things they can do for your charity, such as providing sector insights, that will add value to the role? List them below.			
B	**Firm or individual employed by a firm, where relevant** (what elements are important?)			
	Size (mid-tier, member of the 'Big Four' accounting firms, etc.) **1 2 3 4 5 6 7 8 9 10** State what size is ideal:	Reputation **1 2 3 4 5 6 7 8 9 10** List any factors of importance:	Charity team size **1 2 3 4 5 6 7 8 9 10** State what size is ideal:	
	Diversity **1 2 3 4 5 6 7 8 9 10** List any factors of importance:	Culture **1 2 3 4 5 6 7 8 9 10** List any factors of importance:	Personality of individuals **1 2 3 4 5 6 7 8 9 10** Do you like/can work with them?	
	Need to work to a specific time frame **1 2 3 4 5 6 7 8 9 10** State any deadlines:			

C	Experience (is it important that the firm has experience of the following?)
	Charities of a similar size or nature **1 2 3 4 5 6 7 8 9 10**
	Entities operating with a similar business model **1 2 3 4 5 6 7 8 9 10**
	(For example, if your charity has retail activities or buildings, or heavily relies on a particular type of income, it would be good to know the firm's first rodeo won't be with you!)

Section 2: Identify who in your charity will be involved		**Completed**
Circle the party or parties that will be involved in reviewing the responses and making the selection.		**(yes/no)**
A	**Staff/executive**		
	CEO	Finance representative	Other (list)
B	**Trustees/governance**		
	Chair	Finance committee	Other (list)

Section 3: Identify any key dates your process needs to work to (such as board meetings or filing dates)	**Completed**
Set out a process for selection and a timeline which works to these dates, ensuring sufficient time is left for getting any appropriate sign-off within your charity (appointment of auditors is usually a decision reserved to the board).	**(yes/no)**

Section 4: Identify a longlist of firms/individuals that your trustees might wish to invite to tender for the role	**Completed**
	(yes/no)
Undertake some basic due diligence (checking them out) based on your charity's criteria. Factors such as size of firm/team, reputation and internal diversity should be easily gleaned from a check on a candidate's website.	

Longlist	Commentary/notes	Due Diligence
1		(yes/no)
2		
3		
4		
5		

Section 5: Shortlisting		**Completed**
Whittle the list down to the names your trustees will invite to tender for the role. Make sure the list is not too long because some firms and individuals won't submit a response to a process that includes a high number of participants. As a rule of thumb, three is sufficient.		**(yes/no)**
Shortlist	**Commentary/notes**	
1		
2		
3		
Section 6: Draft an invitation to tender (ITT) This should:		**Completed** **(yes/no)**
A Set out your process for conducting the 'beauty parade' (Will it be based on written responses only? Will there be an interview element? Is there someone who can answer questions about the process and/or your charity before the invited firms/individuals submit their bids? How many stages are there? Will your charity have a shorter list to call for interview? Is there anything else you need to consider?)		
B Give a brief background of your charity (size; history; area of activity; any relevant features of your business model, such as use of a trading subsidiary, etc.)		
C Set out relevant timeline and key accounting information (Such as year-end dates, previous qualified opinions issued, instances of late filing, etc.)		
D Set out any crucial selection criteria on which trustees will make their choice (For example, everyone's time will be saved if you set out a limit on what you can pay, in case a firm/individual's fees are completely out of line with what your charity can pay. This information doesn't need to be shared externally if you don't want to.)		

9. External scrutiny

Section 7: Decide whom to interview		
Review the responses and decide whether you want to invite each firm/individual for an interview (the decision on whom to invite is down to the trustees, as is the decision on whom to appoint). **Make sure you agree the questions internally beforehand** (as this helps to target the conversation and gain consistent information from the firms/individuals, making it easier to decide who meets the brief the best).	ITT response review	**Interview?**
	1	(yes/no)
	2	
	3	
Section 8: Check compliance		
Make sure any internal governance considerations – such as any resolutions required to formally appoint auditors – are met. Then confirm the appointment.		**Completed** (yes/no)

Maintaining a good relationship

Your charity has made the appointment – now what? Depending on the nature of the scrutiny, it may be that the big event happens once a year (review of your year-end position) or there may be a number of assignments during the year. However, as with all relationships, you get out what you put in. If, for example, the only time your staff or trustees speak to your scrutineer is as they rock up to examine your charity's finances at year end, then it is likely to be a less pleasant experience than if time has been taken to get to know them.

For example, how do they like to work? Do they use particular e-solutions, such as a portal, where your charity's staff can submit documents and the scrutineer will highlight queries? If so, can your team be trained so that they are familiar with the systems? Who are the key people you will be liaising with (in the case of a firm)? Can informal introductions be made to key members of staff within your charity?

Similarly, there may be times when you need expert input (sometimes between formal reviews), when your scrutineer may become a trusted advisor. In the case of an independent examination, your independent examiner may not be a qualified accountant so they may be limited in the professional input they can give, but others may be highly expert. In the case of a statutory audit, your auditor is likely to be expert in all manner of things. In the case of an internal audit, those conducting the audit are also likely to be able to share their expertise with you. What kind of advice might you seek from your scrutineer and could it help with maintaining a positive working relationship? For example, you might need guidance on how those examining your charity's information might perceive a particular transaction. Or the finance team might be wrestling with whether a particular item should appear in your charity's accounts – perhaps a legacy or grant has been received for the first time and your staff are unfamiliar with the relevant SORP requirements.

These touchpoints can assist in building a relationship. Building rapport should not compromise independence. I'm not suggesting that your staff and trustees start going out regularly for social time with your scrutineer. However, communication and strong working relationships can help to smooth your passage through difficult conversations if problems are encountered or differences of opinion arise.

However, it isn't always possible to work through those differences of opinion with your scrutineer. There are areas within the accounting rules where professional judgement is required and, even if you disagree or have a different view, you may not be able to change your scrutineer's opinion. There can be variations between what different professionals think regarding, say, the treatment of a charity's pension liability or valuation. I recall one situation where a charity disagreed with its audit team on how an investment should be treated. The audit team was adamant that a certain approach ought to be taken, but the charity's finance team felt this approach would put the charity at a disadvantage. The charity took advice from a third party and pushed back with an alternative view. The auditors acknowledged a different interpretation was possible and did not insist on their position being adopted. However, the incident soured the relationship and the charity and auditor parted company at the end of the audit.

Differences of opinion, in my experience are particularly evident in internal audits. I have seen instances where the management didn't think a recommendation being made was appropriate, proportionate or achievable when taking into account all factors. With appropriate push-back, further information and explanation, I've seen internal auditors accept the management's position.

Likewise, before an auditor has formed their opinion, there will be areas where they seek information, express their views and question the executive. There will be certain topics where discussion will bring about an agreement on how to treat a certain transaction or set of transactions in the accounts. In other situations, it is clear that the scrutineer is fixed in their view and disagreeing could result in a comment being made in a final opinion if adjustments are not made to reflect that view.

Be clear about whether something is or is not up for debate. Some topics – for example, whether an auditor believes your charity can continue to operate as a going concern – will be serious issues and some even impact the ability of the auditor to remain in post. Do not assume whether something is more or less serious – ask.

It is entirely possible for the relationship between your charity and your scrutineer to be convivial, warm, supportive and constructive. Aim to avoid relationships which are cold and overly formal. In my experience, trying for the former rather than the latter aids ongoing working and also helps when the time comes to part company. Make sure everyone at your charity is aware that having a scrutineer in can consume a lot of time and resources. Your finance team may need to call on them at short notice for information, and the team may also be less available to the rest of your charity because their attention is elsewhere. Ensuring this is understood can smooth relationships within your charity as well as with your scrutineer.

Parting company

There is a range of reasons why your charity might part company with a scrutineer. The most common is that it's simply time for a fresh set of eyes. Here the parting of ways should be uneventful. But the end can also be more acrimonious as a result of a falling-out about costs or simply a breakdown in relationships. Sometimes it is down to unreconciled differences of opinion, and occasionally a scrutineer will deem it legally, ethically or professionally necessary to resign from their post.

It is important to have a good end to a relationship where possible. If your charity has managed the relationship well and nothing comes from left field to derail it – such as a sudden change in personnel – it is advisable to let your scrutineer know before your trustees start the process of replacement. However, sometimes a bad end is unavoidable.

Where an independent examiner or auditor does find a serious issue – something typically called a 'matter of material significance' – they may have to resign and may be obliged to report your charity to its regulator(s) and/or other bodies. I couldn't find an exhaustive list of what would give such a 'cause to resign'. However, within *Matters of Material Significance Reportable to UK Charity Regulators: Guidance for auditors and independent examiners*, the three UK regulators set out a number of areas where a duty arises. Issues in one of those areas may lead to a resignation. Such matters can range from dishonesty and fraud to failure to have good controls or keep appropriate accounting records where this could give rise to a loss of charitable funds. These are serious issues, not just spats between parties, and your scrutineer could get into trouble if they don't report to the appropriate regulator(s). There may also be other duties to report to other bodies or agencies – such as the police, in the case of crime.

It is worth pointing out that internal auditors generally do not have the same duty to report as they are under contract to an internal audience. They ought not to act in a way which may give rise to a breach of that contract, and the legal protection afforded to auditors and independent examiners (who make reports to the charity regulators) does not extend to internal auditors. However, there may be circumstances where it is justifiable for an internal auditor to breach a contract because of the serious nature of what they have uncovered. Something like money laundering or fraud could prompt an internal auditor to become a whistle-blower. It's impossible to give a comprehensive list of such circumstances so just be aware that where someone is scrutinising your information, they may owe duties to entities other than the one paying the bill.

Independence

One common area that charities spend a disproportionate amount of time worrying about is the independence of their scrutineer. While it is entirely appropriate for your charity to do some basic checks so the trustees are satisfied about whether a firm or individual is sufficiently independent, it is actually the duty of the firm or individual being appointed to make sure they can accept the appointment.

When it comes to independent examination, because your charity is appointing an individual, it could be argued that there is a greater responsibility on trustees to make sure they ask the right questions. This may be particularly true if the person being asked is not qualified: in such circumstances, I would recommend signposting the candidates to relevant information available from the charity regulators, and trustees should require potential appointees to confirm they believe they meet the rules.

Once your charity gets to audit level, the duty to ensure independence rests solely with the auditor. Auditors are required by their regulator and the underlying audit standards to be and remain independent. Trustees don't need to spend too much time worrying about things like the length of time a firm can be in post or the services it can provide alongside the audit, as the rules on these matters are set down in the standards of practice which govern auditors. Each firm will have to follow the industry rules on how long someone can be the audit partner before they have to hand over the reins to a colleague (so-called audit rotation rules) and on the nature and extent of other services they may provide to your charity. However, if your charity is deemed to be a 'public interest entity' (listed entities and regulated industries such as banks and insurance) as set out in company law, the auditors must stand down after ten years.

Some audit firms remain the auditors of charities for years, even decades. Provided the individuals involved in the work meet the independence requirements, there is nothing inherently wrong with this. However, trustees may feel that the credibility of the appointment is reduced if the length of service is very long or the relationship could be perceived to be too close. In such cases, they may decide to change scrutineer regularly. My advice is not to make the intervals too short. It takes time for a professional to really get to know your charity. Change scrutineer too frequently and it will drive up the cost, potentially compromise quality and perhaps even reduce the pool of candidates prepared to do the work. Plus, undertaking a 'beauty parade' and establishing a new relationship with a firm or individual can be time-consuming and unsettling for your charity's team. Don't underestimate the work involved in making the change – and think about other big moments in your charity's life that may generate unusual levels of work, and might make changing your scrutineer at the same time ill-advised, before making a move.

In one charity I knew of, the auditors had expressed a desire to stand down: they were changing their firm's mix of clients and had determined the charity was too small to fit the new profile and anticipated income level. However, an event occurred within the charity which gave rise to media criticism of its finances, despite its clean audit. After a discussion, the firm agreed to extend its tenure for an additional year to avoid speculation about the reasons for its departure. Neither party wished for anything to be read into the end of the relationship. This was possible because of – and is a good illustration of – the importance of taking time to build a positive relationship with your scrutineer.

Opinions and reports

What a scrutineer says in an assurance report – or their 'opinion' – will be a key piece of information your charity's stakeholders will take into consideration when reviewing your accounts. Opinions can also be of interest to journalists – particularly for high-profile charities or in the light of scandal or intrigue. So, what might your scrutineer's opinion or report say? It's helpful to know the typical language your charity could encounter.

A typical 'clean' report of an independent examiner may read as follows:

> I have completed my examination. I confirm that no material matters have come to my attention in connection with the examination which give me cause to believe that, in any material respect:
> - accounting records were not kept in accordance with section 130 of the Charities Act 2011 or
> - the accounts do not accord with the accounting records.
>
> I have no concerns and have come across no other matters in connection with the examination to which attention should be drawn in order to enable a proper understanding of the accounts to be reached.

If something is discovered by an independent examiner, they will write to the trustees to set out expressly what that matter is and why it is of concern. The Charity Commission guidance *Independent Examination of Charity Accounts: Examiners* (CC32) sets out a number of examples where the independent examiner should (or in some cases must) raise concerns, which I will not set out here.

An auditor's final opinion can contain many elements and often runs to a few pages as the auditor sets out their opinion, the basis for it and other standard content they are required to include. I don't intend to repeat all of this here either, you'll be pleased to know. However, I think it helps to familiarise yourself with the standard phrasing of some bits, such as this one:

> We have audited the financial statements of [name] (the 'charity') for the year ended [date] which comprise the Consolidated Statement of Financial Activities, the Consolidated and Charity Balance Sheets, the Consolidated Statement of Cash Flows and notes to the financial statements, including a summary of significant accounting policies. The financial reporting

framework that has been applied in their preparation is applicable law and United Kingdom Accounting Standards, including FRS 102 'The Financial Reporting Standard applicable in the UK and Republic of Ireland' (United Kingdom Generally Accepted Accounting Principles).

In our opinion, the financial statements:

- give a true and fair view of the state of the charity and the group's affairs as at [date] and of the group's income and expenditure for the year then ended;
- have been properly prepared in accordance with United Kingdom Generally Accepted Accounting Principles;
- have been prepared in accordance with the requirements of the Companies Act 2006.

Where an auditor is not satisfied, you may get what is known as an 'emphasis of matter' or your charity's audit opinion may be 'qualified'. I will explain these concepts in more detail, but first let's quickly look at the question of going concern.

Going concern

Going concern is a judgement that an entity has sufficient resources to continue operating into the foreseeable future without incurring debt it has no ability to pay. An external auditor, or an independent examiner where relevant, will ordinarily consider a reasonable period for the 'foreseeable future' to be 12 months from the date a set of accounts is signed when judging whether the trustees' conclusions have legitimacy. It's important to note that this period doesn't run from the financial year end but rather from the date the opinion is given.

The wording you will likely see in a going concern statement where your auditors have decided they agree with your trustees that your charity will be able to operate into the foreseeable future without running out of money is as follows:

> In auditing the financial statements, we have concluded that the trustees' use of the going concern basis of accounting in the preparation of the financial statements is appropriate.
>
> Based on the work we have performed, we have not identified any material uncertainties relating to events or conditions that, individually or collectively, may cast significant doubt on the charity's ability to continue as a going concern for a period of at least 12 months from when the financial statements are authorised for issue.
>
> Our responsibilities and the responsibilities of the trustees with respect to going concern are described in the relevant sections of this report.

You'll notice the words 'we have not identified any material uncertainties' in this statement. Where an auditor does identify things that they believe cast serious doubt on a charity's conclusion that it is a going concern, they will say so in their audit report. As with other conclusions, an auditor will have had conversations with the executive and trustees beforehand, so this won't just happen without those running the charity knowing.

Materiality
The concept of materiality will come up when your charity is scrutinised. What is considered to be a material sum (one that is big or important enough to make a difference to the financial picture of your charity) is determined by the scrutineer. They will set out what the amounts in any given items of income and expenditure, or area of activity, individually or collectively, they consider to be material before they start their work. This is an important accounting principle that determines whether a discrepancy, such as something missing or something that's incorrect, needs to be absolutely right in the accounts because it could impact the decision-making of a user of those accounts. It also gives the trustees and executive a good idea of the relative importance of different figures.

Emphasis of matter
Auditors have a responsibility to draw users' attention to anything they think is critical to understanding the financial statements, even when the auditor has concluded that the technical reporting of it is correct. This is known as an 'emphasis of matter'. The text an auditor is obliged to include in their report will refer to:

> a matter appropriately presented or disclosed in the financial statements that, in the auditor's judgement, is of such importance that it is fundamental to users' understanding of the financial statements.

Such matters may be about uncertainty that exists because of litigation or regulatory action against the charity, or a major catastrophe that has had (or continues to have) a significant effect on the charity's financial position. An auditor has an obligation to tell those 'charged with governance' if they conclude there is something that requires an emphasis of matter disclosure. This is likely to have been discussed during the audit so shouldn't come out of the blue for your trustees when they receive the final audit report.

Qualification
If your charity's audit is 'qualified', what does this mean? An opinion or report is said to be qualified where an auditor cannot confirm that, in their view, your charity's accounts give a completely true and fair view of the state of the charity's affairs at year end, or where they have reservations about whether the numbers and/or records have been properly prepared. Qualification is, therefore, not a good thing. However, there are different degrees to which this may be a nightmare.

Sometimes, this conclusion arises because an auditor cannot get enough appropriate evidence, or if they find (or think there is a good chance that there are) material misstatements in your charity's numbers. In such situations, you might see words which reflect concern limited to a specific set of balances, transactions or disclosures. In this case, the auditor is reporting that, other than for those specific items, they have concluded that your financial statements are true and fair. While this is not a brilliant state of affairs, it is not completely awful. In addition, the auditor may well be content to remain in post.

However, where an auditor is prevented from obtaining sufficient appropriate audit evidence by, say, the management of the charity, this is really serious. In such circumstances, they are likely to withdraw from the engagement, give a qualified opinion or disclaim their opinion (meaning they are distancing themselves from providing any opinion at all related to the financial statements). If this happens to your charity, this is likely to be a serious issue and it could lead to reputational damage, undermine your funding prospects and draw the attention of the regulators.

An independent examiner doesn't express an opinion on whether your financial statements are true and fair. But, similarly to an auditor's qualification of an opinion, if they discover differences between the accounting records and the financial statements, their report will be qualified in relation to those matters.

Assurance relating to your charity's management

During an assurance engagement, the scrutineer may seek assurance from the executive and trustees about a number of things. The executive and trustees may be asked to provide a letter of representation setting out and confirming that full disclosure has been given to the scrutineer. Your trustees will be asked for evidence of key decisions and calculations relating to things like reserves and the conclusion that the charity is financial sustainable. Before the work starts, the scrutineer will provide your trustees with an outline of the things they will look at and the evidence they are likely to test. They should also be clear which documents, such as a letter from the executive and/or trustees, they will need. But, in addition to these process elements, it is worth highlighting the importance of the opportunity the trustees have to obtain an insight into the processes, performance and procedures of their executive.

In the case of an external audit, when it comes to the relevant meeting to receive the final report and formally sign off the accounts (sometimes known as 'adopting the accounts'), it is good practice for the trustees to have a closed session with the auditors. This provides an opportunity, without the executive, for the trustees to raise concerns with or hear from the auditors regarding the wider issues and conduct of the audit. I have known executives to be incredibly concerned about this discussion. Indeed, although I know I should have nothing to be concerned about when it comes to Charity Finance Group's board meeting with its auditors, my heart is sure to skip a beat! But I would always recommend this opportunity is taken. Trustees benefit from hearing comments from an external auditor, as they can be sure these comments won't be filtered or affected by working relationships with the executive. It's worth the moment of discomfort to provide that extra layer of good governance.

Some last words before ye walk the plank

There is no doubt that assurance, whatever the nature of your scrutineer, is an important part of understanding your charity's numbers. It is definitely worthwhile to know what to expect, take time to get the best out of the relationship, and embrace scrutiny not just as a compliance exercise to be endured but an opportunity to be reassured. Once you know what to expect and have familiarised yourself with the very formal language of the reports, instead of thinking that you'll be stepping out into the unknown, you should be able to stride forward confidently.

Main chapter takeaways

- Build a good relationship with your charity's scrutineer and, where relevant, between your staff and the firm's personnel.
- Don't waste too much time on considering independence – verifying this is mainly the scrutineer's responsibility, not yours!
- Make sure your charity's trustees don't change scrutineers too frequently: tenders for reappointment can consume a lot of time and resources.
- Familiarise yourself with the wording used in assurance reports.
- Take time to provide evidence when requested and explain your charity's position if queries arise – this can help you avoid costly misunderstandings.
- Recognise that having someone scrutinise your charity's numbers can be stressful and time-consuming, so be kind to your colleagues (and yourself) when you have the scrutineers in!

10 Pearls of wisdom

Share your knowledge. It is a way to achieve immortality. Dalai Lama

In this chapter, a range of charity finance professionals share their thoughts and lessons. A fantastic feature of the charity finance community is people's generosity and willingness to share their insight and wisdom. They do this not because they know it all and wish to dispense their faultless expertise, but because they have personally grown on the 'immortality' of those who came before, added their own experiences and challenges. Now, they are happily passing the baton to the next runner.

Nicki Deeson, leadership coach and charity mentor, former Finance Director of Amnesty International

- As Finance Director of the secretariat at Amnesty International, I learned it's vital to know where your charity's money comes from and where it goes to. Write it down in a few sentences, draw it on one page, or model it using Lego or Post-its.
- Most of our money came from partner Amnesty organisations around the world. When one large partner suffered a financial crisis in 2019 and couldn't pay its contribution, the secretariat found itself in a significant savings and redundancy drive, damaging staff morale and the leadership's ability to achieve strategic goals. In retrospect, we should have deliberately asked ourselves where the biggest spanners could be thrown in the works.
- Risk registers can provide false reassurance. At Amnesty, we didn't see the problems coming because our risk register assumed the other partner organisations had high trust and commitment in the secretariat and would bail us out.
- It's important to know the reality: at Amnesty, our partner organisations' trust in us was actually near rock bottom.
- If we had identified that we were vulnerable around our partners' financial sustainability, and that we needed to build trust, great relationships and supportive commitments, then when difficult times came, the Amnesty movement could have come together to best manage our partner's financial challenges and be stronger for the future.

*Note: This recollection is my personal views on my experience at the time.

Rui Domingues, Director of Finance, Property and Technology, London City Mission and former Director of Finance and Operations, Charity Finance Group

- Regular management information tells staff and trustees where to look for stories they may be missing in your charity and helps them to see where course corrections might be needed. But the management information often lags behind the stories, because it is backward looking.
- Build indicators to help you see your charity's key activities as quickly as possible and use the management information as a safety net to catch those stories that might be missed.
- The finance tail should never wag the organisational dog! If your charity's processes, procedures and policies aren't supporting what trustees and staff are trying to do, and how they are trying to do it, change them.
- Reserves are an umbrella to help you weather a storm. When the rain's pouring, use the umbrella!
- The trustees' annual report and accounts are a great way to publicly share your charity's story with a wider audience. Think about who will be listening and write the document with them in mind.

Andrew Hind, former CEO of the Charity Commission for England and Wales and Senior Visiting Fellow at Bayes Business School

- The most important person around the board table is not the treasurer (if you have one) but the finance director (or equivalent finance professional on the staff). This person has front-line responsibility, with the CEO, for steering the financial ship in line with the board-approved approach.
- The treasurer is there to act as a sounding board to the financial director and, most importantly, to help engage non-financial trustees in board discussions about the numbers. Of course, if the treasurer is unhappy about the charity's finances, they must make this known. But this should be discussed with the financial director and CEO in advance, and never for the first time in a board meeting.
- Don't forget the balance sheet. Your management information is not just about tracking budget variances against income and expenditure. You must also closely monitor your charity's cash-flow health. If you are about to run out of cash, it's best to know in advance. Without a monthly balance sheet, you have no chance of knowing how close you are to hitting the rocks.
- If you have an audit committee, bring a lay trustee onto it. An audit committee's financially expert members and attendees – the treasurer, the finance director, the external auditor, etc. – can sometimes get themselves tied up in too many intricate financial knots and lose sight of the big strategic picture. A non-financially expert trustee can make an important contribution by asking apparently naive questions, such as 'Why do we do it that way?'

10. Pearls of wisdom

- It's not the financial director's job to write the trustees' annual report. They are likely to draft your charity's annual financial *accounts*, but the trustees should take the lead in drafting their trustees' annual report – 'their' being the operative word.

Simon Hopkins, originating author of the Finance Journey

- Charity finance often combines the more complex ends of both commercial and government money management. And charity personnel have to get their heads around lots of aspects of finance that are unique to the charity sector, such as restricted funds, endowments and legacies. Make sure your charity finds people who understand charity finance at the truly big-picture level and learns from them.
- Look beyond the assumption that charities all operate in an identical or interchangeable fashion. Whatever your role, you'll need to understand the underlying business model behind *your* charity. There is as much difference between a foundation trust that awards institutional grants and a traditional fundraiser that runs services as there is between a fashion retailer and a travel agent.
- Whatever you do, make sure you are as familiar with impact reporting as you are with the accounts. Qualitative measures such as case studies – which will describe the difference your charity makes – can help you make sense of the financials.
- Have a strategic view of charity finance as something that drives organisational effectiveness and transformation rather than simply processes transactions and passively reports on the charity. Make sure you understand the true, underlying financial resilience of your charity. You won't necessarily get this from looking at one year's accounts in isolation.
- Trustees and the executive will need to decide what role they want finance to play and recruit people who 'fit'. There is no point recruiting a disrupter or strategic change agent if a back-office admin service is what is really wanted. Similarly, an out-and-out technician might not give your charity much by way of organisational strategy or transformational change.

Bob Humphreys, Chair of the Audit and Finance Committee at the Education Development Trust

- Every year at the helm of an organisation is like setting off in a large yacht on a trans-oceanic voyage – there will be cross-winds and strong currents pulling and pushing you in various directions. Some might help you along, while others will throw you off course or spin you around. Waves will crash over your bows and give you a good drenching now and then.
- Your crew is a team – nothing will go right unless everyone does their part, so stay close, with open and honest communication, and always listen to what the lookout is telling you.

- You need to be constantly taking sextant readings to establish your position and direction of travel. When challenges inevitably sweep in from the horizon, the later you leave it to make course corrections, the further you will drift and the longer the voyage will be.
- Plan ahead so you don't risk running out of supplies before you get to your destination or foundering on uncharted rocks.
- Use your soundings and observations to make timely small adjustments to your sails and the rudder as soon as possible, to maximise your chances of a smooth crossing.

Joyce Materego-Woodall, Director of Finance and Operations, Global Greengrants Fund

- Focus on relationships with those around you:
  - with the essential trio of funders (to bring in as much unrestricted funds as possible), the operations team (including fundraisers) and (if you are on the board) the CEO (who should support your charity's vision);
  - with the treasurer, as the link between the board and the financial executives (the treasurer is the lead custodian of financial well-being of the charity as far as the board is concerned, so it is crucial to ensure that this link is strong);
  - with your auditors, who are critical friends and guides;
  - with your bankers (keep your bankers informed and updated on your financial performance beyond bank transactions and balances; and never rule out the need for an overdraft or a loan!);
  - with your sector peers, to keep abreast of current issues and the corresponding emerging thoughts around solutions.
- Have more honest conversations with your funders and donors. Remember that you serve and know your beneficiaries, and therefore you have and are part of the solutions.
- Try to steer funders away from acting as power-brokers and gatekeepers – again, your charity is a solutions broker.
- Use audiovisual technology to show and share your impact over time. Most charities deal with social issues, so written reports only go so far.
- Organisations fail due to a lack of cash to fulfil their financial obligations, not due to a year-end deficit. Cash really is king.

Kevin O'Brien, Chair of Charity Finance Group and former CFO in a number of charities

- The charity sector above all is the one where the numbers are everybody's business.
- The most important role I played as CFO was to ensure we could tell the charity's financial story in simple terms, in plain English, whether this was to the board, the employees or external stakeholders (such as funders).

- Staff and trustees have to understand how all the bits of your charity function and how they fit together.
- Try to explain your charity's finances to a friend or family member. If they don't get it, you need to keep working on your understanding.
- Understanding your charity's finances is just as important when the finances are looking healthy as when they are not.

Ian Theodoreson, former Chair of Charity Finance Group, former CFO at the Church of England, and now trustee of the Bath and Wells Diocesan Board of Finance

- There is no such thing as a stupid question when it comes to understanding your charity's finances.
- The best question I was ever asked, which resulted in the charity re-evaluating its approach, came from a colleague who worked as our receptionist. She saw the organisation from her unique perspective and rightly challenged the 'group think' that had set in. The glory of this is that she didn't even know she was asking such an insightful question – she was just being curious!
- At the start of every year, spend some time thinking about the management information your charity routinely produces. Is it still fit for purpose?
- Also think about who is using the information. What do they get out of it? Is there information being produced that no one uses any more? Do people need you to report on new issues?
- If you are a trustee, check who you are getting your information about your charity from. Is it always the same few voices? If so, widen your sources and preferably see things directly for yourself.

Main chapter takeaways

- There is no such thing as a stupid question.
- Use financial information to make adjustments so you keep delivering for your charity's beneficiaries.
- A risk register is no substitute for understanding what's going on in your charity.
- If your charity's policies, procedures and systems don't help drive your charity's work – change them!
- Don't underestimate the power of great relationships.
- Bring non-finance people into conversations on the numbers. There are big differences between different charities – they are not all the same – so take time to understand the business model of your charity.
- Ensure charity's finances are explained in plain English. Finance people who understand charity finance well should be able to explain it to a non-specialist.

Appendix 1

Table of thresholds

Legal form	Minimum requirements in England and Wales (Charity Commission for England and Wales)	Minimum requirements in Scotland (Office of the Scottish Charity Regulator)	Minimum requirements in Northern Ireland (Charity Commission for Northern Ireland)*
Gross income less than £10,000			
Unincorporated	✓ **Receipts and payments** ✗ File trustees' **annual report** and accounts ✗ File **annual return** ⚲ No examination or audit	✓ **Receipts and payments** ✓ File trustees' **annual report** and accounts ✓ File trustees' **annual return** ⚲ **Independent examination** by person with *requisite skills*	✓ **Receipts and payments** (if governing document is silent on form of accounts) ✓ File trustees' **annual report** and accounts ✓ File **annual monitoring return** ⚲ **Independent examination** by person assessed as *being capable*
Company	✓ **Accrual accounts** ✗ File trustees' **annual report** and accounts ✗ File **annual return** ⚲ No examination or audit	✓ **Accrual accounts** ✓ File trustees' **annual report** and accounts ✓ File trustees' **annual return** ⚲ **Independent examination by** a *qualified* person	✓ **Accrual accounts** ✓ File trustees' **annual report** and accounts ✓ File **annual monitoring return** ⚲ **Independent examination** by person assessed as *being capable*

Legal form	Minimum requirements in England and Wales (Charity Commission for England and Wales)	Minimum requirements in Scotland (Office of the Scottish Charity Regulator)	Minimum requirements in Northern Ireland (Charity Commission for Northern Ireland)*
Charitable incorporated organisation (CIO or SCIO in Scotland)	✓ **Receipts and payments** ✓ File trustees' **annual report** and accounts ✓ File **annual return** ⚑ No examination or audit	✓ **Receipts and payments** ✓ File trustees' **annual report** and accounts ✓ File trustees' **annual return** ⚑ **Independent examination** by person with *requisite skills*	n/a**

* Charities that are not registered with the Charity Commission for Northern Ireland are not required to report until they are placed on the register.

** It is not possible to set up a charitable incorporated organisation in Northern Ireland at present as the relevant section of the Charities Act (Northern Ireland) 2008 is not yet in force.

Appendix 1

Legal form	Minimum requirements in England and Wales (Charity Commission for England and Wales)	Minimum requirements in Scotland (Office of the Scottish Charity Regulator)	Minimum requirements in Northern Ireland (Charity Commission for Northern Ireland)*
Gross income greater than £10,000 up to £25,000			
Unincorporated	✓ **Receipts and payments** ✗ File trustees' **annual report** and accounts ✓ File **annual return** ⚲ No examination or audit	✓ **Receipts and payments** ✓ File trustees' **annual report** and accounts ✓ File **annual return** ⚲ **Independent examination** by person with *requisite skills*	✓ **Receipts and payments** (if governing document is silent on form of accounts) ✓ File trustees' **annual report** and accounts ✓ File **annual monitoring return** ⚲ **Independent examination** by person assessed as *being capable*
Company	✓ **Accrual accounts** ✗ File trustees' **annual report** and accounts ✓ File **annual return** ⚲ No examination or audit	✓ **Accrual accounts** ✓ File trustees' **annual report** and accounts ✓ File **annual return** ⚲ **Independent examination by** a *qualified* person	✓ **Accrual accounts** ✓ File trustees' **annual report** and accounts ✓ File **annual monitoring return** ⚲ **Independent examination** by person assessed as *being capable*

Legal form	Minimum requirements in England and Wales (Charity Commission for England and Wales)	Minimum requirements in Scotland (Office of the Scottish Charity Regulator)	Minimum requirements in Northern Ireland (Charity Commission for Northern Ireland)*
Charitable incorporated organisation (CIO or SCIO in Scotland)	✓ **Receipts and payments** ✓ File trustees' **annual report** and accounts ✓ File **annual return** ○ No examination or audit	✓ **Receipts and payments** ✓ File trustees' **annual report** and accounts ✓ File **annual return** ○ **Independent examination** by person with requisite skills	n/a**

* Charities that are not registered with the Charity Commission for Northern Ireland are not required to report until they are placed on the register.

** It is not possible to set up a charitable incorporated organisation in Northern Ireland at present as the relevant section of the Charities Act (Northern Ireland) 2008 is not yet in force.

Appendix 1

Legal form	Minimum requirements in England and Wales (Charity Commission for England and Wales)	Minimum requirements in Scotland (Office of the Scottish Charity Regulator)	Minimum requirements in Northern Ireland (Charity Commission for Northern Ireland)*
Gross income greater than £25,000 up to £250,000			
Unincorporated	✓ **Receipts and payments** ✓ File trustees' **annual report** and accounts ✓ File **annual return** ⚲ **Independent examination** by person with *requisite skills*	✓ **Receipts and payments** ✓ File trustees' **annual report** and accounts ✓ File **annual return** ⚲ **Independent examination** by person with *requisite skills*	✓ **Receipts and payments** (if governing document is silent on form of accounts) ✓ File trustees' **annual report** and accounts ✓ File **annual monitoring return** ⚲ **Independent examination** by person assessed as *being capable*
Company	✓ **Accrual accounts** ✓ File trustees' **annual report** and accounts ✓ File **annual return** ⚲ **Independent examination** by person with *requisite skills*	✓ **Accrual accounts** ✓ File trustees' **annual report** and accounts ✓ File **annual return** ⚲ **Independent examination** by *qualified* person	✓ **Accrual accounts** ✓ File trustees' **annual report** and accounts ✓ File **annual monitoring return** ⚲ **Independent examination** by person assessed as *being capable*

Legal form	Minimum requirements in England and Wales (Charity Commission for England and Wales)	Minimum requirements in Scotland (Office of the Scottish Charity Regulator)	Minimum requirements in Northern Ireland (Charity Commission for Northern Ireland)*
Charitable incorporated organisation (CIO or SCIO in Scotland)	✓ **Receipts and payments** ✓ File trustees' **annual report** and accounts ✓ File **annual return** ⚑ **Independent examination** by person with requisite skills	✓ **Receipts and payments** ✓ File trustees' **annual report** and accounts ✓ File **annual return** ⚑ **Independent examination** by person with requisite skills	n/a**

* Charities that are not registered with the Charity Commission for Northern Ireland are not required to report until they are placed on the register.

** It is not possible to set up a charitable incorporated organisation in Northern Ireland at present as the relevant section of the Charities Act (Northern Ireland) 2008 is not yet in force.

Appendix 1

Legal form	Minimum requirements in England and Wales (Charity Commission for England and Wales)	Minimum requirements in Scotland (Office of the Scottish Charity Regulator)	Minimum requirements in Northern Ireland (Charity Commission for Northern Ireland)*
Gross income greater than £250,000 up to £500,000			
All (unincorporated, companies and charitable incorporated organisations**)	✓ **Accrual accounts** ✓ File trustees' **annual report** and accounts ✓ File **annual return** ⚲ **Independent examination** by *qualified* person	✓ **Accrual accounts** ✓ File trustees' **annual report** and accounts ✓ File **annual return** ⚲ **Independent examination** by *qualified* person	✓ **Accrual accounts** ✓ File trustees' **annual report** and accounts ✓ File **annual monitoring return** ⚲ **Independent examination** by a member of a body listed in section 65(4) of the Charities Act (Northern Ireland) 2008

Legal form	Minimum requirements in England and Wales (Charity Commission for England and Wales)	Minimum requirements in Scotland (Office of the Scottish Charity Regulator)	Minimum requirements in Northern Ireland (Charity Commission for Northern Ireland)*
Gross income greater than £500,000 up to £1 million***			
All (unincorporated, companies and charitable incorporated organisations**)	✓ **Accrual accounts** ✓ File trustees' **annual report** and accounts ✓ File **annual return** ⚲ **Independent examination** by *qualified* person	✓ **Accrual accounts** ✓ File trustees' **annual report** and accounts ✓ File **annual return** ⚲ **Audit** by registered auditor	✓ **Accrual accounts** ✓ File trustees' **annual report** and accounts ✓ File **annual monitoring return** ⚲ **Audit** by an auditor compliant with section 65(2) of the Charities Act (Northern Ireland) 2008

* Charities that are not registered with the Charity Commission for Northern Ireland are not required to report until they are placed on the register.

** It is not possible to set up a charitable incorporated organisation in Northern Ireland at present as the relevant section of the Charities Act (Northern Ireland) 2008 is not yet in force.

*** The above figures assume that gross assets do not exceed £3.26 million. An audit will also be needed if total assets (before liabilities) exceed £3.26 million, and the charity's gross income is more than £250,000 per year. (See appendix 3 of the Charities Statement of Recommended Practice (SORP) for more detail.)

Appendix 1

Legal form	Minimum requirements in England and Wales (Charity Commission for England and Wales)	Minimum requirements in Scotland (Office of the Scottish Charity Regulator)	Minimum requirements in Northern Ireland (Charity Commission for Northern Ireland)*
Gross income greater than £1 million***			
All (unincorporated, companies and charitable incorporated organisations**)	✓ **Accrual accounts** ✓ File trustees' **annual report** and accounts ✓ File **annual return** **Audit** by registered auditor	✓ **Accrual accounts** ✓ File trustees' **annual report** and accounts ✓ File **annual return** **Audit** by registered auditor	✓ **Accrual accounts** ✓ File trustees' **annual report** and accounts ✓ File **annual monitoring return** **Audit** by registered auditor

* Charities that are not registered with the Charity Commission for Northern Ireland are not required to report until they are placed on the register.

** It is not possible to set up a charitable incorporated organisation in Northern Ireland at present as the relevant section of the Charities Act (Northern Ireland) 2008 is not yet in force.

*** The above figures assume that gross assets do not exceed £3.26 million. An audit will also be needed if total assets (before liabilities) exceed £3.26 million, and the charity's gross income is more than £250,000 per year. (See appendix 3 of the Charities Statement of Recommended Practice (SORP) for more detail.)

Appendix 2

Glossary of terms

Accounts payable – money that you owe to suppliers, people selling stuff, or **creditors** for goods or services bought on credit, such as a photocopier you are paying for over a period of time.

Accounts receivable – money owed to you for goods or services you have delivered.

Accrual concept – the figures entered in your charity's accounting records for (a) money that has not yet been spent but that you have committed to spend and (b) income that you are entitled to receive but have not yet received in the month or period where the figures are entered. For example, your charity has received stationery and the supplier hasn't invoiced you yet, but you know the invoice is coming. Under the accrual concept, the cost of the stationery would be recorded in the month it is received even though you haven't been invoiced for it yet. Figures that you enter into your accounts for such situations are said to have been 'accrued'.

Allocation – the process of assigning **core costs** to particular activities. For example, you might 'allocate' one-third of your CEO's salary to your fundraising expenditure to show a truer cost of fundraising than just including the direct cost of, say, a postal campaign.

Amortisation – the process of spreading the value of an intangible **asset** (such as software or a website) over its useful lifetime. For example, you've spent £20,000 on a new software system. The cash goes out of your bank as soon as you pay the bill, but your management information will show the money as being spent over the time period that the product still works and you don't need a new one. So if you decide to amortise over five years, your accounts will show that each year you have 'spent' £4,000 on the software.

Asset – a thing of economic value that your charity owns. Assets tend to be categorised by length of use: less than a year and it's current (or short term); more than a year and it's fixed (or non-current).
- **Current asset:** 'Current' as a description of an asset is helpful because current means now in general speak. A current asset is often one a charity can convert into cash quickly.
- **Fixed asset:** 'Fixed' may conjure up the image of an immovable object, and that's quite handy for remembering that a fixed asset is often something you can't turn into cash quickly. These assets will ordinarily be tangible things like land, buildings, vehicles and equipment. But they

might also be things which you cannot touch physically (referred to as 'intangible'), such as copyright or intellectual property.

Audit (external audit) – a charity's accounts belong to the trustees: it is their report and their financial information. An external audit reviews various aspects of your charity's accounts and financial information to check whether everything stacks up, appears truthful and has been accounted for properly. An external audit will test whether your accounts are 'true and fair' (i.e. provide an accurate picture of your charity's financial health); whether your accounts are legitimately drawn up on a **going concern** basis (i.e. that you can keep running without going bust); and whether there are any **material** uncertainties in your accounting information. It will be carried out by a registered auditor. Chapter 9 contains more information on different types of audit.

Bad debt – money that you are owed but which you discover will not be paid.

Balance sheet – a snapshot of how funds are held at a particular point in time, often the year end. It shows both long- and short-term **assets** and **liabilities**. Your balance sheet is not just for you as an organisation. It also tells your stakeholders how much your charity is worth, how much cash it has, how much it owes, whether it has things it can easily sell to meet its bills, and whether or not you are in good financial health and can be relied on to pay your bills.

Big Four – the largest four accounting firms in the UK by total UK fee income, namely PwC, Deloitte, EY and KPMG.

Break even – where money in and money out are evenly matched. It is often discussed in tandem with **budget** – as in 'break-even budget'.

Budget (including zero-based budgeting) – put simply, a budget is a document which plans what your charity is going to spend and what income it expects to come in. This can be for your whole organisation or for a particular project. It is a guide so you can plan what you do with your charity's money more effectively. It is the best guess at how much money will come in from all sources and how much money will be spent in total. Budgets can be built up based on previous performance and by looking at future plans. Most frequently, you will have information from past activities to give you a good guide to what the figures might look like. Sometimes you will start the process from scratch because the budget is for a new activity or service – this is called 'zero-based' budgeting. See chapter 3 for more information.

Capital (expenditure/investment) – money spent or invested to purchase or enhance a fixed **asset**. For example, you might spend £20,000 of your money on turning a therapy room into a multi-sensory environment or on a new website for your charity. Capital expenditure is typically spending that will make something more valuable or will in some way help you to generate more **revenue**.

Cash flow (projection or forecast) – describes how cash flows in and out of your charity, usually by month (i.e. how much cash is going to be paid into your bank account and how much will be paid out in any given period). Maybe your salaries are due to be paid out on the last day of the month and your charity receives a set amount from a grant every quarter on the 1st of the month. A cash flow will track these movements. Your cash flow is separate from but supplements your management information.

Cash-flow statement – a statement providing information about how your charity uses cash. It is part of the statutory accounts for charities of a particular size and is not the same thing as a cash-flow forecast (see chapter 3).

Closing the books – an accounting procedure that happens at the end of financial periods, whether a month, quarter or **financial year**. Closing the books will bring an end to the recording of transactions in your accounts for the relevant period. Anything coming to light after the accounts have been closed – for example, if an invoice is received for the period – will usually be recorded in the next period. Alternatively, if there are technical reasons for doing so (such as if the invoice makes a material difference to the picture of your charity's financial health), the numbers might be adjusted to include the new information (see **post-balance-sheet events (adjusting and non-adjusting)**).

Core costs (including back-office costs) – sometimes also referred to as 'overheads', 'running costs' or 'operating costs', these are the costs which are required to run a charity (such as staff salaries, electricity, telephones and cleaning contractors) that are not related to the charity's purpose or its specific activities (such as providing advice). For example, the CEO's salary would be an example of a core cost and the therapists a charity employs would be an example of a non-core cost. 'Back-office costs' are a subset of core costs and relate to supporting functions such as IT, HR and finance.

Cost centre – a department or activity to which a cost is attributed, such as HR, the finance team or the facilities team.

Creditors – the people or organisations to which your charity owes money. They have effectively given your charity credit by allowing it to use a product or service which it hasn't paid for yet.

Debtors – the people or organisations that owe money to your charity. They are in debt to your charity because they have used a product or service from it which they haven't paid for yet.

Deferred income – money you have received but haven't yet earned and which is therefore shown in the accounting records of the period in which the service or activity will be delivered. For example, you might have advertised a conference for June and it is now February. When people book to attend, they pay the invoice straight away, so you have the cash, but you cannot 'count' the money as belonging to you until you have run the conference.

Deficit – a loss your charity has made, where money spent is more than the money that came in.

Depreciation – the reduction of the recorded cost of a fixed **asset** year on year (over its useful lifetime) until it reaches zero value, rather like **amortisation** for an intangible asset. For example, you buy a minibus worth £10,000. The cost of the fixed asset can be spread in your records according to your accounting policy, which might set the life of the minibus as five years. Each year you record a smaller amount (it is depreciated) and the sum is reduced over time until it reaches zero. So, in year two it might be recorded as £8,000, in year three £6,000 and so on.

Designated funds/reserves – amounts of **reserves** that have been deliberately set aside or earmarked for a particular activity. For example, trustees might designate some funds to spend on an IT project in the coming year.

Double-entry bookkeeping (just because I mentioned it and not because you're likely to use it in everyday conversations!) – the process by which a transaction is recorded as both a credit and a debit. For example, if you took out a loan, the amount would be shown as both a credit (the money in) and a liability (the money owed).

EBITDA (earnings before interest, tax, depreciation and amortisation) – a measure of operating profitability which is arrived at by taking the income of your charity after all deductions (net income) and adding back in these specific deductions: interest, tax, **depreciation** and **amortisation**. This is not a term you will commonly hear in general charities, although it will frequently be used in some areas of the not-for-profit sector, such as housing associations. It is also a term which non-charity folk may be familiar with and may refer to when looking at the contribution or cost an activity makes to your charity's finances. (See also **net income**.)

Endowments – essentially, legal structures. The donor has specified at the time of the gift that the donated **capital** either cannot be spent at all (which refers to permanent endowment) or can be spent only in particular circumstances (which refers to expendable endowment). Endowments can generate **restricted** or unrestricted income depending on the donor's wishes.

Engagement letter – a letter which sets out the basis on which you have engaged a professional, such as an external auditor or independent examiner, to do some work (i.e. carry out an 'engagement').

Appendix 2

Financial year – your charity's financial year is the 12-month period (starting again each year) for which you record your financial transactions for accounting purposes. It will not automatically be a calendar year and will more typically end in March, June, September or December.

Forecasting – much like with the weather, this is the process of predicting. In this case, you're not thinking about wind and snow. Instead, you're showing your charity's financial position at the end of a period – often the **financial year** – based on your actual transactions to that point (referred to as your 'actuals'), how your charity is performing against **budget** and your best guess as to what is going to happen in the coming months. Forecasting is one of the most useful tools you have for making decisions about priorities.

Full cost recovery – when you include all costs in the pricing of a service (whether by grant or contract). This includes not just the physical costs of pens, paper, etc. but also staff time, premises costs and anything else that would be used to deliver the activity being paid for. This is hugely important, especially in bids for grants and contracts, so that you don't end up unwittingly subsidising activities that the entity commissioning the activity ought to cover or find yourself running out of funds because you didn't spot that the money coming in wouldn't be sufficient to cover all the costs associated with the activity.

Going concern – when we talk about an organisation being a going concern, we mean that it has enough money, or the reasonable expectation of money coming in, or that it has **assets** which are worth more than its debts and can be sold, so that it can continue operating into the foreseeable future without incurring debt it has no ability to pay. In other words, it has a reasonable prospect of not going bust any time soon.

Goods receipts – these work in conjunction with **purchase orders**. Goods receipts record in your charity's systems that goods or services have been received so that payment can be made.

Gross – often used in business when talking about costs or profit. Gross costs would be the total costs of something without any deductions. Gross profit would be the amount of profit after deducting the cost of delivery (rent, staff, etc.) but before you deducted tax, expenses and interest. We don't tend to speak in terms of profit in the charity sector, but those coming at charity accounts with business experience may talk in these terms. Knowing the difference between gross and net is helpful because it can help you determine what an activity's true cost or contribution might be to your charity. For example, if you generated £15,000 from a fundraising event, the staff time accounted for £1,500, the venue cost you £6,000 and the advertising a further £1,000, you would want to consider the contribution from that event as being £6,500, not the gross income of £15,000.

Incoming resources (charitable activities, trading activities, investments, etc.) – means all resources which have been earned by or donated to your charity. Incoming resources from charitable activities arise when a charity can charge for the services it provides. 'Trading' incoming resources are services that arise from things your charity sells – for example, through retail operations. Incoming resources can also come from other sources, such as investments held.

Independent examination – an independent review of year-end financial information and accounting records, limited to a set of tasks your independent examiner sets out in its **engagement letter**, which are governed by the relevant charity regulator's guidance for independent examiners. Independent examination is only available for those charities not requiring an **audit**. It is a much lighter touch than an audit, providing a lesser level of assurance to those reading the accounts. (See also **audit (external audit)**.)

Irrecoverable VAT (or unrecoverable VAT) – there is a myth that charities don't pay VAT, or that VAT rules just don't apply to them. But they do, and charities are required to comply with the rules around VAT. Within a glossary of terms, it is impossible to give you a complete picture, so here are a couple of links to guides that (at the time of writing!) might help provide more information on VAT:
- Sayer Vincent, *VAT Made Simple*, www.sayervincent.co.uk/wp-content/uploads/2021/08/SV-MS-VAT-Jan2021.pdf.
- Charity Tax Group, 'VAT', www.charitytaxgroup.org.uk/tax/vat.

The key thing to realise is that the VAT rules set out what can be claimed back and what cannot. Some of the VAT you get charged by your suppliers will be irrecoverable and therefore a cost. This is often missed in bids and **budgets**, which can lead to problems.

Journals – simply a physical or digital record of your transactions in chronological order (usually held in spreadsheets, accounting software or sometimes a physical document).

Liabilities – money that you owe, such as loans, mortgages, invoices you have yet to pay and expenses built up over a period of time.

Liquidity – the ease with which your charity can meet its short-term financial obligations (i.e. the ease with which you can pay your bills). Cash is the most liquid of **assets**. In contrast, investments that are tied up for a fixed long term (for example, to secure a better deal) or assets that you might not easily be able to convert into cash (known as 'realised') without impacting their value could be said to be 'illiquid'.

Management accounts/information – financial reports produced, often on a monthly or quarterly basis, by management. These provide broad information about your charity's financial performance to assist in the management of your charity and help trustees and staff to make decisions. They are usually much more detailed than the information in the accounts you are required to submit to your regulator and potentially Companies House (statutory accounts), and they are not required to follow the **SORP** (see chapter 3).

Margin – the difference between what you earn in providing a product or service and what it costs you to provide it.

Market rate – the usual rate for a product or service that someone buying something would be willing to pay.

Material – an amount of money is considered material when it is big enough to change the overall picture of your charity's finances. For example, if your charity has an income of £100 million, leaving out or including an item worth £10,000 wouldn't make a difference to the financial picture. But let's say your charity has an income of £100,000 – that £10,000 now has a much bigger impact. Materiality in the context of an external **audit** will be determined by your external auditor. They will look at the amounts in any item of income or expenditure, or area of activity, individually or collectively, to decide if they think any of those amounts might impact the decision-making of a reader of the accounts.

Natural classification – the classification of income and expenditure against headings that may feel natural, like salaries, paper and premises, as opposed to the classification of income and expenditure by reference to what charitable activity the money relates to – for example, allocating all the costs associated with delivering a befriending service.

Net income – an amount of money after all deductions for tax, interest, etc. have been applied.

Out-turn – the result achieved in a particular period.

Post-balance-sheet events (adjusting and non-adjusting) – events that happen after your reporting period (see **closing the books**) but before you have issued your official financial statements. Some events will require you to make an amendment to your statements because leaving out the information would make the overall position misleading (called an 'adjusting' post-balance-sheet event). Others do not require such an amendment because, for example, the sum is not **material** (called a 'non-adjusting' post-balance-sheet event). A positive adjusting event might be a large legacy that arises after your accounting period and which makes a big difference to your numbers. A negative example might be a debtor who owes you loads of money going bust, meaning you're not likely to get paid.

Prepayments – amounts paid in advance of receiving a good or service.

Procurement – the process of finding, and agreeing terms for, goods or services from an external source.

Profit and loss – often referred to by the shorthand 'P&L', this is a statement of profit or loss made in a specified period (usually a quarter or full **financial year**) taking into account all **revenue** (income), expenses and costs. In charities, we tend to refer to **surplus** and **deficit** instead of profit and loss, but people more familiar with business accounts might default to the term P&L.

Provision – a sum set aside or allowed for a specific debt or reduction in the value of an asset. For example, a **bad debt** provision would put a figure against the amount of debt owed to your charity which you anticipate will not be paid.

Purchase order (or PO) – a document which shows the intention to buy an item. Within accounting software, this usually means a 'PO number' is given to a supplier to quote when they send you their invoice. This helps with authorising payments and matching invoices to **cost centres** (see also **goods receipts**).

Receipts and payments – sometimes called 'cash accounting'. It is a method of recording cash in and cash out, and does not make provision for money your charity owes, or that is owed to it, that is yet to be paid.

Recurring and non-recurring costs – recurring costs are costs that happen regularly. For example, if you rent an office, the expenditure to pay the lease monthly would be a recurring cost. Conversely, non-recurring costs are one-off costs that are not expected to reoccur. For example, paying to have the office painted when you need to would be a non-recurring cost.

Reserves – the term 'reserves' has a variety of technical and ordinary meanings. People will use terms such as 'general', 'free' or 'cash' reserves interchangeably to describe monies left when a charity has taken out all the restrictions, tied-up monies and monies trustees have earmarked for other stuff. But these terms can mean different things to different people and thus this whole topic is a source of confusion. That's why there is a whole chapter on reserves in this book (see chapter 5)!

Restricted/unrestricted funds – funds your charity holds can be said to be restricted when you can spend them only on specific things, because the person or organisation gave you the money for that specific activity. Conversely, unrestricted funds are money your charity can spend on whatever it likes – subject to your charity's objects, of course (that rules out the trip to the Caribbean – sorry!).

Return on investment – the amount of money that an investment generates as income. For example, if you spend £100 on fundraising that generates £150, the return on investment is £50. The same idea is sometimes expressed as, for example, 'for every £1 spent, £1.50 is returned'. Or it may be expressed as 1:1.5.

Revenue – the total amount of income generated from all sources.

SoFA – the statement of financial activities. It is a table in your accounts which sets out your income from donations, legacies, charitable activities, investments and other income, and your expenditure on raising funds, delivering your charitable activities and anything else.

Solvent – you are solvent when you can pay your bills on time.

SORP – the Charities Statement of Recommended Practice (see chapter 1).

Surplus – if at the end of a period or project your charity has received more money than it has spent, this is called a surplus. In business terms, this would be called profit.

Trial balance – a document prepared at the end of a period – usually the **financial year** – which brings together the balance of all **debtors** and **creditors** from across all the different parts of your charity and provides totals for different types of income and expenditure across your various **cost centres**.

True and fair – a technical term which has been around accounting for many decades. There is no statutory definition of it, but it means the accounts are more than just a set of documents prepared in accordance with accounting standards. True and fair accounts must provide an accurate picture of the financial health of the charity.

Variance – the difference between any set of figures. Often shown as the differences between what was planned (the **budget**), what was predicted (forecast) and what the charity got (actual). A variance can be positive or negative.

VAT invoice – an invoice that includes VAT. Not all services are 'vatable' and the rates or exemptions which apply to charities are many and varied. VAT can only be charged by VAT-registered entities, too. See Alastair Hardman and Kaye Sayer's *The Complete Charity VAT Handbook*, also published by DSC.

Voluntary income – money donated to your charity, whether by the public, philanthropists, grant-makers, foundations, or companies, or through legacies.

References and notes

Page 1 – **Chapter 1 epigraph:** Ian Theodoreson, former CFO of the Church of England and former chair and founder member of Charity Finance Group (CFG), shared this quote in his outgoing speech as the chair of CFG.

Page 3 – **The Institute of Chartered Accountants in England and Wales research report:** Peter Bird and Peter Morgan-Jones, *Financial Reporting by Charities*, London, Institute of Chartered Accountants in England and Wales, 1981.

Page 3 – **The SORP:** *FRS 102: The financial reporting standard applicable in the UK and Republic of Ireland* [PDF], Chartered Institute of Public Finance and Accounting, 2022, https://media.frc.org.uk/documents/FRS_102_The_Financial_Reporting_Standard_applicable_in_the_UK_and_Republic_of_Ireland_ns2SqGY.pdf, accessed 17 April 2024.

Page 3 – **The constitution of the charity sector:** Nayara Tabassum 'UK Civil Society Almanac 2023' [web article], NCVO, www.ncvo.org.uk/news-and-insights/news-index/uk-civil-society-almanac-2023/profile/how-many-voluntary-organisations-are-there, 12 October 2023.

Page 4 – **The SORP application:** The SORP-making body includes representatives from the four UK nations and the Republic of Ireland, and it is the intention for the SORP to become a legal requirement in the Republic of Ireland too when the relevant legislation is laid (it is currently voluntary). The Republic of Ireland is outside the scope of this book.

Page 5 – **Noel Hyndman quote:** Noel Hyndman, *The Charities SORP: An 'engine' for good?* [PDF], Queen's University Belfast, 2018, https://pureadmin.qub.ac.uk/ws/portalfiles/portal/155631755/PMM_Charities_SORP_Engine_for_Good_Accepted_Manuscript_April_2018_Pure.pdf, accessed 17 April 2024.

Page 7 – **Quote from *It's a Battle on the Board*:** Debra Allcock Tyler, *It's a Battle on the Board*, London, Directory of Social Change, 2020, p. 14.

Page 9 – **Debra's quote:** Debra Allcock Tyler, *It's Murder in Management*, London, Directory of Social Change, 2018, p. 6.

Page 9 – **Feel the fear and do it anyway:** This phrase was popularised by Susan Jeffers in *Feel the Fear and Do It Anyway: How to Turn Your Fear and Indecision into Confidence and Action*, London, Century, 1987.

Page 11 – **Chapter 2 epigraph:** Charity Finance Group annual dinner speech, 2018.

Page 13 – **The Finance Journey model:** Simon Hopkins, 'The Finance Journey' [web page], 2014, Charity Finance Group, https://cfg.org.uk/resources/finance_journey, accessed 17 April 2024.

Page 21 – **Chapter 3 epigraph:** J. A. Hammerton, *Barrie: The Story of a Genius*, New York, Dodd, Mead and Company, 1929, p. 337.

Page 24 – **Guidance on financial controls:** *Internal Financial Controls for Charities* (CC8) [PDF], Charity Commission for England and Wales, 2023, www.gov.uk/government/publications/internal-financial-controls-for-charities-cc8, accessed 17 April 2024.

Page 38 – **Questions to consider when viewing management information:** Debra Allcock Tyler, *It's a Battle on the Board*, London, Directory of Social Change, 2020, p. 146.

Page 42 – **Definition of cash equivalents:** *Charities SORP (FRS 102): Accounting and reporting by charities: statement of recommended practice applicable to charities preparing their accounts in accordance with the Financial Reporting Standard applicable in the UK and Republic of Ireland* [PDF], The Chartered Institute of Public Finance and Accountancy 2019, https://assets.publishing.service.gov.uk/media/5e6102c286650c513b442f14/charities-sorp-frs102-2019a.pdf, s. 14.3, accessed 17 April 2024.

Page 47 – **Hilary Seaward's work:** Hilary Seaward, *More of the Wood, Less of the Trees: A trustee-centred approach to management accounts* [PDF], Charity Finance Group, 2013, http://smallcharityfinance.org.uk/wp-content/uploads/2016/06/Wood-For-The-Trees-Resource.pdf, accessed 17 April 2024.

Page 53 – **Chapter 4 epigraph:** Rudyard Kipling, 'If', in *Rewards and Fairies*, London, Macmillan, 1910.

Page 54 – **Guidance on risk management:** *Charities and Risk Management* (CC26) [PDF], Charity Commission for England and Wales, 2010, www.gov.uk/government/publications/charities-and-risk-management-cc26It, accessed 17 April 2024.

Page 57 – **Donald Rumsfeld's speech:** Donald H. Rumsfeld, 'DoD news briefing' [transcript], https://web.archive.org/web/20160406235718/http://archive.defense.gov/Transcripts/Transcript.aspx?TranscriptID=2636, 12 February 2002.

Page 63 – **Risk likelihood scoring system:** Reproduced from *Charities and Risk Management* (CC26) [PDF], Charity Commission for England and Wales, 2010, www.gov.uk/government/publications/charities-and-risk-management-cc26, accessed 17 April 2024.

Page 63 – **Risk impact scoring system:** Reproduced from *ibid*.

Page 64 – **CC26 quote:** *Ibid*.

Page 66 – **CC26 heat map:** *Ibid*.

References and notes

Page 68 – **TEDx Talk:** Gerd Gigerenzer, 'Risk Literacy' [speech], TEDx Talks, www.youtube.com/watch?v=g4op2WNc1e4, 9 December 2013.

Page 72 – **Quote on what is required in a financial review:** *Charities SORP (FRS 102): Accounting and reporting by charities: statement of recommended practice applicable to charities preparing their accounts in accordance with the Financial Reporting Standard applicable in the UK and Republic of Ireland* [PDF], The Chartered Institute of Public Finance and Accountancy 2019, https://assets.publishing.service.gov.uk/media/5e6102c286650c513b442f14/charities-sorp-frs102-2019a.pdf, s. 1.46, accessed 17 April 2024.

Page 72 – **Quote on the requirement for a risk management statement:** Charities (Accounts and Reports) Regulations 2008, s. 40(2). For Scotland see the Charities Accounts (Scotland) Amendment Regulations 2018 and for Northern Ireland see the Charities (Accounts and Reports) Regulations (Northern Ireland) 2015.

Page 72 – **Definition of a small company:** 'Prepare annual accounts for a private limited company' [web page], Gov.uk, www.gov.uk/annual-accounts/microentities-small-and-dormant-companies, accessed 17 April 2024.

Page 72 – **Reporting requirements for charities that are also companies:** See the Companies (Miscellaneous Reporting) Regulations 2018.

Page 74 – **Serious incident reporting requirements:** For the English and Welsh regime, see *Examples Table: Deciding what to report* [PDF], Charity Commission for Egland and Wales, https://assets.publishing.service.gov.uk/media/5bd706d9ed915d789dcd63ef/RSI_guidance_what_to_do_if_something_goes_wrong_Examples_table_deciding_what_to_report.pdf, accessed 17 April 2024; for the Northern Irish regime, see *Serious Incident Reporting: A guide for charity trustees* [PDF], Charity Commission for Northern Ireland, 2022, www.charitycommissionni.org.uk/concerns-and-decisions/serious-incident-reporting-a-guide-for-charity-trustees, accessed 17 April 2024; for the Scottish regime, see 'Raise a concern' [web page], Office of the Scottish Charity Regulator, www.oscr.org.uk/about-charities/raise-a-concern, accessed 17 April 2024.

Page 74 – **Guidance on serious incidents:** 'How to report a serious incident in your charity', Charity Commission for England and Wales, 2019, www.gov.uk/guidance/how-to-report-a-serious-incident-in-your-charity, accessed 17 April 2024.

Page 75 – **List of triggers to report serious incidents**: *Ibid.*

Page 78 – **Author's story of having twins:** Debra Allcock Tyler, *It's a Battle on the Board*, London, Directory of Social Change, 2020, p. 181.

Page 78 – **Kaplan and Mikes's risk management model:** Robert S. Kaplan and Anette Mikes, 'Managing risks: A new framework' [web article], *Harvard*

Business Review, https://hbr.org/2012/06/managing-risks-a-new-framework, June 2012.

Page 83 – **Chapter 5 epigraph:** 'Talking about… Charity reserves' [podcast], Charity Finance Group, 2023, https://audioboom.com/posts/8322535-talking-about-charity-reserves, accessed 17 April 2024.

Page 84 – **Figure summarising categories of funds:** *Beyond Reserves: How charities can make their reserves work harder* [PDF], ACEVO, Charity Finance Group, Institute of Fundraising and Sayer Vincent, 2012, http://smallcharityfinance.org.uk/wp-content/uploads/2016/06/SV_Reserves_Final.pdf, accessed 17 April 2024.

Page 84 – **Guidance on reserves for England and Wales:** *Charity Reserves: Building resilience* (CC19) [web page], Charity Commission for England and Wales, 2023, www.gov.uk/government/publications/charities-and-reserves-cc19, accessed 17 April 2024.

Page 84 – **Guidance on reserves for Scotland and Northern Ireland:** See 'Charity reserves factsheet' [web article], Office of the Scottish Charity Regulator, www.oscr.org.uk/guidance-and-forms/charity-reserves-factsheet, 10 May 2017; *Developing a Reserves Policy* [PDF], Charity Commission for Northern Ireland, 2018, www.charitycommissionni.org.uk/manage-your-charity/developing-a-reserves-policy, accessed 17 April 2024.

Page 85 – **Requirement for trustees to spend income:** Charities Act 2011, part 6.

Page 85 – **Guidance on reserves:** *Charity Reserves: Building resilience* (CC19) [web page], Charity Commission for England and Wales, 2023, www.gov.uk/government/publications/charities-and-reserves-cc19, accessed 17 April 2024.

Page 86 – **SORP requirements for the review of reserves:** *Charities SORP (FRS 102): Accounting and reporting by charities: statement of recommended practice applicable to charities preparing their accounts in accordance with the Financial Reporting Standard applicable in the UK and Republic of Ireland* [PDF], The Chartered Institute of Public Finance and Accountancy 2019, https://assets.publishing.service.gov.uk/media/5e6102c286650c513b442f14/charities-sorp-frs102-2019a.pdf, s. 1.48, accessed 17 April 2024.

Page 86 – **SORP requirements for showing reserves in the accounts:** *Ibid.*, s. 2.

Page 86 – **SORP requirements for larger charities regarding reserves:** *Ibid.*, ss. 1.46 and 1.48.

Page 87 – **UK Civil Society Almanac:** Nayyara Tabassum, *UK Civil Society Almanac* [web page], NCVO, 2023, www.ncvo.org.uk/news-and-insights/news-index/uk-civil-society-almanac-2023, accessed 17 April 2024.

References and notes

Page 90 – **Guidance on the level of reserves:** *Charity Reserves: Building resilience* (CC19) [web page], Charity Commission for England and Wales, 2023, www.gov.uk/government/publications/charities-and-reserves-cc19, accessed 17 April 2024.

Page 90 – **Restricted funds:** Pesh Framjee, *Reserves Policy: Setting and implementing weather protection* [PDF], Crowe, 2016, www.crowe.com/uk/-/media/crowe/firms/europe/uk/croweuk/pdf-publications/reserves-policy-setting-and-implementing.pdf, accessed 17 April 2024.

Page 101 – **Chapter 6 epigraph:** Joe Lazauskas and Shane Snow, *The Storytelling Edge: How to Transform Your Business, Stop Screaming into the Void, and Make People Love You*, Hoboken, NJ, Wiley, 2018, p. xviii.

Page 102 – **SORP's description of good reporting:** *Charities SORP (FRS 102): Accounting and reporting by charities: statement of recommended practice applicable to charities preparing their accounts in accordance with the Financial Reporting Standard applicable in the UK and Republic of Ireland* [PDF], The Chartered Institute of Public Finance and Accountancy 2019, https://assets.publishing.service.gov.uk/media/5e6102c286650c513b442f14/charities-sorp-frs102-2019a.pdf, s. 1, accessed 17 April 2024.

Page 103 – **Quote on the objective of the trustees' annual report**: *Ibid.*, p. 3.

Page 108 – **Young Lives vs Cancer admitting failure:** *Our Impact 2018* [PDF], Young Lives vs Cancer, 2018, www.clicsargent.org.uk/wp-content/uploads/2018/10/CLIC_Sargent_Our_Impact_2018_LR.pdf, p. 21, accessed 17 April 2024.

Page 108 – **Morrisons sponsorship of Young Lives vs Cancer:** 'Morrisons enter 4th year of fundraising for young people with cancer' [web article], Young Lives vs Cancer,www.younglivesvscancer.org.uk/morrisons/morrisons-enter-4th-year-of-fundraising-for-young-people-with-cancer, 11 February 2020.

Page 108 – **Opera company impact measurement example:** Jim Collins, *Good to Great and the Social Sectors. Why business thinking is not the answer*, New York, Harper Business, 2005, p. 10.

Page 111 – **Chapter 7 epigraph:** Harold Geneen and Alvin Moscow, *Managing*, New York, Avon Books, 1985, p. 203.

Page 113 – **R&P regimes in Scotland and Northern Ireland:** For Scotland see 'Receipts and Payments Accounts Work Pack' [web page], Office of the Scottish Charity Regulator, www.oscr.org.uk/managing-a-charity/charity-accounting/receipts-and-payments-accounts-work-pack, accessed 17 April 2024; for Northern Ireland see 'Accounting and reporting essentials' [web page], Charity Commission for Northern Ireland, www.charitycommissionni.org.uk/manage-your-charity/annual-reporting/accounting-and-reporting-essentials, accessed 17 April 2024.

Page 114 – **Charities that shouldn't use R&P accounting method:** *Receipts and Payments Accounts Introductory Notes* [PDF], Charity Commission for England and Wales, 2017, https://assets.publishing.service.gov.uk/media/5a7f7d0fed915d74e622ac49/CC16b.pdf, p. 1, accessed 17 April 2024.

Page 117 – **Guidance on R&P accounts:** 'Receipts and payments accounts pack (CC16)' [web page], Charity Commission for England and Wales, 2017, www.gov.uk/government/collections/receipts-and-payments-accounts-pack-cc16, accessed 17 April 2024; 'Receipts and Payments Accounts Work Pack' [web page], Office of the Scottish Charity Regulator, www.oscr.org.uk/managing-a-charity/charity-accounting/receipts-and-payments-accounts-work-pack, accessed 17 April 2024; 'Accounting and reporting essentials' [web page], Charity Commission for Northern Ireland, 2014, www.charitycommissionni.org.uk/manage-your-charity/annual-reporting/accounting-and-reporting-essentials, accessed 17 April 2024.

Page 117 – **SORP definition of SoFA:** *Charities SORP (FRS 102): Accounting and reporting by charities: statement of recommended practice applicable to charities preparing their accounts in accordance with the Financial Reporting Standard applicable in the UK and Republic of Ireland* [PDF], The Chartered Institute of Public Finance and Accountancy 2019, https://assets.publishing.service.gov.uk/media/5e6102c286650c513b442f14/charities-sorp-frs102-2019a.pdf, s. 4, accessed 17 April 2024.

Page 118 – **Deficit on a restricted fund:** *Ibid.*, paragraph 2.15.

Page 119 – **Rules on movements in pension schemes and investments:** See *FRS 102: The financial reporting standard applicable in the UK and Republic of Ireland* [PDF], Chartered Institute of Public Finance and Accounting, 2022, https://media.frc.org.uk/documents/FRS_102_The_Financial_Reporting_Standard_applicable_in_the_UK_and_Republic_of_Ireland_ns2SqGY.pdf, accessed 17 April 2024.

Page 121 – **Objective of the balance sheet:** *Charities SORP (FRS 102): Accounting and reporting by charities: statement of recommended practice applicable to charities preparing their accounts in accordance with the Financial Reporting Standard applicable in the UK and Republic of Ireland* [PDF], The Chartered Institute of Public Finance and Accountancy 2019, https://assets.publishing.service.gov.uk/media/5e6102c286650c513b442f14/charities-sorp-frs102-2019a.pdf, s. 10.2, accessed 17 April 2024.

Page 124 – **SORP requirements on notes to the accounts:** For more information on what notes to the accounts are required by the SORP, see *Charities SORP (FRS 102): Accounting and reporting by charities: statement of recommended practice applicable to charities preparing their accounts in accordance with the Financial Reporting Standard applicable in the UK and Republic of Ireland* [PDF], The Chartered Institute of Public Finance and Accountancy 2019, https://assets.publishing.service.gov.uk/media/

5e6102c286650c513b442f14/charities-sorp-frs102-2019a.pdf, paragraph 26, accessed 17 April 2024.

Page 131 – **Chapter 8 epigraph:** 'Henry Ford quotations' [web page], The Henry Ford, www.thehenryford.org/collections-and-research/digital-resources/popular-topics/henry-ford-quotes, accessed 17 April 2024.

Page 131 – **Advice on charity investment in different UK jurisdictions:** For England and Wales see 'Investing charity money: A guide for trustees (CC14)' [web page], Charity Commission for England and Wales, 2023, www.gov.uk/government/publications/charities-and-investment-matters-a-guide-for-trustees-cc14, accessed 17 April 2024; for Scotland see 'Charity investments: Guidance and good practice' [web page], Office of the Scottish Charity Regulator, 2018, www.oscr.org.uk/guidance-and-forms/charity-investments-guidance-and-good-practice, accessed 17 April 2024. The Charity Commission for Northern Ireland has not yet issued any investment-specific guidance, but its full list of guidance publications can be found at 'View all guidance' [web page], Charity Commission for Northern Ireland, www.charitycommissionni.org.uk/charity-essentials/view-all-guidance, accessed 17 April 2024.

Page 131 – **Detailed exploration of charity investing:** James Brooke Turner, *Investing for Charities*, London, Directory of Social Change, 2024.

Page 135 – **Church of England's support to a campaign:** See 'Church Commissioners for England voice support for activist campaign targeting ExxonMobil' [web article], The Church of England, www.churchofengland.org/news-and-media/finance-news/church-commissioners-england-voice-support-activist-campaign-targeting,10 December 2020 and Jillian Ambrose, 'ExxonMobil and Chevron suffer shareholder rebellions over climate' [web article], *The Guardian*, www.theguardian.com/business/2021/may/26/exxonmobil-and-chevron-braced-for-showdown-over-climate, 26 May 2021.

Page 138 – **Duties of a trustee:** See 'The Essential Trustee: what you need to know, what you need to do (CC3)' [web page], Charity Commission for England and Wales, 2018, www.gov.uk/government/publications/the-essential-trustee-what-you-need-to-know-cc3/the-essential-trustee-what-you-need-to-know-what-you-need-to-do, accessed 17 April 2024 and 'Investing Charity Money: A guide for trustees (CC14)' [web page], Charity Commission for England and Wales, 2023, www.gov.uk/government/publications/charities-and-investment-matters-a-guide-for-trustees-cc14, accessed 17 April 2024.

Page 138 – **Questions to consider around investing:** For England and Wales, see 'Investing Charity Money: A guide for trustees (CC14)' [web page], Charity Commission for England and Wales, 2023, www.gov.uk/government/publications/charities-and-investment-matters-a-guide-for-trustees-cc14, accessed 17 April 2024; for Scotland, see, *Charity Investments: Guidance and good practice* [PDF], The Office of Scottish Charity Regulator, www.oscr.org.uk/media/3352/2018-11-19-investments-guidance.pdf, accessed 17 April 2024.

Page 139 – **Guidance on charity investing:** 'Investing Charity Money: A guide for trustees (CC14)' [web page], Charity Commission for England and Wales, 2023, www.gov.uk/government/publications/charities-and-investment-matters-a-guide-for-trustees-cc14, accessed 17 April 2024.

Page 140 – **Detailed exploration of charity investing:** James Brooke Turner, *Investing for Charities*, London, Directory of Social Change, 2024.

Page 143 – **Possible ESG evaluation mechanisms:** See, for example, https://eirisfoundation.org or www.ethicalscreening.co.uk.

Page 143 – **Significance of ESG in company performance:** For example, see *ESG and Financial Performance: Uncovering the relationship by aggregating evidence from 1,000 plus studies published between 2015–2020* [PDF], Rockefeller Asset Management and NYU Stern Center for Sustainable Business, www.stern.nyu.edu/sites/default/files/assets/documents/NYU-RAM_ESG-Paper_2021%20Rev_0.pdf, accessed 17 April 2024.

Page 143 – **Comic Relief investments scandal:** Ben Quinn, 'Comic Relief accused of investing in tobacco, alcohol and arms firms' [web article], *The Guardian*, 2013, www.theguardian.com/tv-and-radio/2013/dec/10/comic-relief-tobacco-arms-alcohol-panorama#:~:text=The%20co-founder%20of%20Comic,the%20best%20possible%20financial%20return, accessed 17 April 2024.

Page 144 – **Ethical investment policy:** *Charities SORP (FRS 102): Accounting and reporting by charities: statement of recommended practice applicable to charities preparing their accounts in accordance with the Financial Reporting Standard applicable in the UK and Republic of Ireland* [PDF], The Chartered Institute of Public Finance and Accountancy 2019, https://assets.publishing.service.gov.uk/media/5e6102c286650c513b442f14/charities-sorp-frs102-2019a.pdf, s. 21.13, accessed 17 April 2024.

Page 144 – **Case law that lead to Charity Investment Governance Principles:** See 'Butler-Sloss v Charity Commission: Understanding trustee investment duties and powers in the new landscape' [web article], Bates Wells, 2022, https://bateswells.co.uk/updates/butler-sloss-v-charity-commission, accessed 17 April 2024.

Page 144 – **Charity Investment Governance Principles steering group:** The principles have been developed by a steering group made up of Charity Finance Group, Association of Charitable Foundations, NCVO, Wales Council for Voluntary Action and the Secretariat of the Charities Responsible Investment Network, and with input from charity lawyers, chartered accountants, investment managers and advisers, and other relevant individuals and organisations. The Social Justice Collective and The Social Investment Consultancy provided support on equality, diversity and inclusion across the project, and representatives from the Charity Commission for England and Wales joined the project as independent observers. See 'Sector experts join

References and notes

forces on charity investment governance' [web article], Charity Finance Group, 2023, https://cfg.org.uk/news/charity_investment_governance_principles_project_launched, accessed 17 April 2024.

Page 147 – **Chapter 9 epigraph:** George Jean Nathan, *Materia Critica*, New York, Alfred A. Knopf, 1924, p. 5.

Page 149 – **Bodies that can carry out external audits in Northern Ireland:** Charities Act (Northern Ireland) 2008, s. 65(2).

Page 159 – **Duties in relation to matters of material significance:** *Matters of Material Significance Reportable to UK Charity Regulators: Guidance for auditors and independent examiners* [PDF], Charity Commission for England and Wales, Office of the Scottish Charity Regulator and Charity Commission for Northern Ireland, 2020, https://assets.publishing.service.gov.uk/media/5e96e7b186650c2ddb2da8b4/20200129_-_Matters_of_Material_Significance_guidance_April_2020__FINAL_.pdf, accessed 17 April 2024.

Page 160 – **Information for independent examiners:** For England and Wales, see 'Independent Examination of Charity Accounts: Examiners (CC32)' [web page], Charity Commission for England and Wales, 2021, www.gov.uk/government/publications/independent-examination-of-charity-accounts-examiners-cc32, accessed 17 April 2024; for Scotland, see *Independent Examination: A guide for independent examiners* [PDF], The Office of Scottish Charity Regulator, www.oscr.org.uk/media/4612/independent-examination-a-guide-for-independent-examiners.pdf, accessed 17 April 2024; for Northern Ireland, see *Independent Examination of Charity Accounts: Examiner's guide* [PDF], The Charity Commission for Northern Ireland, www.charitycommissionni.org.uk/media/1411/20190703-arr07-guidance-for-independent-examiners-v20.pdf, accessed 17 April 2024.

Page 160 – **Public interest entities:** See *Revised Ethical Standard 2024* [PDF], Financial Reporting Council, https://media.frc.org.uk/documents/Revised_Ethical_Standard_2024.pdf, accessed 17 April 2024.

Page 161 – **Examples where independent examiners need to raise concerns:** 'Independent examination of charity accounts: Examiners' (CC32) [web page], Charity Commission for England and Wales, 2021, www.gov.uk/government/publications/independent-examination-of-charity-accounts-examiners-cc32, accessed 17 April 2024.

Page 167 – **Chapter 10 epigraph:** These words are commonly attributed to Dalai Lama, although their origin is unconfirmed.

Page 188 – **Guidance for independent examiners:** For England and Wales, see 'Independent examination of charity accounts: Examiners' (CC32) [web page], Charity Commission for England and Wales, 2021, www.gov.uk/government/publications/independent-examination-of-charity-accounts-examiners-cc32, accessed 17 April 2024; for Scotland, see *Independent Examination: A guide for charity trustees* [PDF], Office of Scottish Charity

Regulator, 2020, www.oscr.org.uk/media/3533/independent-examination-a-guide-for-charity-trustees.pdf, accessed 17 April 2024; for Northern Ireland, see *Independent Examination of Charity Accounts: Examiner's guide* [PDF], Charity Commission for Northern Ireland, 2019, www.charitycommissionni.org.uk/media/1411/20190703-arr07-guidance-for-independent-examiners-v20.pdf, accessed 17 April 2024.

Index

Page numbers in *italics* refer to figures and illustrations and in **bold** refer to tables. Glossary items are indicated by a 'g'.

accounts 101–3, 105, 111–12, 128–9, 144
   accounts payable and receivable 183g
   accrual concept 112–13, 114–16, 117, 121, 183g
   balance sheets 117, 121–3, **122,** 168, 184g
   cash-flow statements 42–3, 117, 185g
   Generally Accepted Accounting Principles (GAAP) 3, 4
   method used 112–17, **173–81**
   notes 117, 122–3, 124–8, **125, 126, 128**
   SoFA (statement of financial activities) 117–21, **120,** 127, 191g
accuracy
   of budget 26–9
   of forecast 39, 42
activism, shareholder 135
actuals 36, 39, 191g
advice 133, 138, 139–40, 145, 157–8
aims, charitable *see* objects, charitable
Allcock Tyler, Debra 7, 38, 78
allocation 183g
Amnesty International 167
amortisation 183g
analysis, Finance Journey 15
annual reports 72–3, 86, 144–5, 168, 169, **173–81**
   accounts 111–23
   narrative reporting 101–9, 123
   notes 117, 124–8, **125, 126, 128**

appetite, risk 66–71, *70*
appointment planning checklist **154–7**
assets 42, 132–3, 183–4g
   statement of assets and liabilities 121
assumptions, budget 25–6, 28–9
assurance 148, 165
   from executive and trustees 164–5
   external audits 8, 149–50, 157, 184g
   independent examination 148–9, 188g
   internal audits 150–1, 157, 158, 159–60
   reports 161–5
   table of thresholds **173–81**
audiovisual technology 170
auditors 160, 170
audits 153, 157, 161–2, 168, 184g
   external 8, 149–50, 157
   internal 150–1, 157, 158, 159–60

back-office costs 87–8, 106, 185g
bad debt 184g
balance sheets 117, 121–3, **122,** 168, 184g
banks 170
Beyond Reserves 84, 99
big four, accounting firms 184g
Bird, Peter 3
black-swan events 91–2
bonds 136
break even 184g
Brooke Turner, James 131, 140

203

budgets 16, 23, 24–34, *25*, **30–1,** *32,* **33,** *34,* 39, 42, 184g
business models 7, 13, 16, 23, 88, 169

capital 89, 118, 132–3, 184–5g
case studies 105, 169
cash accounting 4, 112–16, 121, 190g
cash flow 9, 168, 170
    forecasts 43–6, **44–5,** *46,* 185g
    statements 42–3, 117, 185g
charitable objects *see* objects, charitable
Charities and Risk Management (CC26) 54, 62–4
Charities (Accounts and Reports) Regulations 2008 for England and Wales 72
The Charities SORP: An 'engine' for good? 5
Charities Statement of Recommended Practice (SORP) *see* SORP (Charities Statement of Recommended Practice)
Charity Commission for England and Wales 24, 54, 62–4, 74–5, 84, 85, 114, 117, 131, 168–9
Charity Commission for Northern Ireland 84, 117, 131
Charity Finance Group (CFG) 1, 6, 11, 75, 84, 99, 104, 141, 168, 170–1
Charity Governance Code 144
Charity Investors Group 141
Charity Reserves: Building resilience (CC19) 84, 90
classification, of income and expenditure 116–17, 126, 189g
Cleverdon, Dame Julia 11
closing the books 185g
collective investment funds 136–7
Comic Relief 143
commodities 137

communication 169
    budget 29–34, *32,* **33,** *34*
    management information 36–8
    with scrutineers 157–9
companies 72, 104, 112, 117, 137
conflicts of interest 7, 138, 140
consolidated figures 121
contingencies 29, 78, 88
controls 14–15, 23–4, 55–6, 73, 150–1
Cooper, Rachel 21
costs 105–6, 118
    cost centres 185g
    full cost recovery 187g
    operating 87–8, 106, 185g
    recurring 190g
COVID-19 pandemic 63, 91, 93
creditors 86, 122, 185g
culture, and risk management 75–8, **77**
current assets 183g

data 15, 22, 36, 47, 108, 109 *see also* information
debt (bad) 184g
debtors 122, 185g
Deeson, Nicki 167
deferred income 185–6g
deficits 112, 117–18, 186g
delegation, scheme of 8, 22–4
deposit accounts 137
depreciation 31, 43, 186g
designated funds 84, 91, 118, 121, 122, 123, 186g
Directory of Social Change (DSC) 6, 90
disclosure 104, 124, 164
Domingues, Rui 168
double-entry bookkeeping 3, 186g

EBITDA (earnings before interest, tax, depreciation and amortisation) 186g *see also* income

Education Development
  Trust 169–70
emphasis of matter 163
endowments 118, 133, 169, 186g
engagement letters 186g
equities 135–6
ethical investment 142, 143–4
    ESG (environmental, social and
      governance) 3, 134
examination, independent *see*
  independent examination
expenditure analysis (note) 126, **126**
expert advice 133, 138, 139–40, 145,
  157–8
external audits 8, 149–50, 157, 184g
external risks 78, 79

Finance Journey, model 13–19, 169
financial advisers 140
Financial Conduct Authority 140
financial management 7–8, 12–19,
  114–16, 167, 169, 170–1
    budgets 16, 23, 24–34, *25*, **30–1,**
      32, **33,** *34,* 39, 42, 184g
    cash-flow forecasts 43–6, **44–5,**
      46, 185g
    forecasting 9, 16, 38–42, **40,**
      187g
    management information 34–8
    processes and controls 22–4
    reporting to the board 46–50,
      49–50
financial year 28, 39, 112, 117, 118,
  187g
fixed assets 183–4g
forecasting 9, 16, 38–42, **40,** 187g
    cash flow 43–6, **44–5,** *46,* 185g
Framjee, Pesh 90
full cost recovery 187g
funds
    collective investment 136–7
    designated 84, 91, 118, 121, 122,
      123, 186g
    movements in (note) 124–5, **125**

funds—*continued*
    restricted 84, 89, 90–1, 117–18,
      169, 190g

general funds 118, 190g
Gigerenzer, Gerd 68
gilts 136
Global Greengrants Fund 170
going concern 115, 149, 158, 162–3,
  187g
goods receipts 187g
governance 5–8, 9, 53, 56, 138–45
    see also trustees
governing documents 7, 23, 85, 113,
  118, 151
grant-making foundations 118
gross 187g

Harvard Business Review 78–9
heat maps, risk management 65–6,
  66
Hind, Andrew 168–9
Hopkins, Simon 12, 169
Humphreys, Bob 169–70
Hyndman, Noel 5

impact statements 103–4, 169
impacts 101, 106–9
income 89, 123, 133, 189g, 191g
    deferred 185–6g
    incoming resources 188g
independent examination 148–9,
  151, 153, 157, 160, 161, 188g *see*
  also external audits
Independent Examination of Charity
  Accounts: Examiners (CC32) 161
independent financial advisers
  (IFAs) 140
inflation 71, 132–3, 136
information 25 *see also* data;
  management information
    display of *32,* 32–4, **33,** *34,* 46,
      46, 47
inputs 101, 106–9

205

insurance 71, 89, 92
interest rates 136, 137
internal audits 150–1, 157, 158, 159–60
Internal Financial Controls for Charities (CC8) 24
Investing Charity Money: A guide for trustees (CC14) 139, 144
Investing for Charities 131, 140
investment managers 139–41, 143, 144
investment policies 141–4, **142–3**
investment sub-committees 138–9
investments 119
    governance 138–45
    reasons to invest 131–4
    types of investment 135–7
invitation to tender (ITT) **156**
It's a Battle on the Board 7, 38, 78

jargon 12, 48, 50, 57, 145, 170–1
journals 188g

Kaplan, Robert 78–9

land 136
legacies 123, 169
legal form, of charity 112–13, **173–81**
legal requirements 7
    investments 132, 138, 140–1
    reserves 85–8
    risk 71–4, **73**
letters
    engagement 186g
    of representation 164
liabilities 121, 188g
liquidity 42–3, 83, 84, 89, 142, 188g
    policies 95
loss 117, 190g

management information 9, 34–8, 48–9, 168, 171, 188–9g
margins 189g

market rates 18, 189g
Materego-Woodall, Joyce 170
materiality 144, 163, 189g
    material uncertainties 149, 162–3
matrix, of risks 64, 64–5
matter, emphasis of 163
matters of material significance 159
Mikes, Anette 78–9
mission *see* objects, charitable
More of the Wood, Less of the Trees 47
Morgan-Jones, Peter 3
movements in funds (note) 124–5, **125**

narrative reporting 101–9
natural classification 116–17, 126, 189g
net income 189g
notes, to accounts 117, 122–3, 124–8, **125, 126, 128**

objectives, investment 132, 141, 142
objects, charitable 7, 26, 48, 103, 106
    and investments 133, 138
    and reserves 84, 95, 99
    and risk 56, 61
O'Brien, Kevin 170–1
Office of the Scottish Charity Regulator 84, 117, 131
Oneirocritics, Society of *see* Society of Oneirocritics (fictional charity)
operating costs 87–8, 106, 185g
operational functions 8–9, 9–10 *see also* staff
operational risks 59–60
opinion
    in assurance report 161–5
    differences of 158, 159
opportunities 7, 56, 69, **77**, 80–1
out-turn 189g
outcomes/outputs 101, 106–9
overheads 87–8, 106, 185g

Index

pay 89, 127–8, **128**
pension schemes 119, 127
performance, Finance Journey 9, 15–16
permissions 22, 23
planning, budgets 24–5
policies 168
  investment 141–4, **142–3**
  liquidity 95
  reserves 88–98, **97, 98**
pooled funds 136–7
post-balance-sheet events 189g
premises 23, 89, 126, 133
prepayments 189g
preventable risks 78–9
processing, Finance Journey 14, 22–4
procurement 190g
professional bodies and qualifications **152–3**
profit and loss 117, 190g
property 136
provision 190g
purchase orders (PO) 190g *see also* goods receipts

qualification, in an audit 163–4
qualifications, professional **152–3**

real estate 136
receipts and payments (R&P) accounting 4, 112–16, 121, 190g
recruitment 99, 104, 169
recurring costs 190g
relationships 167, 170
  with scrutineers 157–61
reports 15 *see also* annual reports
  assurance 161–5
  to the board 46–50, **49–50**
  for investments 132, 143, 144–5
  serious incidents 74–5
representation letters 164
reputation
  damage 164

reputation—*continued*
  and investments 139
  and reserves 92–5
reserves 83–5, *84*, 137, 168, 190g
  designated 84, 91, 118, 121, 122, 123, 186g
  legal requirements 85–8
  policies 88–98, **97, 98**
  reducing level of 99
resignation issues, for scrutineers 159, 164
responsible investment *see* ethical investment
restricted funds 84, 89, 90–1, 117–18, 169, 190g
returns on investment 133–4, 136, 190–1g
revenue 89, 123, 133, 189g, 191g
risk 7, 9, 23, 43, 86, 89
  appetite 66–71, *70*
  and investments 132, 133–4, 136, 138, 139, 142
  and reserves 86, 89, 91–2, 94, 96, 98, 99
  risk management 53–7, 75–81, **77,** *79*
  risk management statements 71–4, **73**
  risk management tools 57–71
risk registers 58–62, **59,** 167
  rating systems 62–6, **63,** *65, 66*
roles and responsibilities 5–9
running costs 87–8, 106, 185g

salaries 89, 127–8, **128**
savings accounts 137
scrutiny 147, 165
  assurance 148–51
  opinions and reports 161–5
  relationship with scrutineer 152–61
  selection of scrutineer **152–3,** 152–7, **154–7**
Seaward, Hilary 47–9

207

serious incident reporting 74–5
shares 132, 133, 134, 135–6
social returns 133, 136
Society of Oneirocritics (fictional charity) 9
    accounts **120**, 121, **122**, 122–3
    budget **30–1**, *32*, *33*, *34*
    forecasting **40**, **44–5**, *46*
    notes, to accounts **125**, **126**, **128**
    reserves 95–8, **97**, **98**
    risk **59**, *65*, 76–7, **77**
SoFA (statement of financial activities) 117–21, **120**, 127, 191g
solvency 43, 191g
SORP (Charities Statement of Recommended Practice) 3, 4–5, 34, 144, 191g
    annual reports and accounts 102–3, 104, 113, 116–17, 121, 123, 124
    cash-flow statement 42–3
    reserves 85, 86
    risk management statements 71–4, **73**
    table of thresholds **173–81**
staff 8–9, 18–19, 23
statements *see also* SORP (Charities Statement of Recommended Practice)
    assets and liabilities 121
    cash flow 42–3, 117, 185g
    of financial activities (SoFA) 117–21, **120**, 127, 191g
    impact 103–4, 169
    risk management 71–4, **73**
statutory audits 8, 149–50, 157, 184g
stocks and shares 132, 133, 134, 135–6
strategic risks 59–60, 79
sub-committees, investment 138–9
subsidiaries, trading 121
surpluses 112, 191g
synthesis, Finance Journey 16

templates 25–6, 42
tendering, invitation **156**
Theodoreson, Ian 1, 171
thresholds, table of **173–81**
tied agents 140
timescale of investment 142
trading subsidiaries 121
transactions, processing and control 14–15
transformation, Finance Journey 16
treasurers 5–6, 168, 170
trial balance 191g
true and fair accounts 115, 149, 163–4, 191g
trustees 2, 5–8, 10, 171 *see also* annual reports
    and audits 164–5, 168
    and investments 138–41
    and risk management 77–8

unrestricted funds 118, 190g

variance 36, 124, 168, 191g
VAT invoices 191g
vision 8, 16, 17
volatility 26, 89, 93, 99, 136
voluntary income 191g

working capital 89, 96, 137
Writing Your Investment Policy 141

zero-based budgeting 26, 184g

Why not catch up with the rest of the series

www.dsc.org.uk/mur

www.dsc.org.uk/ppn

www.dsc.org.uk/itt

www.dsc.org.uk/bob